Hannah Arendt
and Theology

OTHER TITLES IN THE PHILOSOPHY AND THEOLOGY SERIES INCLUDE

Adorno and Theology, Christopher Craig Brittain
Badiou and Theology, Frederick Depoortere
Derrida and Theology, Steven Shakespeare
Foucault and Theology, Jonathan Tran
Girard and Theology, Michael Kirwan
Habermas and Theology, Maureen Junker-Kenny
Hegel and Theology, Martin J. De Nys
Kant and Theology, Pamela Sue Anderson and Jordan Bell
Kierkegaard and Theology, Murray Rae
Levinas and Theology, Nigel Zimmerman
Lyotard and Theology, Lieven Boeve
Merleau-Ponty and Theology, Christopher Ben Simpson
Nietzsche and Theology, Craig Hovey
Simone Weil and Theology, A. Rebecca Rozelle-Stone
Vattimo and Theology, Thomas G. Guarino
Wittgenstein and Theology, Tim Labron
Žižek and Theology, Adam Kotsko
Heidegger and Theology, Judith Wolfe

Hannah Arendt and Theology

John Kiess

Bloomsbury T&T Clark
An imprint of Bloomsbury Publishing Plc

B L O O M S B U R Y
LONDON • OXFORD • NEW YORK • NEW DELHI • SYDNEY

Bloomsbury T&T Clark
An imprint of Bloomsbury Publishing Plc

Imprint previously known as T&T Clark

50 Bedford Square	1385 Broadway
London	New York
WC1B 3DP	NY 10018
UK	USA

www.bloomsbury.com

BLOOMSBURY, T&T CLARK and the Diana logo are trademarks of Bloomsbury Publishing Plc

First published 2016

© John Kiess, 2016

John Kiess has asserted his right under the Copyright, Designs and Patents Act, 1988, to be identified as Author of this work.

All rights reserved. No part of this publication may be reproduced or transmitted in any form or by any means, electronic or mechanical, including photocopying, recording, or any information storage or retrieval system, without prior permission in writing from the publishers.

No responsibility for loss caused to any individual or organization acting on or refraining from action as a result of the material in this publication can be accepted by Bloomsbury or the author.

British Library Cataloguing-in-Publication Data
A catalogue record for this book is available from the British Library.

ISBN: HB: 978-0-56745-093-7
PB: 978-0-56722-227-5
ePub: 978-0-56762-851-0
ePDF: 978-0-56766-653-6

Library of Congress Cataloging-in-Publication Data
Names: Kiess, John.
Title: Hannah Arendt and theology / John Kiess.
Description: New York : T&T Clark Bloomsbury US, 2016. | Includes bibliographical references and index.
Identifiers: LCCN 2015024317 | ISBN 9780567450937 (hardback) | ISBN 9780567222275 (pbk.)
Subjects: LCSH: Arendt, Hannah, 1906–1975. | Philosophical theology.
Classification: LCC B945.A694 K54 2016 | DDC 191--dc23 LC record available at http://lccn.loc.gov/2015024317

Typeset by Fakenham Prepress Solutions, Fakenham, Norfolk NR21 8NN

For Austin—
Initium ut esset homo creatus est

CONTENTS

Acknowledgments ix
Abbreviations xi
Introduction 1

1 A Public Philosopher: The Life and Thought of Hannah Arendt 11
  I. Beginnings 13
  II. Philosophical Formation 16
  III. The Turn to the Political 22
  IV. "The Burden of Our Time" 27
  V. Thinking What We Are Doing 30
  VI. The Eichmann Controversy 35
  VII. *The Life of the Mind* 37

2 The Problem of Evil Reconsidered 51
  I. Radical Evil 55
  II. The Banality of Evil 63
  III. The Ironies of Thinking without Bannisters 72
  IV. The Fearful Imagination 80

3 *Amor Mundi*: Worldliness, Love, and Citizenship 95
  I. The Human Condition of Worldliness 99
  II. Christian Worldlessness? Arendt's Assessment of the Christian Legacy 106
  III. Contending with Arendt on Worldliness and Love 112

IV. Revisiting Arendt's Vision of *Amor Mundi* 119
V. "This-Worldliness" 125

4 **"That a Beginning Be Made": Natality, Action, and the Politics of Gratitude** 139
   I. The Human Condition of Natality 144
   II. Pearl Diving in the *City of God* 150
   III. Arendt's Theory of Action 157
   IV. Pelagianism Redux? 164
   V. Political Freedom and the Limits of Action 168
   VI. The Grace of Natality 176

5 **In the Region of the Spirit: Thinking Between Past and Future** 189
   I. "The Spark of Fire Between Two Flint Stones" 192
   II. The Activity of Thinking 198
   III. The Virtue of Thinking 202
   IV. The Location of Thinking 205
   V. Theology Between Past and Future 212

Bibliography 229
Index 239

ACKNOWLEDGMENTS

It is fitting that the first word in a book about Hannah Arendt should be gratitude. I am particularly grateful for the company of my colleagues in the Department of Theology at Loyola University Maryland: Frederick Bauerschmidt, Jim Buckley, Angela Christman, John Conley, David Decosimo, Rebekah Eklund, Steve Fowl, Claire Mathews McGinnis, Trent Pomplun, Joseph Rossi, and Arthur Sutherland. Many of them generously read parts of the manuscript, and all of them served as conversation partners at various stages of the writing of this book.

I also owe a debt of gratitude to the teachers who first introduced me to Arendt: Romand Coles, Joshua Foa Dienstag, and Stanley Hauerwas. Arendt's writings are an acquired taste, and I am not sure I would have ventured very deeply into her thought if it were not for their assurance that it would be worth it. They were right. I now have the privilege of sharing her work with students myself, and I am especially grateful to Loyola students who have helped me think through Arendt's views on evil, refugees, human rights, and many other topics. This is a better book because of them.

My understanding of Arendt has also benefitted from the rich and welcoming community of Arendt scholars. Parts of Chapter 3 were presented as "Hannah Arendt and the Politics of Immortality" at the Arendt Circle in March 2012. I am grateful for the comments of those gathered and for many subsequent conversations with participants. Thanks also to Lisa Stenmark, Deborah Galaski, and Mavis Biss, close readers of Arendt from whom I have learned much.

Parts of this project were funded with the generous assistance of a Loyola Summer Research Grant. Special thanks to Craig Hovey for alerting me to T&T Clark's Philosophy and Theology series and to Thomas Kraft, former Associate Editor, for his early interest in the book. Anna Turton has served as my editor throughout this project and has provided an unending supply of support and encouragement. Thanks also to Miriam Cantwell and Kim Storry for assistance in bringing the manuscript to press.

My thanks finally to family and friends who have journeyed with me throughout this project, including Eddie Howard, Nicole Hurd, Charles Marsh, Rydell Payne, Peter Slade, Sam Wells, and Matthew Whelan. Above all, I owe the greatest debt of gratitude to my wife, Ana. Arendt once wrote of her husband, Heinrich Blücher: "It is so seldom that people are able to help each other, mutually; but in our case I think it really is true that both of us would, without the other, scarcely have survived." Ana's generosity of spirit can be felt on every page of this book. She helped me sort through the ideas, find the words, and bring the project to completion. The book is as much a conversation with Ana as it is with Arendt, and I imagine Arendt herself would have envied my good fortune in being able to think alongside such a companion.

During this project we welcomed our first son, Austin. If the reader detects a little too much enthusiasm for Arendt's concept of natality in this book, I attribute that to his arrival. His presence has confirmed every grain of truth contained in those words of Augustine that Arendt was so fond of quoting: "that a beginning be made, man was created." This book is dedicated to him.

ABBREVIATIONS

BPF   *Between Past and Future.* New York: Penguin Books, 1977 [1st edn Viking Press, 1961].

CR   *Crises of the Republic.* New York: Harcourt Brace & Company, 1972.

EJ   *Eichmann in Jerusalem: A Report on the Banality of Evil.* New York: Penguin Books, 1977 [1st edn Viking Press, 1963].

EU   *Essays in Understanding, 1930-1954: Formation, Exile, and Totalitarianism.* Edited by Jerome Kohn. New York: Schocken Books, 1994.

HAKJ   *Hannah Arendt and Karl Jaspers: Correspondence, 1926–1969.* Edited by Lotte Kohler and Hans Saner. New York: Harcourt Brace & Company, 1992.

HC   *The Human Condition.* Chicago: University of Chicago Press, 1958.

JW   *The Jewish Writings.* Edited by Jerome Kohn and Ron H. Feldman. New York: Schocken Books, 2007.

KPP   *Lectures on Kant's Political Philosophy.* Edited by Ronald Beiner. Chicago: University of Chicago Press, 1982.

LMT   *The Life of the Mind*, vol. 1, *Thinking*. New York: Harcourt Brace Jovanovich, 1978.

LMW   *The Life of the Mind*, vol. 2, *Willing*. New York: Harcourt Brace Jovanovich, 1978.

LSA   *Love and Saint Augustine.* Edited by Joanna Vecchiarelli Scott and Judith Chelius Stark. Chicago: University of Chicago Press, 1996.

MDT	*Men in Dark Times.* New York: Harcourt Brace & Company, 1968.
OR	*On Revolution.* New York: Viking Press, 1963.
OT	*The Origins of Totalitarianism.* New York: Harcourt Brace Jovanovich, 1968 [1st edn 1951].
OV	*On Violence.* New York: Harcourt Brace & Company, 1970.
PP	*The Promise of Politics.* Edited by Jerome Kohn. New York: Schocken Books, 2005.
RJ	*Responsibility and Judgment.* Edited by Jerome Kohn. New York: Schocken Books, 2003.
RV	*Rahel Varnhagen: The Life of a Jewess.* Edited by Liliane Weissberg. Baltimore: Johns Hopkins University Press, 1997.

Introduction

The New Yorker's Adam Kirsch recently observed that Hannah Arendt's "scholarly and popular profile is higher today than at any time since she died ... It is hard to name another thinker of the twentieth century more sought after as a guide to the dilemmas of the twenty-first."[1] Arendt is relevant today for reasons as diverse as her rich and absorbing thought. Political theorists looking to reinvigorate democratic life in the face of an eroding public sphere are returning to her analyses of revolutions, resistance movements, and other forms of collective action. Scholars in international relations responding to terrorism, ethnonationalism, and new ideological movements are revisiting her arresting studies of totalitarianism and evil. Human rights activists are reexamining her eerily prescient reflections on refugees and statelessness to tame the sovereign prerogatives of nation-states and address shortcomings in their own attempts to defend the vulnerable. Debates surrounding civil liberties and the relation between the public and the private have made Arendt a conspicuous figure again in legal theory and feminist studies, and Arendt "the Jewish pariah" is as controversial today in Jewish thought and Holocaust studies as she was when her *Eichmann in Jerusalem* first ignited a firestorm in the 1960s.

It is a testament to the breadth of Arendt's thought that her work has found a growing audience in Christian theology as well. Theologians wrestling with the problem of evil in the modern age have found her insights into the moral psychology of perpetrators and the destructive potential of bureaucratic organization an essential resource for their own thinking. Several Augustinian theologians in particular have drawn attention to the parallels between Arendt's conception of the banality of evil and Augustine's account of evil as the privation of the good, suggesting that her thought demonstrates the ongoing relevance of a venerable, if largely misunderstood, tradition.[2] The recent publication of her doctoral dissertation on Augustine's concept of love has stimulated broader interest in Arendt as a reader of Augustine and reopened the question of his influence upon other areas of her thought (it was from Augustine that Arendt took her much-beloved phrase, "that a beginning be made, man was created").[3] Moral theologians have been drawn to Arendt as a guide in navigating the various challenges of modernity, from growing world-alienation to the triumph of instrumental rationality, while still others have found in her theory of action vital resources for church-based community organizing and other forms of democratic engagement.[4]

Yet not everyone is convinced that Arendt is such a reliable guide. She was, after all, a fierce critic of Christianity, famously tracing the roots of many of modernity's most disturbing pathologies to trends she believed were set in motion by Christian thinkers and practices. Theologians have come to Arendt's work not only eager to contest these claims, but to show how her misjudgments on these questions illumine troubling features of her own thought. They argue that her desire to maintain a sharp distinction between public and private leaves her inadequately attentive to questions of need and social justice.[5] They point to the worrying implications of her apparent rejection of love and goodness from politics and her ostensibly Nietzschean attempt to judge action solely on the basis of greatness of performance. And in appealing to such ideals as the Greek striving for immortality and the human capacity for spontaneity, they suggest she falls victim to precisely the Pelagian pride and optimism that Augustine and others warned against long ago.[6]

Thus Arendt's work is generating as much appreciation, criticism, and controversy in Christian theology as in other fields. Yet despite Arendt's rising profile, scholars and students of theology still only have a fragmentary picture of her work. Theological engagement with her thought remains selective, often concentrating upon one or two topics, leaving the connections between these and other themes unexplored—and thus potentially misunderstood. This has produced a rather muddled picture of Arendt herself. She is the faithful Augustinian on evil and natality but the anti-Augustinian on worldliness and neighbor-love; she is the political realist who can be cited in defense of the war on terror and the radical democrat who can help Christians envision local forms of nonviolent action.[7] It seems the higher Arendt's profile has risen, the more elusive she has become.[8]

There is a need for a fuller, more integrated picture of Hannah Arendt, one that situates her engagement with theology within the broader contours of her thought, and one that can help readers navigate the various responses her work has generated, as well as consider new directions in which it might be taken. The aim of this book is to provide that picture. It offers a comprehensive overview of her thought, surveying her major influences, the key political experiences that shaped her constructive outlook, the relationship between her various works, and the distinctive method that unites them. It proceeds to offer a close reading of four specific areas in which theological themes and thinkers figure prominently: evil, worldliness, natality, and the life of the mind.[9] Taking stock of how Arendt appropriates or criticizes theological perspectives in the course of developing original positions on these questions, it then considers how these areas of her work have been received in Christian theology, highlighting the chief points of agreement and contention, as well as offering fresh appraisals of her views where lingering confusion remains. In each of these four areas, I consider the unmet challenges of her work and how they can help set a constructive agenda for theology moving forward.

In Chapter 1, I begin with a survey of Arendt's life and thought, journeying from her philosophical formation in the 1920s to her final work, *The Life of the Mind*, which she was working on until her death in 1975. My chief aim is to trace the emergence of Arendt's distinctive intellectual voice and establish a sense for the overall shape of her work, to guide the more specific topical investigations that follow in subsequent chapters. I discuss the early influence of Martin Heidegger as well as her dissertation on Augustine, arguing that both thinkers remain important interlocutors throughout her career as she both appropriates and criticizes their work. I then consider the decisive impact of her experience of totalitarianism, which interrupts her budding academic career and thrusts her into a life of activism, reshaping her outlook and stirring a desire for a way of thinking more responsive to the formidable challenges of her times. In the course of discussing her years as a stateless person in Paris, I emphasize the significance of her friendship with Walter Benjamin, whose notion of "pearl diving" helps to shed considerable light upon Arendt's method of textual criticism and appropriation. I then show how Arendt's investigations into totalitarianism inform her major political works of the 1950s and early 1960s, where she makes her signature appeals to the importance of inhabiting the "gap between past and future" and "thinking what we are doing." Nowhere is the public impact of such thinking more evident than in the controversy generated by her coverage of the Eichmann trial in 1961, at the center of which was her account of Eichmann as a banal, thoughtless bureaucrat, confounding conventional assumptions about the nature of evil. It is this connection between evil and thoughtlessness that leads to her later work on "thinking," which I explore in the final section of the survey and show how it relates to her accounts of willing and judging.

With a sense for the overall shape of Arendt's thought, I then turn to more in-depth investigations of her engagement with theological themes and thinkers, beginning with the area that is most well-known to her Christian readers—her writings on evil. As mentioned above, this area of Arendt's work has attracted widespread interest among Augustinian theologians who see important parallels between Arendt's concept of the banality of evil and Augustine's account of evil as the privation of the good. This has led some to suggest that Arendt can fruitfully be read as a modern representative of the Augustinian tradition on evil. Yet standing in the way of such a reading are Arendt's own strong claims about the limits of tradition in accounting for the specific evil of totalitarianism. Throughout her writings on evil, Arendt consistently maintains that totalitarianism "broke" the thread of tradition and could not be understood through any traditional categories, moral, legal, or theological. Thus what initially appears to be an area of convergence turns out to be an area of considerable tension. Yet as I argue in Chapter 2, this is ultimately a fruitful tension, as it invites a deeper conversation about the nature of tradition and its capacity to meet the challenge of evil in the modern era. At one level, I argue that Arendt was right: she points to dimensions of totalitarianism that were genuinely unprecedented, and in this sense holds up an important challenge for theologians to reflect upon and respond to the unique features of evil in any age. Yet at another level, Arendt inadvertently confirms the ongoing relevance of many features of the Augustinian account, belying her own claims about the irrelevance of traditional approaches. Arendt's disavowals of tradition appear to be based upon a rather static conception of tradition, one that is incapable of change or innovation. I argue that this is hardly the only way to conceive tradition, and that her own writings effectively model what tradition-based innovation can look like. I conclude that we do not have to accept Arendt's rejection of tradition to take up her important challenge to discern the distinctive marks of evil today and marshal creative responses to them, a challenge I take up in the final section of the chapter.

One of the most haunting lessons that Arendt took away from her studies of evil and her specific analysis of the concentration camps was that some of our most basic features and capacities as human beings are not simply given but contingent upon certain conditions which totalitarianism proved more than capable of destroying. The deprivations of the camps, as well as the broader plight of refugees, taught Arendt the particular importance of "worldliness," or membership in an enduring, common world. In Chapter 3, I explore her vision of worldly belonging and the civic virtue she holds up as vital for sustaining it: *amor mundi*, or love for the world. An area of her work that offers a number of suggestive resources for thinking about the deeper conditions that sustain democratic life, it is also where we encounter some of Arendt's strongest criticisms of the Christian tradition. I focus upon her specific criticisms of Augustine, whose commitment to the love of God she takes to enjoin an instrumental outlook on the world, and whose appeals to charity she believes reduce politics to a narrow focus upon meeting basic needs, to the neglect of fostering structures of more enduring worldly permanence. I review how Augustinians have responded to these claims and the shortcomings they reveal about Arendt's own account, especially the costs of her premature dismissal of a variety of forms of love from politics. Yet the fact that Arendt continues to frame her own vision in terms of *amor mundi* will invite further investigation into her views on the relationship between love and citizenship. I show how she not only criticizes Augustine, but also carries forward certain core Augustinian commitments, including the assumption that the world is a product of our loves, as well as his critique of inordinate self-love. I go on to argue that when we look at the actual substance of *amor mundi* as she lays it out in her writings on education, culture, and the needs of the stateless, it entails a vision of citizenship rooted in everyday practices of care, which I compare to Sheldon Wolin's notion of "tending." While falling short of the love of God and neighbor, *amor mundi* is not the same as the love of self that defines the earthly city, and in this sense Arendt raises the possibility of a civic virtue that Augustine appears to have overlooked, a non-possessive outlook that sustains the world in a manner consistent with its fragility. I conclude by considering how the church can contribute to the democratic task of world-building, both by serving as a worldly space itself and by partnering with other institutions to extend the common world to those denied a place within it.

In Chapter 4, I turn to what is arguably Arendt's most original contribution to political thought, her concept of natality. For Arendt, natality refers most broadly to the human condition of birth, but it also has a close association with the faculty of action, which she frames as our capacity to make new beginnings. It is in this area that Arendt draws most widely and appreciatively from theological sources, convinced that her own political tradition has arbitrarily excluded the political insights of religious figures and texts on account of their "allegedly exclusively religious character." In laying out her theory of action, we see her appealing to the Genesis account of creation, the Abrahamic notion of covenant, and Jesus' teachings on forgiveness. If in her writings on worldliness Arendt remained wary of Augustine's love of God, here she finds in his creation theology a powerful ontological basis for supporting the view that each human being is a beginner, routinely citing the passage from the *City of God* mentioned above, "that a beginning be made, man was created." Appreciative as Arendt may have been of theological sources in this area of her work, readers in Christian theology have generally approached these writings with caution. As Charles Mathewes sees it, the basic link that Arendt establishes between natality and action, with its humanistic overtures to the seemingly limitless capacity for new beginnings and spontaneity, sounds less like Augustine than the Pelagianism he rejected. Yet when we trace Arendt's concept of natality to its roots in her dissertation on Augustine and her biography of Rahel Varnhagen, a more complex picture emerges. We see that the question of beginnings also has to do with how birth limits our existence, and how we come to terms with all the things that we do not choose but are given to us. Under totalitarianism the question of natality for Arendt becomes an intensely personal wrestling with her own Jewishness, and how one retains the freedom to act when differences of birth have become the basis of one's exclusion. In her mature work, the relationship between action and natality remains the central lens through which she explores the tension between our freedom and our conditionedness, as she frames action as the process through which we acknowledge, disclose, and re-discover our unique identities in the company of others. In shifting the traditional focus in political theory from mortality to natality, Arendt provides a set of rich resources for re-envisioning politics as the discipline of remaining opening to the unexpected, the fruitfulness for a politics of grace I explore in the chapter's conclusion.

In Chapter 5, I turn to an area of Arendt's thought that has received less attention in Christian theology, her later work on thinking. Arendt had been preoccupied with the question of thinking her entire life, but the connection between evil and thoughtlessness that she observed in Eichmann renewed a desire to follow up her account of the active life in *The Human Condition* with a sequel that would deal with the life of the mind and bring the various strands of her work together. Taking as her point of departure an elusive quote from Cato, "Never is he more active than when he does nothing, never is he less alone than when he is by himself," Arendt conceives thinking as the inner dialogue with the self, made possible by the fact that in solitude, we are not simply one, but "two-in-one." Arendt's model for such thinking is Socrates, who, rather than attempt to transform thinking into a way of life, a *bios theoretikos*, remains a "citizen among citizens," equally at home in action and thought, with his questions generated by the experiences of those around him. Such engaged thinking subjects unexamined opinions to scrutiny, "unfreezing" concepts and narrowing the distance between our minds and reality. Arendt's most absorbing reflections come when she turns to the "time" of thinking, which, as mentioned above, she frames in terms of the gap between past and future, a gap that cannot be inherited but must be taken up by each new generation as their own. I consider what such a vision of thinking might mean for the task of theology, following up on leads that Arendt herself provides (the active searching of medieval meditation, the dialogical character of Augustine's *Confessions*), as well as considering parallels in more recent theological movements such as *ressourcement* theology, which likewise seeks to leverage the resources of the past in responding to the challenges of the modern age.

Arendt is sought after as a guide for many reasons today, but as I hope will become clear in the pages that follow, what is most timely and compelling is not any one position or reading that she gives us, but her overall model as a thinker—the disciplines she bridged, the multiple audiences for which she wrote, and above all, the responsiveness of her thought to the major crises of her century. Her reflections on evil arose out of a meticulous historical investigation of totalitarian government, a searing analysis of the concentration camps, and the concrete discipline of attending the trial of one of the chief architects of the Holocaust; her writings on the plight of refugees emerged out of her own experience as a stateless Jew and the intimate knowledge of what it is to be denied a place in the world; and her theory of action was born from events such as the Hungarian Revolution and French Resistance and the inspiration of such individuals as Rosa Luxemburg and Anton Schmidt. This is why we read Arendt. We read her because we sense something vital in her voice, something not only daring, but profoundly invested in healing divides between theory and practice, between the rulers and the ruled, a voice that is eminently public and engaged, which enlivened existing debates and launched entirely new ones, many of which continue to this day. She is the conversation partner charitable enough to inhabit our traditions and yet honest enough to voice criticisms that demand we rearticulate our most basic assumptions and advance positions worthy of our deepest beliefs. Most of all, she is the intellectual companion who challenges us not to be content merely to repeat what our predecessors have said but to do the thinking that our predecessors now demand of us. This book is an attempt to take up that invitation. It extends that invitation to its readers, which is Arendt's abiding challenge to all of us.

Notes

1 Adam Kirsch, "Beware of Pity: Hannah Arendt and the Power of the Impersonal," *The New Yorker*, January 12, 2009, 62–4.

2 See, for example, Jean Bethke Elshtain, "Augustine's Evil, Arendt's Eichmann," in *Augustine and the Limits of Politics* (South Bend, IN: University of Notre Dame Press, 1998), 69–87, and Charles T. Mathewes, *Evil and the Augustinian Tradition* (Cambridge: Cambridge University Press, 2001).

3 See Joanna Vecchiarelli Scott and Judith Chelius Stark, eds., *Love and Saint Augustine* (Chicago: University of Chicago Press); Stephan Kampowski, *Arendt, Augustine, and the New Beginning: The Action Theory and Moral Thought of Hannah Arendt in the Light of Her Dissertation on St. Augustine* (Grand Rapids, MI: Eerdmans, 2008); and John von Heyking, *Augustine and Politics as Longing in the World* (Columbia, MO: University of Missouri Press, 2001), 9–12.

4 On Arendt's relevance for navigating modernity, see Michael S. Northcott, *A Moral Climate: The Ethics of Global Warming* (Mary Knoll, NY: Orbis Books, 2007), 45–156, and Bernd Wannenwetsch, *Political Worship* (Oxford: Oxford University Press, 2004), 207–18. On the relevance of Arendt's theory of action for radical democracy and community organizing, see Stanley Hauerwas and Romand Coles, *Christianity, Democracy, and the Radical Ordinary* (Eugene, OR: Cascade Books, 2008) and Luke Bretherton, *Christianity and Contemporary Politics* (Oxford: Blackwell, 2010).

5 See Thomas Breidenthal, "Jesus is My Neighbor: Arendt, Augustine, and the Politics of the Incarnation," *Modern Theology* 14:4 (October 1998): 489–503, and Eric Gregory, *Politics and the Order of Love* (Chicago: University of Chicago Press, 2008), 197–240.

6 For a critique of her appeals to immortality, see Rowan Williams, "Politics and the Soul," *Milltown Studies* 19/20 (1987): 55–72. On the potential dangers of Pelagianism in her account of action, see Mathewes, *Evil and the Augustinian Tradition*, 149–97.

7 In *Just War Against Terror* (New York: Basic Books, 2004), Jean Bethke Elshtain observes that in response to those who would minimize the threat posed by terrorism, "Hannah Arendt would have had a sharp retort. 'Politics is not the nursery,' she liked to say. Practicing a reasonableness based on the calculations of the 'humanist' world of infinite negotiation and 'logical' explanation is often of little use in helping us to face harsh evidence before our eyes. Moreover, naiveté—including the conviction that horrific

events are momentary setbacks and will surely be brought to heel by 'reasonable' persons (who shrink from speaking of evil)—can get thousands of innocents killed" (2). On Arendt's relevance for sustaining local, nonviolent forms of politics, see Hauerwas and Coles, *Christianity, Democracy, and the Radical Ordinary*, 6, 54, 304.

8   In *Politics, Philosophy, Terror: Essays on the Thought of Hannah Arendt* (Princeton: Princeton University Press, 1999), Dana Villa observes a similar phenomenon in other disciplines, noting a "dizzying proliferation of Arendts, some familiar (the civic republican Arendt), some novel (the Habermasian Arendt; the postmodern Arendt), some revisionist (the feminist Arendt), and some more than a little ironic (the empathic Arendt). Of course, the writings of any great thinker generate numerous and conflicting interpretations ... But there is clearly something specific to Arendt's writing which invites creative interpretation and (just as often) misinterpretation" (4).

9   While I take these areas to be most central to her thought as a whole, an exhaustive study of the question of her relationship to theological sources is beyond the scope of this book. For more on this relationship, see Mara Willard, "'Recasting the Old Questions': Theological Reliance and Renunciation in the Political Thought of Hannah Arendt" (Ph.D. diss., Harvard University, 2011); Susannah Young-ah Gottlieb, *Regions of Sorrow: Anxiety and Messianism in Hannah Arendt and W.H. Auden* (Stanford: Stanford University Press, 2003), 135–60; and Mavis Louise Biss, "Arendt and the Theological Significance of Natality," *Philosophy Compass* 7/11 (2012): 762–71. On Arendt's relationship to Jewish thought more generally, see Richard Bernstein, *Hannah Arendt and the Jewish Question* (Cambridge: MIT Press, 1996).

1

A Public Philosopher: The Life and Thought of Hannah Arendt

When asked to describe her role among the philosophers during a 1964 interview, Hannah Arendt famously replied: "I am afraid I have to protest. I do not belong to the circle of philosophers ... I neither feel like a philosopher, nor do I believe that I have been accepted in the circle of philosophers ... I have said good-bye to philosophy once and for all" (EU 1–2).[1] In the 1920s, she had studied philosophy under Martin Heidegger and Karl Jaspers, the two most prominent representatives of the phenomenological school of German philosophy, but abandoned her promising academic career in 1933, when the rise of the Nazi regime forced her to flee to Paris and later the United States. Disillusioned with philosophy after seeing so many of her intellectual acquaintances collaborate with the Nazis, including most infamously Heidegger himself, Arendt turned to a life of activism. She worked for the German-Zionist movement, spearheaded efforts to recover Jewish cultural objects scattered during WWII, served as a journalist for *Aufbau* (a German-language newspaper for Jews), and later became an editor at Schocken books. Arendt's first major book, *The Origins of Totalitarianism*, a historical study of anti-Semitism, imperialism, and totalitarian domination, marked her return to academic scholarship in 1951, but she would remain largely an outsider in academic circles, never settling into any permanent intellectual home.² Instead, she held a number of visiting professorships, lectured widely, and wrote for such periodicals as *The Review for Politics* and *The New Yorker*. The books for which she is most famous—*The Human Condition, On Revolution, Between Past and Future,* and *Eichmann in Jerusalem*—defy easy classification or genre, serving as largely unsystematic attempts to wrestle with specific political events as they occurred. The common thread tying these projects together was Arendt's sense that the events and major trends of the twentieth century, whether totalitarianism itself, the advent of nuclear warfare, or revolutions in science and technology, threatened our very capacity to think and speak about them. "Wherever the relevance of speech is at stake," she wrote, "matters become political by definition, for speech is what makes man a political being" (HC 3). For Arendt, no task was more politically urgent than "to think what we are doing," to try to reconcile ourselves to realities that increasingly outpace our ability to comprehend.

This, evidently, was not "philosophy." She preferred to characterize her thinking as political theory, which she believed was based, as Margaret Canovan summarizes, "on the authentically political experience of acting among others" rather than "the experience of the philosopher, who thinks in solitude and then has to cope with an uncomprehending world when he emerges from his reflections."³ Surveying her works, this distinction seems largely to hold, yet there is at least one dimension of Arendt's thinking that suggests she remained a philosopher at heart—namely, that her thinking began where all philosophy begins: in wonder. She frequently quotes with approval the words Plato voices through Socrates in the *Theaetetus*: "For this is chiefly the passion of the philosopher, to wonder. There is no other beginning of philosophy than this one" (PP 32).⁴ She explains that for Plato and his followers, wonder or *thaumazein* was no mere puzzlement or ignorance to be cured through learning. It was a *pathos*, something suffered, an inexhaustible, speechless awe experienced at the perception of the invisible harmony behind appearances that could only be translated "in unending variations [of] what we call the ultimate questions—What is being? Who is man? What meaning has life? What is death? etc.—all of which have in common that they cannot be answered scientifically" (33). The problem, as Arendt saw it, is that philosophy as a discipline has traditionally withheld this wonder from the realm of human affairs. While philosophers certainly wondered at Man in the singular, they rarely wondered at men and women in their plurality. Yet speechlessness was exactly the sensation that Arendt felt when she turned her attention to the major events of her lifetime, a speechlessness prompted not only by the ingenuity and daring manifested in revolutions, acts of civil disobedience, and technological innovations, but also the horror of the concentration camps, the slaughter of the world wars, and the specter of nuclear annihilation. "For the speechless horror at what man may do and what the world may become," she wrote in 1954, "is in many ways related to the speechless wonder of gratitude from which the questions of philosophy spring" (EU 445). Arendt's questions sprang from both, from the horror at what human beings can destroy and the wonder at what they can create. This made her a philosopher, but it made her a very different kind of philosopher: one whose thinking arose from events that transpired in the public realm, and whose thinking helped enrich and ennoble that realm. In rare moments, we hear Arendt herself expressing a longing for a different kind of political philosophy. This, she says, is what it would look like:

> Philosophy, political philosophy like all its other branches will never be able to deny its origins in *thaumazein*, in the wonder at that which is as it is. If philosophers, despite their necessary estrangement from the everyday life of human affairs, were ever to arrive at a true political philosophy, they would have to make the plurality of man, out of which arises the whole realm of human affairs—in its grandeur and misery—the object of their *thaumazein*. (PP 38)

That is what Arendt set out to do.

I. Beginnings

Hannah Arendt was born in 1906, in Hanover, Germany.[5] She spent most of her childhood in Königsberg, the former capital of East Prussia and birthplace of Immanuel Kant. Arendt would later say that when she sat down to write, she felt as if Kant was "looking over her shoulder."[6] She devoured the *Critique of Pure Reason* at the age of fourteen and named Kant as one of her early inspirations for studying philosophy. Although critical of his work in many places, she continued to return to Kant throughout her career, developing his concept of radical evil in her work on totalitarianism, appropriating his notion of the "enlarged mentality" for her thinking on political judgment, and structuring her final work around a version of his tripartite division of mental faculties, thinking, willing, and judging.

During the nineteenth century, Königsberg served as an important refuge for Jews fleeing persecution in Russia, and Arendt's maternal great-grandfather arrived in 1851. He established a successful tea-trading company that supported the family until WWI.[7] Arendt's father died when she was young, leaving her mother to raise her on her own. Growing up, Arendt remembers lively conversations about socialism and German politics, but little talk about Jewish identity or religion. "My mother was completely a-religious," she recalls. "My grandfather was the president of the liberal Jewish community and a civil official of Königsberg. Nevertheless, the word 'Jew' never came up when I was a small child. I first met up with it through anti-Semitic remarks—they are not worth repeating—from children on the street. After that I was, so to speak, 'enlightened'" (EU 6).

When a teacher made similarly offensive remarks during her teenage years, Arendt organized a boycott of his classes and was promptly expelled.[8] Her mother arranged for her to audit classes for two terms at the University of Berlin, and a wider world opened up to her. She studied Greek and Latin, read widely in poetry and psychology, and eventually found her way to the lecture hall of Romano Guardini, a leading Catholic theologian whose eclectic interests ranged from Bonaventure and Dante to Kierkegaard and Dostoevsky.[9] Some of the brightest religious minds of the twentieth century would pass through this same lecture hall, including Josef Pieper and Hans Urs von Balthasar. They would each be exposed to a lively, existentialist brand of Christianity conversant with other disciplines that was critical both of the reigning school of Neo-Scholasticism and the growing anomie of modern technological society.[10] For the young Arendt, this vision struck a chord, enough to inspire her to study theology at Marburg University in 1924.

There she studied under Rudolf Bultmann, the noted New Testament scholar whose own theological outlook was shaped by existentialism.[11] Yet if existentialism manifested itself in Guardini in the form of a socially conscious, outward-facing Christianity, it took the form of an inward, demythologized Christianity in Bultmann. In a later letter to Karl Jaspers, Arendt summarized her disappointment, noting that demythologization effectively reduced Christianity to "a radicalized Paulinism" and exhibited "an exclusive regard for the functional and a pushing aside of the real 'substance'" (HAKJ 221). "Jesus," she went on to write, "remains interesting only in his function within God's work of salvation on earth, not as a 'preacher' who says: You should or should not do this or that" (221). Arendt's criticisms of Bultmann anticipate what will become a familiar pattern in her later writings: a general sympathy for Jesus and those who aspired to live like him, and an impatience with Christian thinkers who ventured too far from his call to action. In her remarks to the Society of Christian Ethics near the end of her life, Arendt observed:

> I told you I am not a Christian ... [but] I may feel a loyalty to Jesus, because that is indeed an example, what Jesus did, and his whole life, the *logoi*, and all the stories, this can indeed become an example. That is, as he said when someone asked, "What should I do?" he said, "Come on and follow me."[12]

No one in her lifetime took this call more seriously, she believed, than Pope John XXIII, one of the figures she features in *Men in Dark Times*. "I think Luther once said: the word of Jesus still makes the world shake. And this shaking I felt very directly when Roncalli was Pope."[13]

But Arendt's future in theology was not to be. Back in Marburg, word was spreading about a young professor who had recently arrived in the philosophy department. Curiously, he had not written anything of consequence, but his name traveled "like the rumor of the hidden king."[14] His name was Martin Heidegger.

II. Philosophical Formation

Looking back on her time in Marburg, Arendt remembers a general dissatisfaction among her peers with the reigning philosophical schools and areas of study. As she put it, they had heard enough talk "*about* philosophy" and wanted to learn how to *think* philosophically.[15] Heidegger, the rumor had it, could teach them how. She writes:

> The rumor about Heidegger put it quite simply: Thinking has come to life again; the cultural treasures of the past, believed to be dead, are being made to speak, in the course of which it turns out that they propose things altogether different from the familiar, worn-out trivialities they had been presumed to say. There exists a teacher; one can perhaps learn to think.[16]

In the 1924/25 winter semester, Arendt followed the rumor to Heidegger's seminar on Plato's *Sophist* and was quickly converted to the study of philosophy.

The question of Heidegger's influence upon Arendt's thinking is one of the most contentious issues in Arendt scholarship, no doubt complicated by the fact that he was not only her teacher but, for a time, her lover.[17] In the seminars that Arendt attended, Heidegger was working through material that would eventually become *Being and Time*, and several aspects of this project would prove to have a lasting impact upon Arendt. Foremost among these was Heidegger's sweeping critique of the Western philosophical tradition. *Being and Time* famously begins with the claim that the question of the meaning of being has been "forgotten," buried under the weight of a metaphysical tradition that failed, in his view, to theorize existence as it is actually lived in time.[18] While Arendt's interests would eventually draw her away from metaphysics to political philosophy, there is a striking similarity in the way she conceived her own project: she too believed a fundamental question had been forgotten, not the meaning of being, but the meaning of action, and she also emphasized the importance of breaking the hold of traditional categories over our thinking. For her, like Heidegger, this did not mean abandoning the past, but learning to look upon the past with "new eyes," to discover the original spirit behind concepts and to read thinkers against the grain of their traditional interpretation.[19] Heidegger's influence is felt most strongly in *The Human Condition*, where Arendt applies his phenomenological method to describe the existential grounds of political life. She acknowledges her debt to him in a letter written shortly after its publication, noting that the book "grew right out of the first days in Marburg and so is in all respects indebted to you."[20]

The circumstances surrounding Arendt's affair with Heidegger prevented her from continuing her studies in Marburg, and in 1925 she relocated to Heidelberg to write her dissertation under Karl Jaspers, another key figure in the German phenomenological tradition and someone who became an important mentor and lifelong friend.[21] She wrote on the problem of love in Augustine. That Arendt would choose to write on Augustine is not entirely surprising, given her interest in theology and his popularity in philosophy departments at the time.[22] He was a particularly logical choice for Arendt because in his thought converged two of her main interests: the social teachings of Jesus, particularly his command to love the neighbor, and her more recent interest in the impact of Greek categories upon the Western metaphysical tradition. Indeed, as she saw it, there was no other thinker in whom the tension between the two was greater.

The dissertation is a fascinating document on many levels: as a glimpse into a young, developing thinker, a window into the influence of Heidegger and Augustine, and a lens for understanding Arendt's own views on the significance of the dissertation for her later thinking.[23] On the latter point, Arendt actually returned to the dissertation in the 1960s with the intention of publishing an English version, only to insert a number of revisions, including some key terminology from her mature thought. Her coverage of the Eichmann trial prevented her from completing the project, but her revisions provide revealing insight into what she made of the work many years later.

As mentioned above, Arendt's dissertation is a study in tension. Specifically, she sought to understand how Augustine reconciles his lingering debts to Greek thought, especially the otherworldly imperatives of Neoplatonism, with his commitment to Christianity's this-worldly command to love thy neighbor.

In the introduction, she states that her aim is not to offer "an absolute critique from some fixed philosophical or theological standpoint" (LSA 3), but rather an immanent critique, one that asks how well Augustine succeeds in accounting for the relevance of the neighbor given the overriding priority that he assigns to the eternal. Acknowledging that Augustine does not work with a single concept of love, but several, Arendt proposes to consider the relevance of the neighbor from the vantage point of three different conceptions of love. In the first part of the dissertation, she considers love as *appetitus*, or craving, the most Neoplatonic of the loves that inform Augustine's thinking. *Appetitus* is a future oriented love, grasping for what one does not yet possess. The problem that vexes appetitive love is not so much whether one will obtain the object, but once having attained it, how to deal with the fear of losing it. The only antidote to such fear is the promise of an object that cannot be lost, which for Augustine, as for the Neoplatonists, is the eternal. It is love for the eternal that stills our fears and finally satisfies the craving of *appetitus*. Yet as Arendt sees it, this serenity is purchased at a high cost, for it requires that one adopt an instrumental outlook with respect to everything else, including the neighbor. Referring to his well-known use/enjoyment distinction, Arendt writes: "The love for my neighbor is at best a secondary consideration for a desire whose aim transcends mankind and the world, both of which have a justifiable existence only to the extent that they can be 'used' for the sake of something that is radically different and separated from them" (41).

In the second part of the dissertation, she attempts to ground the relevance of the neighbor in another conceptual context, where love is conceived in the more explicitly theological terms of the creature's love for the Creator. Yet here, she says, we run into similar problems. This love, which requires that "we deny both ourselves and the world" (95), severs the ties that connect us to the neighbor:

> The lover reaches beyond the beloved to God in whom alone both his existence and his love have meaning ... No individual means anything in comparison with this identical source. The Christian can thus love all people because each one is only an occasion, and that occasion can be everyone. (96–7)

This leaves Arendt wondering how "another person can still be considered our neighbor, that is, as someone specifically connected to us," given that one does not love the neighbor "in the concrete and worldly encounter with him," but rather only "in his createdness" (95). She attempts a final solution in the third part of the dissertation, where she examines love construed as the social bond shared between sinners in history, but even here the importance of the neighbor is relativized, as we come to love him or her only in their generic condition as sinner redeemed through grace, not in his or her particularity: "I never love my neighbor for his own sake, only for the sake of divine grace ... This indirectness turns my relation to my neighbor into a mere passage for the direct relation to God himself" (111). Exhausted by the end of the study, Arendt finds herself unable to resolve the tensions and concludes: "We must let the contradictions stand as they are" (7).

In later chapters we will have an opportunity to assess Arendt's reading of Augustine in greater detail, as several theologians have taken issue with her understanding of how the love of God operates in his thought. But for the moment, my primary interest is what the dissertation reveals about this stage of her thinking. One can detect the clear influence of Heidegger in its phenomenological method, suspicion of the corrupting effects of Greek thought, and emphasis upon the future as a condition of our finitude. There are, however, signs scattered throughout the work that suggest that her encounter with Augustine helped her perceive some shortcomings in her teacher's thought and launch some important trajectories of her own.[24]

The first such sign is the structure of the dissertation itself, which moves from the familiar Heideggerian territory of desire and death in the first part to the role of remembrance and creation in the second part. Heidegger famously frames our temporal situation as one determined by the expectation of death, yet in turning to the role of memory, we see Arendt exploring how our finitude is also conditioned by the past. In a paragraph inserted into the revised dissertation, she distinguishes Augustine's approach from Heidegger's on this point: "Since our expectations and desires are prompted by what we remember and guided by a previous knowledge, it is memory and not expectation (for instance, the expectation of death as in Heidegger's approach) that gives unity and wholeness to human existence" (56). "What ultimately stills the fear of death," she observes earlier, "is not hope or desire, but remembrance and gratitude" (52). This emphasis upon remembrance and taking stock of our beginnings anticipates what will become one of her most original contributions to political thought, her concept of natality.[25] As she develops this theme in her mature work, she will repeatedly return to Augustine and credit him with the discovery of the importance of beginnings in its "full significance" (EU 321). In addition to the connection between birth and remembrance, she will expand the concept to include the capacity to make new beginnings, which becomes an important part of her action theory. In *The Human Condition*, Arendt names this as another point of difference between her and Heidegger: "since action is the political activity par excellence, natality, and not mortality, may be the central category of political, as distinguished from metaphysical, thought" (HC 9).

If Arendt's initial encounter with Augustine gave her resources for challenging Heidegger's preoccupation with death, it also gave her tools for critiquing some of the more individualistic strands of his thinking. In a 1946 essay entitled, "What is Existential Philosophy?", Arendt argues that for all of Heidegger's emphasis upon historicity, worldliness, and being-with-others, the picture of the self that emerges is surprisingly isolated.[26] Heidegger's *Dasein* anxiously looks ahead to his own death, which is his alone to bear, and seeks to maintain authenticity against a world constantly threatening to encroach upon his projects. Augustine may have been ambivalent about worldly belonging, but he was deeply attuned to the inherently social character of human existence. In the final part of the dissertation on social life, we see Arendt drawing attention to the many ties that bind us to others, from our different loves to our various historical solidarities, challenging the illusion that we ever act as completely isolated individuals. In her later work, Arendt will speak of this in terms of her concept of "plurality," which refers both to the fact of human difference and the way in which our being in the world is always conditioned by the presence of others. As mentioned earlier, Arendt sought to move political philosophy away from a narrow focus upon the individual to a consideration of human beings in the plural. As she liked to say, "Men, not Man, inhabit the earth." To begin from plurality was to appreciate that our actions are never self-contained, but reverberate into a wider "web of human relationships," which is what lends our deeds both their fragility and great power—another key note in her later theory of action.

Impressed by these early and lasting debts to Augustine, some scholars have spoken of an "Augustinian root" to Arendt's thought.[27] As we will see, Augustine is indeed a pervasive presence in Arendt's writings, someone to whose work subsequent events will cause her to return again and again.[28] He will feature not only in her account of natality and plurality, but also in her response to totalitarianism, her theory of action, her concept of freedom, and her reflections on willing. The core Augustinian temporal imagery of being located "between past and future" plays a foundational role for how she understands our experience of finitude and the specific relationship between thinking and time. As we will discuss in the next chapter, some see strong parallels, if not a direct influence, in her writings on evil as well. At the same time, while Arendt considered Augustine her "old friend" and praised him as "the last to know at least what it once meant to be a citizen" (HC 14) and the "only philosopher the Romans ever had" (LMW 84), she maintained her distance. She continued to express deep reservations about the instrumentalizing effects of his *amor dei* and eventually extended these worries to neighbor-love itself. These points come to play an important role in her much broader critique of Western philosophy and the impact of the Christian tradition upon the way we think about politics.

Thus, as with Heidegger, Arendt appropriated and criticized elements of Augustine's work with the same spirit of independence that will mark her engagement with many other thinkers, including Aristotle, Marx, Nietzsche, Jaspers, and Benjamin. Below I will have more to say about her unique method of textual criticism and appropriation, but for now, it is important to stress that while Arendt was influenced by Heidegger and Augustine, she was neither "Heidegger's child" nor "Augustine's faithful daughter," as some have argued.[29] Such readings underplay not only the important differences between these thinkers, but the decisive impact of Arendt's later experience of totalitarianism, to which I now want to turn.

III. The Turn to the Political

Following the defense and publication of her dissertation in 1929, Arendt received a prestigious fellowship to study German Romanticism, with an eye to making this the subject of her *Habilitationschrift*.[30] Her research eventually focused around the figure of Rahel Varnhagen, a late eighteenth/early nineteenth-century Jewish salon hostess who spent a lifetime trying to assimilate to German society only to utter these final words, "The thing which all my life seemed to me the greatest shame, which was the misery and misfortune of my life—having been born a Jewess—this I should on no account now wish to have missed" (RV 85).[31] If Arendt's encounter with Augustine prompted her to reflect upon the general significance of beginnings, her study of Varnhagen challenged her to wrestle with the more specific question of her Jewish origins, planting the seeds for what would become another significant layer of her concept of natality. The Varnhagen study also challenged her to revisit the question of worldly belonging. If her worry in the dissertation was the risk of becoming so detached from the world that it becomes a desert, Varnhagen's journey revealed that there is a certain advantage to remaining an outsider, a "pariah" who does not assimilate on society's unjust terms.[32] Broadly academic questions prior to 1933, both would now become intensely personal ones.

In the interview mentioned at the outset of this chapter, Arendt was asked if she could date her turn to the political. She responded with an exact day: February 27, 1933, the burning of the Reichstag (EU 4).[33] "That was an immediate shock for me," she said, not because it revealed anything new about the Nazis, but because the general political situation had become "a personal fate" (10)—a striking admission from a thinker famous for unfashionably insisting upon a separation between the personal and political.[34] Being Jewish "had become my own problem, and my own problem was political" (12). Intensifying the personal nature of the problem was the fact that so many of her intellectual acquaintances were collaborating with the Nazis, including Heidegger, who had recently joined the Nazi party and now enjoyed the position of rector at Freiburg University. Arendt recalls, "The problem, the personal problem, was not what our enemies did but what our friends did" (10–11). From that moment on, she remembers, "I felt responsible" (5).

Resolving to act, she put her intellectual gifts to work for her friend Kurt Blumenfeld, a leader in the German Zionist movement.[35] Blumenfeld asked her to document cases of anti-Semitism in professional clubs and other civil society groups, work for which the previously apolitical Arendt was ideally suited because she would not arouse any suspicion. At least for a time. Before long the Gestapo caught on and arrested her, detaining her in a Berlin jail for eight days. Arendt managed to persuade an officer to let her go, but she knew she could not count upon such good fortune in the future. Upon her release, she made immediate arrangements to leave the country.

She and her mother left Germany illegally through the Czech Republic and eventually settled in Paris.[36] For the next eighteen years, Arendt would live as one of the millions of stateless persons whom she later described in *The Origins of Totalitarianism* as "the most symptomatic group in contemporary politics" (OT 277), having "no government to represent and to protect them" (269) and for whom "the rules of the world around them had ceased to apply" (267). Arendt learned firsthand that to be deprived of citizenship entails more than the loss of individual liberties; it is "first and above all ... the deprivation of a place in the world which makes opinions significant and actions effective" (296). To be "worldless," she discovered, was to lack those basic conditions that allow us to appear before one another as distinct individuals; it is to lose the basic social texture in which the moral claim of our lives becomes intelligible to others. Arendt had come to appreciate what would become one of her most enduring insights into the paradoxical nature of human rights: that the moment one is stripped of citizenship and becomes nothing but a human being, one effectively has no rights at all, given that there is no framework in which these rights are binding and no one who feels obligated to enforce them.[37] What the stateless lack, Arendt discovered, is not individual rights, but "the right to have rights," the right to "a community willing and able to guarantee any rights whatsoever" (297).

In Paris, Arendt found employment as a social worker for an organization called Youth Aliyah, which prepared Jewish children to emigrate to Palestine.[38] She also found pockets of community among her fellow pariahs, especially those German émigrés who, like herself, fell outside the academic mainstream. Among them was the playwright Bertolt Brecht, whose language of "dark times" Arendt would later appropriate as a description for the erosion of the public realm and the loss of the light that it casts upon human affairs.[39] The group also included the literary critic Walter Benjamin, whom Arendt had come to know through their mutual friend Theodor Adorno. Meeting regularly, they took stock of their situation, supported one's another work, and began the important task of soliciting visa sponsors from America.

Benjamin would come to exert a particularly important influence on Arendt.[40] Loosely tied to the Frankfurt School, his interests were wide-ranging, including everything from German tragic drama and Proust to questions surrounding language, violence, and history. In Paris, he was working on a massive study he called *Das Passagen-Werk*, or the Arcades Project.[41] The title referred to the remains of the nineteenth-century Parisian arcades, which had once occupied the center of the city's commercial life but now lay in ruins. Benjamin was haunted by how quickly these and other "waves of the future" had been abandoned and forgotten. He grew skeptical about progress narratives that painted history as a smooth, continuous story of advancing civilization. As he famously suggests in his description of Paul Klee's angel of history in the "Theses on the Philosophy of History," progress is better likened to a storm that leaves a pile of wreckage in its wake.[42] Not only did such narratives elide the destructive impact of modern society, but they also conveyed the misleading sense that time is "empty" and "homogenous," with one moment giving way to the next and the past lying safely behind us, dead and buried. The ruins of the arcades suggested otherwise: that time is not so linear, that the past lingers with us, and that it may even continue to speak, if we are prepared to listen. In a later appreciation of his life, Arendt memorably describes Benjamin's method in a passage worth quoting at length:

> Like a pearl diver who descends to the bottom of the sea, not to excavate the bottom and bring it to light but to pry loose the rich and the strange, the pearls and the coral in the depths and to carry them to the surface, this thinking delves into the depths of the past—but not in order to resuscitate it the way it was and to contribute to the renewal of extinct ages. What guides

this thinking is the conviction that although the living is subject to the ruin of time, the process of decay is at the same time a process of crystallization, that in the depth of the sea, into which sinks and is dissolved what once was alive, some things "suffer a sea-change" and survive in new crystallized forms and shapes that remain immune to the elements, as though they waited only for the pearl diver who one day will come down to them and bring them up into the world of the living—as "thought fragments," as something "rich and strange," and perhaps even as everlasting *Urphänomene*. (MDT 205–6)

The imagery here of "pearls," "coral," and the past suffering a "sea-change" is borrowed from Shakespeare's *Tempest*, one of Arendt's favorite plays, and she uses this same imagery in describing her own method.[43] In her political thought, Arendt will apply the spirit of pearl diving to a range of neglected experiences and "lost treasures": Athenian democracy, the Roman experience of founding, the Christian practice of forgiveness, the promise-making of the American founders, Varnhagen's salons, and the French Resistance, among many others. She will also apply it to many forgotten or excluded ideas and concepts: Plato's notion of *thaumazein*, Aristotle's distinction between *praxis* and *poiēsis*, Augustine's *initium* passage from the *City of God*, Kant's concept of radical evil, Montesquieu's theory of political principles, and the American founders' vision of "public happiness." The point of such pearl diving for Arendt was not to try to recover experiences as they were, but to catch something of their still-living spirit, even if they only survived in ruined form. Not the *polis*, but the abiding ruin of the *polis*, inspired her. In her essay on Benjamin, she writes:

> Any period to which its own past has become as questionable as it has to us must eventually come up against the phenomenon of language, for in it the past is contained ineradicably, thwarting all attempts to get rid of it once and for all. The Greek *polis* will continue to exist at the bottom of our political existence—that is, at the bottom of the sea—for as long as we use the word "politics." (MDT 204)

Even if all that we have left are "empty shells" of concepts, they still provide access to the experiences that inspired them, opening the possibility that their original spirit might be applied in new ways. For Arendt, this meant the experience of loss and rupture was also an opportunity, a chance to rediscover the past against the backdrop of the challenges of the present.

Arendt remained in Paris until 1941. The year prior to her departure she married Heinrich Blücher, a gregarious, working-class former Marxist who became a companion and intellectual sparring partner during their Paris years. He would remain so until his death in 1970. Blücher had participated in the Spartacist strike in 1919 and often regaled Arendt with stories of the participatory nature of Rosa Luxemburg's movement.[44] Arendt's later investigations into totalitarianism, Marxism, and revolutionary politics were in many ways joint explorations with Blücher, as she tested and deepened her ideas in conversation with his. She would later write of her relationship with Blücher, "It is so seldom that people are able to help each other, mutually; but in our case I think it really is true that both of us would, without the other, scarcely have survived."[45]

A few months after Arendt and Blücher married, the French government ordered all German-born immigrants to internment camps. Arendt was detained at the local sports stadium, the Vélodrome, and then transported to the internment camp of Gurs, where she remained for several weeks until France was defeated and, in the resulting confusion, she was able to secure liberation papers. Serendipitously, she ran into Blücher in the town of Montauban, where many refugees had been congregating. They moved on to Marseilles, where they secured visas to America. When the Vichy government relaxed its exit-permit policy in 1941, they travelled to Lisbon to board the ship that would take them to New York and a new life in America.

During their stay in Marseilles, they saw their friend Walter Benjamin a final time. He too secured an emergency visa to America, but could not obtain a French exit visa and decided to leave the country through the Pyrenees. Before he left, he gave a number of his manuscripts (including the "Theses on the Philosophy of History") to Arendt with instructions to deliver them to Adorno in New York. Perhaps Benjamin had a premonition that he would not make it there himself. He was subsequently denied entrance at the Spanish border, and during the night of September 26, 1940, committed suicide. Arendt and Blücher read the "Theses" and other essays while they waited for their ship in Lisbon, and Arendt would later edit and publish Benjamin's writings in a volume fittingly entitled *Illuminations*. "Even in the darkest of times," she wrote, "we have the right to expect some illumination, and ... such illumination may well come less from theories and concepts than from the uncertain, flickering, and often weak light that some men and women, in their lives and their works, will kindle under almost all circumstances and shed over the time span that was given them on earth" (MDT ix).

IV. "The Burden of Our Time"

In her preface to *Between Past and Future*, Arendt suggests that if an intellectual history of the twentieth century could be written "in the form of the biography of a single person" (9), such a person would have experienced two reversals: first, from thought into action (as epitomized by existentialism's turn from philosophy to politics) and second, from action back into thought (as reflected in René Char's appeal to the survivors of the French Resistance to think upon and document their experience before it was forgotten). Whatever the usefulness of such an exercise for understanding twentieth-century intellectual history, it certainly illumines the course of Arendt's own life. If the initial shock of 1933 prompted her to turn from thought to action, the dawning realization of the full horror of totalitarianism now demanded a return to thought.

Such a return was necessary because totalitarianism had opened up a gap between thought and reality that no appeal to action could fill. The need now was for understanding. By understanding, Arendt meant the "unending activity by which, in constant change and variation, we come to terms with and reconcile ourselves to reality, that is, try to be at home in the world" (EU 308). Readers will detect a hint of Hegel in these words and the particular echo of his conviction that the owl of Minerva only takes its flight at dusk. Arendt was sympathetic to his view that the need for thought arises out of the experience of disintegration, but she remained doubtful that the gap between thought and the reality of totalitarianism could be closed with a philosophy of history. "Who would dare to reconcile himself with the reality of extermination camps or play the game of thesis-antithesis-synthesis until his dialectics have discovered 'meaning' in slave labor?" (444). There could be no "Hegelian escape from concern with politics into an interpretation of history" (444). True to her training in phenomenology, Arendt wanted to understand the nature of totalitarianism itself, what distinguished this phenomenon from others, rather than where it fit within some broader genealogical narrative. She believed the challenge of totalitarianism was minimized if we attempted to understand it merely as the latest version of tyranny or the outgrowth of the ideas of the Enlightenment, as no shortage of political scientists and philosophers were now attempting to do. As Arendt saw it, Hegelian progress narratives and anti-Enlightenment decline narratives were "two sides of the same medal" (OT vii). She became especially impatient with the latter:

> To hold the thinkers of the modern age, especially the nineteenth-century rebels against tradition, responsible for the structure and conditions of the twentieth century is even more dangerous than it is unjust. The implications apparent in the actual event of totalitarian domination go far beyond the most radical or most adventurous ideas of any of these thinkers. (BPF 27)

Far from being the root of Nazism, she wrote, the broader tradition of European humanism "was so little prepared for it or any other form of totalitarianism that in understanding and trying to come to terms with this phenomenon we can't rely on either its conceptual language or its traditional metaphors."[46] For Arendt, the reality was that totalitarianism "constituted a break with all our traditions" and "exploded our categories of political thought and our standards for moral judgment" (EU 310). It cut "the already outworn thread with which we still might have been tied to a historical entity of more than two thousand years" (160). Understanding totalitarianism required facing this reality, which meant acknowledging that "the very event, the phenomenon, which we try—and must try—to understand has deprived us of our traditional tools of understanding" (310).

Arendt's quest for understanding took the initial form of essays that she wrote as a journalist for *Aufbau* and various lectures and courses she gave in New York. Her investigations culminated in 1951 with the publication of *The Origins of Totalitarianism*. She was never happy with the title, as it suggested that she was offering exactly the kind of genealogical account that she rejected (she preferred the British title, *The Burden of Our Time*). As she tried to clarify to a reviewer, the book "does not really deal with the 'origins' of totalitarianism—as its title unfortunately claims—but gives a historical account of the elements which crystallized into totalitarianism" (403). If totalitarianism was unprecedented, as she insisted, then one could not trace its "origins" for the simple reason that it "did not exist before it had come into being" (405). Yet totalitarianism was obviously a historical phenomenon, arising out of concrete circumstances and the product of human actors and decisions. As she later came to appreciate, this was not a problem limited to totalitarianism alone. It was the paradox that accompanies any genuinely novel event in history, which while conditioned by a range of historical factors, is not reducible to any one of them. As she put the point in "Understanding and Politics":

> Not only does the actual meaning of every event always transcend any number of past "causes" which we may assign to it, but this past itself comes into being only with the event itself. Only when something irrevocable has happened can we even try to trace its history backward. The event illuminates its own past; it can never be deduced from it. (319)

Thus instead of beginning with precedents and working forward to totalitarianism, Arendt proposed to move from the unprecedented back to the precedents. She would start with the phenomenon itself and break it up into its constitutive elements.[47] These included anti-Semitism, imperialism, the emergence of the masses, the rise of European pan-nationalism, the expulsion of minorities and stateless peoples, and new forms of industrial and bureaucratic organization. None of these elements, however, were totalitarian in themselves. What ultimately distinguished totalitarian domination from these elements was the attempt, through a fusion of ideology and terror, to realize a certain purified vision of the human species independent of the individuality and spontaneity of human beings themselves. The concentration camps were the central institution of totalitarian domination because it was there that such individuality and spontaneity could be eliminated. "What totalitarian ideologies therefore aim at," Arendt writes in the penultimate chapter, "is not the transformation of the outside world or the revolutionizing transmutation of society, but the transformation of human nature itself. The concentration camps are the laboratories where changes in human nature are tested" (OT 458). For Arendt, the issue was not ultimately the amount of suffering or the destruction of life that totalitarianism caused, horrible as these were; it was "the ghastly experiment of eliminating, under scientifically controlled conditions, spontaneity itself as an expression of human behavior and of transforming the human personality into a mere thing, into something that even animals are not" (438). We cannot reconcile our minds to such horror, but we must reconcile ourselves to a world in which such things are possible, lest the unprecedented set a new precedent for politics in the age to come.

V. Thinking What We Are Doing

The Origins of Totalitarianism marked Arendt's return to academic scholarship and established her as a major figure on the American intellectual scene. Some early reviewers went as far as to herald the book as the most significant advance in social thought since Marx.[48] Other reviewers were less enthusiastic.[49] The political scientist Eric Voegelin issued a particularly scathing review, dismissing Arendt's style as moralizing, sentimental, and philosophically careless, taking particular exception to her suggestion that totalitarian regimes had the power not merely to destroy, but to change human nature.[50] He did not mince words: "A 'nature' cannot be changed or transformed; a 'change of nature' is a contradiction of terms; tampering with the 'nature' of a thing means destroying the thing. To conceive the idea of 'changing the nature' of man (or of anything) is a symptom of the intellectual breakdown of Western civilization."[51] Arendt saw the matter differently. In what became a famous exchange, she replied:

> [T]he success of totalitarianism is identical with a much more radical liquidation of freedom as a political and as a human reality than anything we have ever witnessed before. Under these conditions, it will be hardly consoling to cling to an unchangeable nature of man and conclude that either man

himself is being destroyed or that freedom does not belong to man's essential capabilities. Historically we know of man's nature only insofar as it has existence, and no realm of eternal essences will ever console us if man loses his essential capabilities. (EU 408)

Arendt's study of totalitarianism convinced her that whatever the final ontological status of human nature might be, our basic human capacities are correlative with certain conditions.[52] By intentionally altering the conditions in the concentration camps so as to deprive human beings of these capacities, the Nazi regime was effectively trying to change human nature. Arendt learned there is a much closer relationship between essence and existence than we may have thought, and that the capacities that many of us take for granted are in fact radically contingent. By destroying the conditions for these capacities, totalitarianism brought them to light. The task now was to name them, take stock of the ways they remain vulnerable after the demise of totalitarianism, and articulate strategies for renewing and sustaining them.

Arendt took up this task in her next major work, *The Human Condition* (1958). In it, she identifies four specific conditions, each of which reflect something fundamental that was lost in the concentration camps. The first of these conditions is what she calls *worldliness*. By worldliness, Arendt means membership in the man-made world, the enduring human artifice that provides a measure of permanence amidst the natural processes of growth and decay. This includes the public realm, that specific region of the world where we move beyond the task of merely staying alive and act in freedom, disclosing our unique identities to one another in word and deed. As Arendt knew well from her experience as a refugee, to rob someone of worldliness was to take away the conditions of possibility for being seen and heard by others; in the camps, it was to take away the grounds for being an agent at all. To go further and attempt to destroy all traces of individuality and exterminate whole ethnic groups was to attempt to deny the human condition of *plurality*, the fact we are always surrounded and enriched by those different from us, others upon whom we rely for our development and fulfillment. To go further still and attempt to shift the focus of politics from individuals to the human race, one that transcends the individual lifespan of human beings and has the potential to last forever, is an attempt to deny the human condition of *mortality*, the fact that human life is finite, that it is subject to decay and eventually comes to an end. Finally, although totalitarianism was itself an expression of the human capacity to do new things, its continued existence depended upon the elimination of this capacity in others, which made it hostile to the very principle of beginning. In this way, it sought to destroy the human condition of *natality*, the basic fact that human beings are born into the world and introduce an inevitable element of surprise and unpredictability into it.

In addition to these, Arendt identifies two more basic conditions that human beings share with other forms of sentient life: the *biological life process*, which imposes upon human beings the task of securing daily sustenance, and the *earth*, the habitat in which living beings "move and breathe without effort and without artifice" (HC 2).[53] Arendt did not think these exhausted all the conditions of human existence, nor did she think that any of these conditioned human life absolutely (atomic energy and space exploration reminded her that not even the earth is an absolute condition). She did regard these conditions as the most general and universal, conditions which were not chosen but, in her words, "given" to us (7). In addition, she went on to identify three basic capacities or activities that correspond to these conditions, which together constitute what she calls the "*vita activa*": *labor* (which sustains the biological life process), *work* (which builds up and protects the man-made world against mortality), and *action* (which presupposes plurality and expresses our natality).

The purpose of Arendt's book was not simply to outline these conditions and activities, but to reconsider them "from the vantage point of our newest experiences and our most recent fears" (5). Totalitarianism was obviously one of these, threatening these conditions and activities in an absolute sense, but by 1958, Arendt had come to appreciate many others: automation, the rise of a "society of jobholders," the conversion of property into abstract wealth, mass consumption, biomedical engineering, and the prospect of nuclear warfare, to name a few. Each of these promised to alter the human condition in fundamental ways: automation offered the real possibility of realizing the ancient dream of freedom from labor; biomedical engineering and nuclear technology gave us the power to "act into nature" and change the life process itself; and the new imperatives of limitless economic growth and an ephemeral consumer economy put the very idea of a durable common world into question. Thus these developments required reflection. They demanded political deliberation and judgment about whether these were directions in which we wanted to venture. Yet these developments proceeded at a pace that seemed to rule out the very possibility of such reflection, rendering us "thoughtless creatures at the mercy of every gadget which is technically possible" (3). As Arendt saw it, the urgent need was to break from this frenetic activity and "think what we are doing" (5), to subject these new trends to scrutiny and strive again to reconcile our minds to reality.

In addition to thinking what we are doing, Arendt also sought to recover a specific kind of doing that she believed had gotten lost in the flurry of activity that characterized the modern age. This was "action," a non-instrumental form of activity that she associated with the words and deeds that citizens perform in the public realm. Influenced by the experience of Athenian democracy and Aristotle's understanding of *praxis*, Arendt took action to entail a kind of second birth, the disclosure of our unique identities to others. This might take the form of a speech, a political demonstration, or an act of forgiveness, but in every action there is an element of newness, rooted in the newness of our first birth, that charges the political realm with its characteristic unpredictability. For Arendt, the functionalization of the modern age has caused us to lose sight of the value of an activity whose chief ends are internal to itself, which include self-discovery, friendship, and the enlarged mentality that comes from seeing the world from a plurality of perspectives. These are the goods that Arendt sought to recover.

Arendt carried this project forward in *Between Past and Future* (1961), a collection of essays addressing specific crises in education, culture, science, and politics, complemented by broader conceptual investigations into the meaning of tradition, authority, history, and freedom. She uses as her point of departure René Char's elusive aphorism, "our inheritance was left to us by no testament," which for him referred to the way in which he and others were thrust into the French Resistance without any categories for describing the challenges they faced or the joys they experienced. Arendt finds the aphorism a helpful way to frame the challenge of thinking more generally, just to the extent that each of us are faced with perplexities that are unique to our times that neither our predecessors nor our heirs can resolve for us. The book, she says, is an attempt to learn how to move in the "gap" between past and future, and she frames her essays as "exercises" in how to think (BPF 14). Guided by the core methodological assumption "that thought itself arises out of incidents of living experience and must remain bound to them as the only guideposts by which to take its bearings" (14), her exercises begin from specific crises and then move "between past and future" by way of historical criticism and experiment. In the spirit of Benjamin, the critical examination of the past traces the empty shells of concepts to their origins in order to recover a sense of their original meaning; the experiment entails a consideration of how such concepts may, under new conditions, crystallize into something strange and new, guiding us into the future. In later years, Arendt will apply these "exercises" to many other issues, including lying in politics, the civil rights movement, and civil disobedience.

Arendt capped this dizzying five-year period of activity with *On Revolution* (1963), in which she explores the quintessential expression of the human capacity to make new beginnings, the political act of founding. Inspired by the Hungarian Revolution and the upheavals in the postcolonial world, Arendt launched into a historical examination of key founding moments in Rome, America, France, and Russia. She sought to challenge the assumption that the founding act of a republic must be a violent one: "The relevance of the problem of beginning to the phenomenon of revolution is obvious," she wrote. "That such a beginning must be intimately connected with violence seems to be vouched for by the legendary beginnings of our history as both biblical and classical antiquity report it: Cain slew Abel, and Romulus slew Remus; violence was the beginning and, by the same token, no beginning could be made without using violence, without violating" (OR 20). Yet Arendt wanted to unsettle our assumptions about "founding violence," pointing instead to the fact that in countless revolutions, violence actually betrays an earlier stage of mutual promising, characterized by such participatory mechanisms as town meetings, councils, and communes. It is the power of concerted action, of joint enterprise, to be distinguished from violence, that builds a democratic culture and gives binding force to a community's laws. She writes, "where and when men succeed in keeping intact the power which sprang up between them during the course of any particular act or deed, they are already in the process of foundation, of constituting a stable worldly structure to house, as it were, their combined power of action" (175). Violence, she says, "by no means [gives] birth to something new and stable but, on the contrary, drown[s] in a 'revolutionary torrent' the beginning as well as the beginners" (209).

Taken together, all three works from this period can be read as ventures in the "new political philosophy" about which Arendt spoke earlier in her career. The questions that she sought to address initially arose from the horror of totalitarianism, but this horror eventually gave way to a no less powerful sense of wonder at the human capacity for action, which Arendt regarded as "the one miracle-working faculty of man" (HC 246). She likely would have continued down the path of developing this new political philosophy if not for the news that she received in the summer of 1960 that the chief architect of the Holocaust, Adolf Eichmann, had been captured.

VI. The Eichmann Controversy

When Arendt learned that the Israeli government intended to put Eichmann on trial in Jerusalem, she wrote to the editor of *The New Yorker* and offered to cover the trial for the magazine. Her series of articles (and later her book *Eichmann in Jerusalem*) ignited a firestorm of controversy. The controversy centered around her characterization of the role of the Jewish councils in the deportation of the Jews and the enigmatic phrase that she used to sum up the lessons of the trial, a phrase that has become synonymous with her name: "the banality of evil."[54] In the eyes of her critics, not only did Arendt appear to be blaming the Jews for their own suffering, but it sounded as if she was calling the most horrifying event in the history of mankind something ordinary, not a big deal.[55] What is more, in suggesting that Eichmann was "banal," she appeared to be suggesting that he was just like the rest of us, that he was just following orders, and that if we were in his shoes we would have done the same thing.

Arendt always insisted she would have welcomed a real controversy over her book, one that rigorously debated its actual claims.

As she said, "There is nothing so entertaining as the discussion of a book nobody has read" (RJ 17). The book she wrote was not a history of the Holocaust or a theory of evil, but more modestly, a "trial report." She wanted to know "the extent to which the court in Jerusalem succeeded in fulfilling the demands of justice" (EJ 298) and "how well our present system of justice is capable of dealing with this special type of crime and criminal it has had repeatedly to cope with since the Second World War" (286). This was a quintessentially Arendtian project. She sought to approach the political event of the Eichmann trial as a signpost for thought and "think what we are doing." She wanted to know if in fact it is possible to do justice when one is dealing with such a crime as genocide and such a criminal as Eichmann.

The problem that became apparent from the opening of the trial was the gross disparity between the gravity of the crimes and the banality of the criminal. The prosecution made Eichmann out to be a monster, but when Arendt looked across the courtroom at the man behind the glass booth, she was struck by how "terribly and terrifyingly normal" he was (276). He was a former vacuum oil salesman who possessed no firm convictions or ambitions beyond career advancement. He had trouble uttering a single word that was not a cliché (48); even his last words—"After a short while, gentlemen, we shall all meet again"—betrayed the superficiality of someone who was so alienated from reality that he did not even realize he was attending his own funeral. "Eichmann was not Iago and not Macbeth," Arendt observes, "and nothing would have been farther from his mind than to determine with Richard III 'to prove a villain'" (287). Neither a monster nor a villain, Eichmann represented a more haunting possibility: "That such remoteness from reality and such thoughtlessness can wreak more havoc than all the evil instincts taken together which, perhaps, are inherent in man—that was, in fact, the lesson one could learn in Jerusalem" (288).

We will have an opportunity to explore Arendt's portrait of Eichmann and her views on the banality of evil in greater detail in the next chapter, but for now a few brief points are in order. First, by "thoughtless" Arendt did not mean Eichmann was unaware of what he was doing. She explicitly states that "he knew quite well what it was all about" (287), "admitted [his] role in it," and "carried out, and therefore actively supported, a policy of mass murder" (278–9). Nor did she mean he was not responsible for his crimes. She calls him "one of the greatest criminals of that period" (288) and rejects his defense of superior orders, observing that "politics is not like the nursery; in politics obedience and support are the same" (279). As for what others might have done in his shoes, she states that "there is an abyss between the actuality of what [he] did and the potentiality of what others might have done" (278), adding that "even if eighty million Germans had done as [he] did, this would not have been an excuse" (278). For Arendt, the issue was not whether he was guilty. The issue was that his actions were not rooted in any deeper diabolical character. Eichmann had no such depth. Instead, he was a "joiner," someone who was content to take his cues from the prevailing legal culture, submitting to whatever happened to be lawful in the name of duty instead of submitting this culture to scrutiny and independent thought. If on the court's account it took a great villain to commit horrendous evil, Arendt was suggesting that it only takes a habituated will and inability to think to open the floodgates of hell.

In a world in which bureaucratic structures make it increasingly easy to surrender one's faculty of judgment and defer to whatever the wider society says is right or legal, the potential for political evil has never been greater. What we are in fact doing when we put criminals such as Eichmann on trial, Arendt concluded, is to demand "that human beings be capable of telling right from wrong even when all they have to guide them is their own judgment, which, moreover, happens to be completely at odds with what they must regard as the unanimous opinion of all those around them" (294–5). Where might such independent judgment come from? It was this question to which Arendt devoted the final chapter of her career.

VII. *The Life of the Mind*

In the spring of 1972, Arendt received an invitation to deliver the Gifford Lectures in Aberdeen.[56] These lectures became the basis of a three-volume project entitled *The Life of the Mind*. Arendt liked to think in threes. In *The Human Condition*, she identified three activities: labor, work, and action. Turning now to the activities of the mind, she again identified three: thinking, willing, and judging. Kant, evidently, was still looking over her shoulder.

In the introduction to the first volume, she explains the bridge between the Eichmann project and her new focus on thinking. Summarizing the lessons of the trial, she writes:

> I was struck by a manifest shallowness in the doer that made it impossible to trace the uncontestable evil of his deeds to any deeper level of roots or motives ... the only notable characteristic one could detect in his past behavior as well as in his behavior during the trial ... was something entirely negative: it was not stupidity but *thoughtlessness*. (LMT 4)

This led her to ask, "Might the problem of good and evil, our faculty for telling right from wrong, be connected with our faculty of thought? ... Could the activity of thinking as such ... be among the conditions that make men abstain from evil-doing or even actually 'condition' them against it?" (5). In asking such questions, Arendt did not mean to suggest that thinking by itself produces ethical behavior. The example of Heidegger and other German intellectuals provided ample evidence against such an illusion.[57] Moreover, Arendt's sense of the complex circumstances that exacerbated Eichmann's thoughtlessness—the role of bureaucratic routine, the inverted legal culture of the Third Reich, the accumulated frustrations of a life of seemingly continual disappointment—made clear that thinking is only one of a range of factors that shape our moral character. But the question remained: what, if anything, is the role of thought in the moral life?

She begins by clarifying that the particular kind of thinking she has in mind is not to be confused with such logical processes as deduction or induction. One could, as Eichmann did, deduce conclusions from ideological premises and still not think in the relevant sense. What she had in mind was thinking as an ongoing dialogue with the self, thinking as a search for meaning that lasts as long as we are alive. In *The Life of the Mind*, she draws upon two well-known sayings from Socrates, both from the *Gorgias*: first, "It would be better for me that my lyre or a chorus I directed should be out of tune and loud with discord, and that multitudes of men should disagree with me rather than I, being one, should be out of harmony with myself" (482c); and second, "It is better to be wronged than to do wrong" (474b). What Arendt finds suggestive about the first saying is that it presents the self not as one, but as two, or a "two-in-one." It suggests that when we are engaged in thought, we carry on a "silent intercourse" with ourselves, enjoying the company of another even when we are alone. For Socrates, sustaining this conversation is essential to the integrity of the self, and the main way we do so is by avoiding contradictions, or as Arendt puts it, not "becoming one's own adversary" (LMT 186). "To Socrates," she observes, "the duality of the two-in-one meant no more than that if you want to think, you must see to it that the two who carry on the dialogue be in good shape, that the partners be *friends*" (187–8).

This is where the second saying comes in. As Arendt sees it, "It is better to suffer wrong than to do wrong, because you can remain the friend of the sufferer; who would want to be the friend of and have to live together with a murderer? Not even another murderer" (188). Those who commit evil will naturally flee their own company and break off the silent intercourse with themselves. This means there is nothing to prevent them from committing additional crimes, since they "can count on its being forgotten the next moment. Bad people—Aristotle to the contrary notwithstanding—are *not* 'full of regrets'" (191). The reason why Eichmann was able to commit his crimes without regrets is because he had long ago ceased to see himself as a friend, no longer carrying on the conversation that would have allowed him to subject his deeds to scrutiny.

Arendt was under no illusions that such thinking formed a sufficient basis for moral character. It offered little help to those like Eichmann who had already surrendered themselves to thoughtless routine, and it could not help one actually perform good acts. For this, she needed to say more about the other two mental faculties, willing and judging.

During the writing of her willing lectures, Arendt confessed to her friend J. Glenn Gray, "The will is not my thing."[58] She had spent a lifetime describing freedom as something tangibly experienced in the company of others and had always been wary of the kinds of fallacies that can arise when freedom is reduced solely to an exercise of the will. Yet here she was delving into a vast literature on the subject and trying to work out her own position on the question. With the exception of a short concluding section, the book is mostly a historical review of different ideas on the will, and by Arendt's own admission, it raises more problems than it solves. She begins by noting the curious fact that we find nothing resembling a faculty of the will in Greek thought. Aristotle's reflections on choice provide a precursor to the will, but it is only with the rise of Christianity that reflection on the will as a separate faculty begins in earnest. She credits the Apostle Paul with the "discovery" of the will and calls Augustine the "first philosopher of the will." She then tracks evolving views on the relationship between will and intellect in Aquinas, Scotus, Kant, and Hegel, before turning to the more recent views of Nietzsche and Heidegger. For her own part, Arendt settles on a view of the will as "the spring of action," the "faculty of being able to bring about something new" (LMW 7). Her discussion echoes many of the broader themes of her action theory, especially the way our willing is said to interrupt chains of causation and transcend the variety of circumstantial factors that condition it.

Augustine comes to play a particularly prominent role in Arendt's discussion, and whatever her misgivings about the will, she clearly relished the opportunity to return to his thought a final time. She notes the centrality of the will for Augustine's account of freedom, but dwells upon the perplexity of what moves the will, especially if the will is itself divided. The problem, as she sees it, cannot be resolved simply by resorting to his views on grace, for even when we account for the way that grace lifts the obstacles that stand in the way of our willing the good, grace cannot so determine the movement of the will that its exercise is no longer free.[59] As in her dissertation, Arendt moves through different texts looking for a solution, only now she is more optimistic that one can be found. She finds it in *De Trinitate*, where Augustine discusses the will not in isolation, but in relationship to the other faculties of intellect and memory. Here the will has the potential to serve as a bonding agent between these faculties, establishing a kind of love between them that unites their collective attention and arrests the fluctuations within the will itself. Arendt notes Augustine's famous formulation of love as the soul's "weight," its center of gravity, what directs a person one way or the other. It is this weight, a weight that can be directed towards good or bad objects, that helps to explain why we will the way we do.

As with several other figures in the book, it is unclear how much of Augustine's views on the will she endorses as her own. What is clear is that she continues to find in his broader creation theology a compelling picture of the human being as a beginner. Perhaps the elusiveness of locating the precise source of our freedom, she speculates in the volume's conclusion, has something to do with the fact that we are beginners by nature. She acknowledges that this sounds "opaque," and "seems to tell us no more than that we are *doomed* to be free by virtue of being born, no matter whether we like freedom ... or prefer to escape its awesome responsibility by electing some form of fatalism" (217). At any rate, the impasse can only be solved, she says, by appealing to another mental faculty, the faculty of judgment.

Unfortunately Arendt did not live to write the third volume on judging. We are left largely to speculate how she would have pulled off the promised synthesis, and many have.[60] Suffice to say, *The Life of the Mind* is radically incomplete without it, a "tale without an ending," in the words of Ronald Beiner.[61] Arendt did, however, provide some clues as to what she might have said. At the end of the volume on thinking, for example, she suggests an important link between thinking and judging. While thinking deals with "the representation of things that are absent" and "judging always concerns particulars and things close at hand" (LMT 193), the two are related in that judging "realizes" thinking by making it "manifest in the world of appearances" (193). As she puts it, "The manifestation of the wind of thought is not knowledge; it is the ability to tell right from wrong, beautiful from ugly. And this, at the rare moments when the stakes are on the table, may indeed prevent catastrophes, at least for the self" (193). What Arendt is saying is that thinking plays an important critical role in relation to existing standards of judgment, subjecting them to scrutiny, which then liberates the faculty of judgment for fresh appraisals of whatever particulars may be at hand. This proves invaluable in political crises because these are the times when our ability to make judgments is most captive to social conventions and when independent judgment is hardest to come by. Thinking frees us to judge, which then frees us to act.

While one can only speculate what Arendt may have said, the theme of judgment is one that runs throughout her work. In her writings on political action, she speaks of the role of the imagination in helping citizens to see goods held in common from a plurality of perspectives, yielding an "enlarged mentality" from which to make political judgments. In her writings on totalitarianism, she speaks of the "fearful imagination" that "dwells upon horrors" in order to arrive at the judgments that are necessary to alleviate the plight of the stateless. Not surprisingly, we find Arendt's most revealing and insightful reflections on judgment in her occasional writings. It is in the character studies of *Men in Dark Times* that Arendt works out how individuals such as Rosa Luxemburg and Pope John XXIII make judgments in the face of new contingencies. It is in such essays as "Lying in Politics" that Arendt makes her own judgments about how truthful speech figures into a healthy democracy. And it is in *Eichmann in Jerusalem* that Arendt fleshes out both the fullest implications of what it means when the faculty of judgment breaks down, and what legal innovations are necessary in order to judge the unprecedented realities of our time.

Hannah Arendt died in her Upper West Side apartment on December 4, 1975. She was sixty-nine years old. Earlier in the day she rolled the first page of "Judging" into her typewriter, where it remained blank, except for the title and two epigraphs from Cato and Goethe. She died a citizen of the United States, having naturalized in 1950. Her experience of statelessness in Europe shaped her understanding of the fragility of the human condition, and her time in America opened her to the varieties of ways that human beings can appear to one another within it. In *Men in Dark Times*, her compilation of essays celebrating some of the leading actors and thinkers of the twentieth century, many of whom Arendt knew as friends, Arendt writes:

> [T]his collection of essays and articles is primarily concerned with persons—how they lived their lives, how they moved in the world, and how they were affected by historical time ... they share with each other the age in which their life span fell, the world during the first half of the twentieth century with its political catastrophes, its moral disasters, and its astonishing development of the arts and sciences. (MDT vii)

Hannah Arendt thought by the light of such men and women. She marveled at what human beings can do when they gather together in joint enterprise. And she made good on her promise to regard the whole realm of human affairs, in its misery and grandeur, an object worthy of wonder.

Notes

1 The October 28, 1964 interview was with Günter Gaus as part of the West German television series *Zur Person*. The full transcript is printed in EU under the title, "What Remains? The Language Remains," 1–23.
2 The closest thing to a home was the New School for Social Research, where she taught as University Professor from 1967 to 1975.
3 Margaret Canovan, "Socrates or Heidegger? Hannah Arendt's Reflections on Philosophy and Politics," *Social Research* 57:1 (Spring 1990), 139.
4 This passage is found in *Theaetetus* 155D. It features prominently in her later account of thinking in LMT (141–51), as well as her essay "Concern for Politics in Recent European Thought" (EU 444–5). For general background on the importance of *thaumazein* for philosophy, see John Llewelyn, "On the saying that philosophy begins in *thaumazein*," in *Post-structuralist Classics*, ed. Andrew Benjamin (London: Routledge, 1988), 173–91, and Mary-Jane Rubenstein, *Strange Wonder: The Closure of Metaphysics and the Opening of Awe* (New York: Columbia University Press, 2008). George Kateb provides a helpful discussion of the role of wonder in Arendt's thought in "Arendt and Individualism," *Social Research* 61:4 (Winter 1994): 765–94. See also Peg Birmingham, *Hannah Arendt and Human Rights* (Bloomington: Indiana University Press, 2006), 7–8.
5 The best source for background on Arendt's life remains Elisabeth Young-Bruehl's biography, *Hannah Arendt: For Love of the World* (New Haven: Yale University Press, 1982). See also Julia Kristeva, *Hannah Arendt: Life is a Narrative* (New York: Columbia University Press, 2001). Briefer but no less illuminating are Hans Morgenthau, "Hannah Arendt 1906-1975," *Political Theory* 4:1 (February 1976): 5–8; Peter Berkowitz, "The Pearl Diver," *The New Republic* 44 (June 14, 1999): 44–52; and Kirsch, "Beware of Pity".
6 "Introduction," in *Hannah Arendt: Twenty Years Later*, eds. Larry May and Jerome Kohn (Cambridge: MIT Press, 1996), 1.
7 Young-Bruehl, *Hannah Arendt*, 6.
8 Young-Bruehl, *Hannah Arendt*, 33–4.

9 Fergus Kerr, *20th Century Catholic Theologians* (Oxford: Blackwell, 2006), 9. For more background on Guardini, see Robert A. Krieg, *Romano Guardini: A Precursor of Vatican II* (South Bend, IN: University of Notre Dame Press, 1997) and Hans Urs von Balthasar, *Romano Guardini: Reform from the Source* (San Francisco: Ignatius Press, 2010).

10 von Balthasar, *Guardini*, 16.

11 See Dermot Moran's discussion of Arendt's views on Bultmann in *Introduction to Phenomenology* (London: Routledge, 2000), 293. Young-Bruehl reports that Arendt also attended Martin Dibelius's New Testament lectures (*Hannah Arendt*, 66).

12 Hannah Arendt, "Remarks to the American Society of Christian Ethics," 1973, Library of Congress MSS Box 70, 011838.

13 Arendt, "Remarks," 011838.

14 Arendt, "Martin Heidegger at Eighty," in Michael Murray, ed. *Heidegger and Modern Philosophy* (New Haven: Yale University Press, 1978), 294.

15 Arendt, "Heidegger at Eighty," 295.

16 Arendt, "Heidegger at Eighty," 295.

17 There is a vast literature on the question of Heidegger's influence on Arendt. For arguments making the case for a strong and enduring influence, see Richard Wolin's *Heidegger's Children* (Princeton: Princeton University Press, 2001), 30–69, and Martin Jay, *Permanent Exiles: Essays on the Intellectual Migration from Germany to America* (New York: Columbia University Press, 1985), 237–56. For perspectives that balance Heidegger's influence with that of others, see Dana R. Villa, *Arendt and Heidegger: The Fate of the Political* (Princeton: Princeton University Press, 1996) and 'Apologist or Critic? On Arendt's Relation to Heidegger' in Steven E. Aschheim, ed. *Hannah Arendt in Jerusalem* (Berkeley: University of California Press, 2001), 325–37; Seyla Benhabib, *The Reluctant Modernism of Hannah Arendt* (Lanham, MD: Rowman & Littlefield, 2003), 102–22; Joanna Vecchiarelli Scott and Judith Chelius Stark, "Heidegger: Arendt Between Past and Future," in *Love and Saint Augustine* (Chicago: University of Chicago Press, 1996).

18 In *Being and Time*, Heidegger writes, "Do we in our time have an answer to the question of what we really mean by the word 'being'? Not at all. So it is fitting that we should raise anew *the question of the meaning of being*. But are we nowadays even perplexed at our inability to understand the expression 'being'? Not at all. So first

of all we must reawaken an understanding for the meaning of this question" (Albany, NY: SUNY Press, 1996), xix.

19 See LMT 12. For more on Heidegger's influence in this respect, see Villa, *Arendt and Heidegger*, 9–10, and Mara Willard, "'Recasting the Old Questions': Theological Reliance and Renunciation in the Political Thought of Hannah Arendt" (Ph.D. diss., Harvard University, 2011), 3–4, 130–2, 169–70.

20 Cited in Benhabib, *Reluctant Modernism*, 117.

21 For more, see their voluminous letter correspondence in HAKJ, as well as Arendt's two essays on Jaspers in MDT 71–94.

22 Scott and Stark report that according to Hans Jonas, another student of Heidegger, "such a topic would not have been all that unusual in the German universities of the time" (LSA xv). The *Confessions* was a "crucial and pivotal text," important to both Heidegger and Jaspers (xv).

23 On the significance of the dissertation for Arendt's later thinking, see the editorial essays included in Scott and Stark, *Love and Saint Augustine*, 115–211. See also Ronald Beiner, "Love and Worldliness: Hannah Arendt's Reading of Saint Augustine," in May and Kohn, *Hannah Arendt: Twenty Years Later*, 269–84; Patrick Boyle, S.J., "Elusive Neighborliness: Hannah Arendt's Interpretation of Saint Augustine," in *Amor Mundi: Explorations in the Faith of Hannah Arendt*, ed. James Bernauer (Dordrecht, Netherlands: Nijhoff Publishers, 1987), 81–113; Eric Gregory, *Politics and the Order of Love* (Chicago: University of Chicago Press, 2008), 197–240; and Stephan Kampowski, *Arendt, Augustine, and the New Beginning* (Grand Rapids: Eerdmans, 2008).

24 See Scott and Stark, LSA, viii, 173–97.

25 Several scholars trace the roots of Arendt's thinking on natality back to the dissertation, a reading Arendt herself encourages by inserting her mature concept into her revisions (see LSA 51–2 and my fuller discussion in Chapter 4). Patricia Bowen Moore observes, "While the 1929 dissertation does not employ the term 'natality' as such, it does give ample evidence for Arendt's implicit concern for the experience of 'beginning' as it comes to bear on creaturely existence." See her essay 'Natality, *Amor Mundi* and Nuclearism in the Thought of Hannah Arendt,' in Bernauer, *Amor Mundi: Explorations in the Faith and Thought of Hannah Arendt*, 138. Stephan Kampowski echoes this judgment in *Arendt, Augustine, and the New Beginning*, 201–9. See also Young-Bruehl, *Hannah Arendt*, 496, and Scott and Stark, LSA, 146–8.

26 In "What is Existential Philosophy?" Arendt writes, "Though death may be the end of *Dasein*, it is at the same time the guarantor that all that matters ultimately is myself. In experiencing death as nothingness as such, I have the opportunity to devote myself exclusively to being-a-Self and, in the mode of axiomatic guilt, to free myself once and for all from the world that entangles me" (EU 181). She adds, "Later, and after the fact, as it were, Heidegger has drawn on mythologizing and muddled concepts like 'folk' and 'earth' in an effort to supply his isolated Selves with a shared, common ground to stand on ... If it does not belong to the concept of man that he inhabits the earth together with others of his kind, then all that remains for him is a mechanical reconciliation by which the atomized Selves are provided with a common ground that is essentially alien to their nature" (181).

27 In their interpretive essay in LSA, Scott and Stark speak of "the Augustinian foundations of Arendt's political thought" (xi) and the "Augustinian root of Arendt's critique of modernity" (115). In *The Broken Middle* (Oxford: Blackwell, 1992), Gillian Rose makes a similar claim: "Arendt's authorship becomes more Augustinian not less as its political focus develops" (228).

28 On the broader question of Augustine's influence on Arendt, see Kampowski, *Arendt, Augustine, and the New Beginning*; Scott and Stark, LSA, 115–211; Joanna Vecchiarelli Scott, "Hannah Arendt's Secular Augustinianism," in *History, Apocalypse, and the Secular Imagination: New Essays on Augustine's* City of God (Bowling Green: Bowling Green State University Press, 1999), 293–310; Scott, "'A Detour through Pietism': Hannah Arendt on St. Augustine's Philosophy of Freedom," *Polity* 20:3 (Spring 1988), 394–425; and Julia Kristeva, *Hannah Arendt: Life is a Narrative* (New York: Columbia University Press, 2001), 30–47.

29 On the first, see Wolin, *Heidegger's Children*, 30–69; on the second, see Jean Bethke Elshtain, "Augustine's Evil, Arendt's Eichmann," in *Augustine and the Limits of Politics* (South Bend: University of Notre Dame Press, 1995), 76–7.

30 Young-Bruehl, *Hannah Arendt*, 77–8.

31 The most probing exploration of the significance of the Varnhagen study for understanding Arendt's work is Benhabib's *The Reluctant Modernism of Hannah Arendt*, esp. 1–61. See also Richard Bernstein, *Hannah Arendt and the Jewish Question* (Cambridge: MIT Press, 1996), 14–45.

32 Kampowski makes this perceptive connection in *Arendt, Augustine, and the New Beginning*, 3-4. On the tension between worldlessness

and pariahdom, see Lisa Stenmark, *Religion, Science, and Democracy: A Disputational Friendship* (Lanham, MD: Lexington Books, 2013), 141–69.

33 On the importance of Arendt's experience of totalitarianism for her constructive political theory, especially for understanding *The Human Condition*, see Margaret Canovan, *Hannah Arendt: A Reinterpretation of Her Political Thought* (Cambridge: Cambridge University Press, 1992). See also Maurizio Passerin d'Entreves, *The Political Philosophy of Hannah Arendt* (London: Routledge, 1994).

34 My thanks to Deborah Galaski for conversation on this point. See her paper, "Between Public and Private: Navigating the Jewishness of Hannah Arendt," presented at the Annual Meeting of the Arendt Circle, April 9, 2011.

35 For background on Kurt Blumenfeld and her involvement in the German-Zionist movement, see Young-Bruehl, *Hannah Arendt*, 70–6, 102–10.

36 Young-Bruehl, *Hannah Arendt*, 107.

37 Peg Birmingham provides a comprehensive treatment of Arendt's view on human rights in *Hannah Arendt and Human Rights* (Bloomington: Indiana University Press, 2006).

38 Young-Bruehl, *Hannah Arendt*, 137, 143–4.

39 See Arendt's memorable appreciation of Brecht in MDT 207–49.

40 On the influence of Benjamin, see Susannah Young-ah Gottlieb, *Regions of Sorrow: Anxiety and Messianism in Hannah Arendt and W. H. Auden* (Stanford: Stanford University Press, 2003), 135–60; Berkowitz, "The Pearl Diver"; and Benhabib, *Reluctant Modernism of Hannah Arendt*, 91–5.

41 Walter Benjamin, *The Arcades Project* (Cambridge: Harvard University Press, 2002).

42 The famous passage reads, "This is how one pictures the angel of history. His face is turned toward the past. Where we perceive a chain of events, he sees one single catastrophe which keeps piling wreckage upon wreckage and hurls it in front of his feet. The angel would like to stay, awaken the dead, and make whole what has been smashed. But a storm is blowing from Paradise; it has got caught in his wings with such violence that the angel can no longer close them. This storm irresistibly propels him into the future to which his back is turned, while the pile of debris before him grows skyward. This storm is what we call progress." See Benjamin, *Illuminations*, ed. Hannah Arendt (New York: Schocken Books, 1968), 257–8.

43 In LMT, Arendt acknowledges that she has taken her place among those who have sought to "dismantle" metaphysics, but having just concluded a book in which she draws appreciatively from many of its representatives, she tries to articulate why she continues to appeal to them. She reiterates her familiar claim about the break in tradition and writes, "What has been lost is the continuity of the past as it seemed to be handed down from generation to generation, developing in the process its own consistency ... What you then are left with is still the past, but a *fragmented* past, which has lost its certainty of evaluation" (212). It is with such fragments, Arendt believes, that we think, and she concludes with a warning to those eager to take up the project of dismantling, "let them be careful not to destroy the 'rich and strange,' the 'coral' and the 'pearls,' which can probably be saved only as fragments" (212). Arendt is influenced both by Heidegger and Benjamin here, but this last statement brings her closer to Benjamin, who approaches texts with more of a preservationist sensibility, even as he expects them to speak in new ways as well. We hear this sentiment expressed most clearly in BPF, where she states that her aim is "to discover the real origins of traditional concepts in order to distill from them anew their original spirit which has so sadly evaporated from the very key words of political language" (15).

44 Young-Bruehl, *Hannah Arendt*, 122–9.

45 Young-Bruehl, *Hannah Arendt*, 250.

46 Young-Bruehl, *Hannah Arendt*, 222.

47 In a 1958 article in *The Meridian*, Arendt wrote, "While I was writing this book, these intentions presented themselves to me in the form of an ever-recurring image: I felt as though I dealt with a crystallized structure which I had to break up into its constituent elements in order to destroy it" (OT [2004 hardcover edition] 617).

48 Dwight MacDonald, "A new theory of totalitarianism,' *New Leader*, May 14, 1951, 17–19.

49 See Philip Rieff, "The Theology of Politics: Reflections on Totalitarianism as the Burden of Our Time," *The Journal of Religion* 32:2 (April 1952): 119–26. In depicting totalitarianism as a kind of judgment for Western hubris, he accuses Arendt of attempting to smuggle in a "covert theology" (120).

50 Eric Voegelin, "The Origins of Totalitarianism," *Review of Politics* 15:1 (January 1953): 68–76.

51 Voegelin, "Origins," 74–5.

52 In *The Human Condition*, Arendt argues that the question of human nature is ultimately a "theological" question because only God could "speak about a 'who' as though it were a 'what'" (HC 10). To know our own nature would be "like jumping over our own shadows" (10). Instead, she limits her analysis to the relationship between those conditions which have been "given" to us as a "free gift from nowhere" (2–3) and "those activities that traditionally, as well as according to current opinion, are within the range of every human being" (5).

53 One may wonder why Arendt thought natality and mortality were distinctively human conditions, and not conditions that we share with other forms of sentient life. The reason has to do with her identification of the natural world with the cyclical life process and the specific meaning that birth and death take on in relation to the common world. I discuss these points at greater length in Chapters 3 and 4.

54 For more background on this aspect of the controversy, see Steven E. Aschheim, 'Nazism, Culture, and The Origins of Totalitarianism: Hannah Arendt and the Discourse of Evil," *New German Critique* 70 (Winter 1997), 120–1. For a full summary of the controversy, see Young-Bruehl, *Hannah Arendt*, 328–78.

55 Jacob Robinson offered the most comprehensive rebuke in *And the Crooked Shall Be Made Straight* (New York: MacMillan, 1965). Peter Berkowitz observes that the controversy revealed an important shortcoming in Arendt's method: "At a minimum, Robinson's criticisms remind us that one of the very features that makes Arendt's political theory distinctive and attractive, the manner in which she wins speculative conclusions from original historical reconstruction, also leaves her work vulnerable, particularly to the charge that she molds or invents history to advance moral and political judgments" ("The Pearl Diver," 49).

56 Young-Bruehl, *Hannah Arendt*, 448.

57 Kampowski considers this objection in *Arendt, Augustine, and the New Beginning*, 94–9.

58 Glenn J. Gray, "The Abyss of Freedom—and Hannah Arendt," in *Hannah Arendt: The Recovery of the Public World*, ed. Melvyn A. Hill (New York: St. Martin's Press, 1979), 225.

59 Arendt writes, "Divine grace would not help once he had discovered that the brokenness of the Will was the same for the evil and for the good will; it is rather difficult to imagine God's gratuitous grace deciding whether I should go to the theater or commit adultery" (LMW 97).

60 See, for example, Maurizio Passerin D'Entrèves, "Arendt's theory of judgment," in Dana Villa, ed. *The Cambridge Companion to Hannah Arendt* (Cambridge: Cambridge University Press, 2000), 245–60.

61 Ronald Beiner, 'Hannah Arendt on Judging,' in Hannah Arendt, *Lectures on Kant's Political Philosophy* (Chicago: University of California Press, 1992), 90.

2

The Problem of Evil Reconsidered

Having reviewed the broad shape of Arendt's life and thought, I now want to turn to a closer examination of her engagement with theological themes and thinkers, as well as the response her work has generated in recent Christian theology. Among many areas that have received attention from theologians, none have captivated quite like her writings on evil. As these writings provide a crucial lens for understanding other features of her thought, from her views on tradition to her constructive vision of worldliness, action, and thinking, they seem an especially good place to begin.

In 1945, Arendt predicted: "The problem of evil will be the fundamental question of postwar intellectual life in Europe" (EU 134). As Richard Bernstein points out, it may have taken other intellectuals longer to come around than she anticipated, but it did become a fundamental question for her.[1] It is a concern that can be traced throughout her postwar writings, from her investigations of totalitarianism to her last work, *The Life of the Mind*. The most well-known source for her views on evil is, of course, *Eichmann in Jerusalem*. The book has been of special interest to Christian theologians, especially Augustinians, who have noted several parallels between Arendt's conception of the banality of evil and Augustine's account of evil as the privation of the good.[2] When Arendt suggests that Eichmann lacked "any diabolical or demonic profundity" (EJ 288) and that his evil could not be traced "to any deeper level of roots" (LMT 4), Jean Bethke Elshtain hears the unmistakable echo of Augustine's view that evil is a "diminution" of being, "a kind of noncreation, a draining away from that which is."[3] Just as Augustine was trying to strip Manichaeism of its mythological power and avoidance of responsibility, Arendt sought to destroy "the legend of the greatness of evil" and insist upon greater accountability in an age when duty and superior orders were regularly cited as ways of escaping it.[4] Elshtain finds the parallels so strong, in fact, that she suspects a direct influence: "Here Hannah Arendt, as elsewhere, is Augustine's faithful daughter. To capture the depth of her horror at the era through which she has lived, she returns to one of her first great teachers, St. Augustine."[5] While Charles Mathewes does not go quite so far, he does consider Arendt a "recent descendant" of his thought, someone who is sufficiently shaped by his work to bring a "recognizably Augustinian" approach to the question of evil.[6] As Mathewes puts it, her approach reveals how "the Augustinian account's conceptual scheme is both theoretically viable and practically applicable in understanding and responding to evil."[7] Interestingly, this is a reading increasingly shared not only among her Augustinian champions, but her critics as well, who fault Arendt precisely for her inability to think about evil beyond the Augustinian terms of privation and original sin. As Alan Wolfe writes, "Like no other twentieth-century writer, Arendt took the idea of original sin and made it part of our everyday vocabulary. Only now, we—Christians and non-Christians alike—refer to it as the 'banality of evil.'"[8]

The irony, of course, is that if there is one point that unites all of Arendt's writings on evil, from her early analysis of the concentration camps to her later coverage of the Eichmann trial, it is that she believed that the specific evil of totalitarianism "broke" the thread of tradition and could not be understood through any traditional categories, legal, moral, or theological. In *The Origins of Totalitarianism*, she makes the point explicit: "we actually have nothing to fall back on in order to understand a phenomenon that nevertheless confronts us with its overpowering reality and breaks down all standards we know" (OT 459). This explains why, when Arendt initially sought to conceptualize this evil, she resorted to the language of "radical evil," a term originally coined by Kant but which she re-appropriated to name what distinguished the horrors of the concentration camps from all previous evils. While she later switched to the language of the banality of evil, she did not back away from her claims about the break in tradition. In the introduction to *The Life of the Mind*, she explains that when she first found herself "in possession" of her new phrase, "I held no thesis or doctrine, although I was dimly aware of the fact that it went counter to our tradition of thought—literary, theological, or philosophic—about the phenomenon of evil" (LMT 3). Moreover, where Arendt does directly engage the privation account of evil, she is actually critical, suggesting that such "time-honored opinions have become dangerous" because they inspire "a treacherous hope used to dispel legitimate fear" (OV 56).[9] "Evil is either denied true reality (it exists only as a deficient mode of the good) or is explained away as a kind of optical illusion" (LMW 34).

Thus we appear to have a rather strange situation: Arendt consistently and emphatically disavows the relevance of tradition in making sense of the unprecedented nature of totalitarian evil, and yet much of what she has to say about evil inadvertently confirms the continued relevance of the Augustinian tradition. What should we make of this? The irony, I think, is ultimately instructive, as it helps to highlight the complexities of responding to evil in the modern age and opens a deeper conversation about the specific role of tradition in this task. On the one hand, Arendt invites us to consider what is genuinely unprecedented about totalitarianism. Here her neglected concept of radical evil, frequently (and mistakenly) assumed to conceive evil in Manichean terms, warrants our closer attention, as this is where she lays out in fullest terms what exactly she finds unprecedented about political evil in the twentieth century. As I discuss in the first section of the chapter, radical evil refers to two specific novelties: a new kind of crime, "the organized attempt to render human beings superfluous," and a new kind of perpetrator, one who lacks the conventional motives we associate with evil-doing and whose psyche is diminished or destroyed under the weight of ideology. In shifting to the later language of the banality of evil, Arendt does not leave these points behind, but builds upon them, as I show in the second part of the chapter. She deepens her account of the novelty of the crime by drawing attention to the way that it represents an attack on human plurality, appropriating the new legal term "crimes against humanity," and she extends her account of the new kind of criminal by depicting Eichmann as thoughtless and acting in an inverted legal context where the ordinary virtue of being a law-abiding citizen becomes a murderous vice. With a sense for what Arendt regards as novel about totalitarian evil, we will then be prepared in the third section to assess her claims about tradition. Arendt's disavowal of tradition is a function of two things: first, her understanding of specific traditional positions on evil, and second, her assumptions about tradition itself. With regard to the first, I argue that while Arendt makes a persuasive case that totalitarianism represents a new kind of crime, she overstates the novelty of her points about Eichmann's moral psychology. Here the parallels that Augustinians identify between her and Augustine are suggestive, as they show that much of Arendt's analysis actually confirms the continued applicability of the Augustinian account. This reveals a tendency in Arendt to dismiss traditional resources too prematurely and, in the case of the privation account, on the basis of a mischaracterization of the position in question. The deeper issue, I argue, is how Arendt conceives tradition itself. Arendt's disavowal of tradition is based upon one rather static conception of tradition, one in which a fixed set of conceptual resources is passed down that either anticipates or fails to anticipate contemporary realities. I argue that this is not the only way to conceive tradition, and that when Arendt endorses the use of a criminal trial, appropriates legal innovations such as the language of crimes against humanity, and unwittingly confirms how many features of the Augustinian tradition continue to apply in radically changed circumstances, her work testifies to the possibility that traditions can develop and innovate in the face of a crisis. The enduring challenge of Arendt's writings on evil, I conclude, is not that they require us to abandon tradition, but to discern anew the distinctive marks of evil in every age, taking seriously its novel institutional and organizational forms, and continuously adapt and re-narrate our traditions so that they reflect and remain responsive to these challenges. In this spirit, I close the chapter by considering how Arendt's analysis of twentieth-century political evil remains relevant today and what new challenges now claim our attention.

I. Radical Evil

To gain a better sense of why Arendt believes traditional categories of evil are inadequate for understanding the nature of totalitarianism, I want to begin with her concept of radical evil. Much confusion has surrounded this term, as it conjures Manichean images of a demonic force invading history and transforming human beings into mere pawns in a cosmic struggle between good and evil. Indeed, Elshtain assumes that Arendt was prey to these very illusions at this stage of her thinking and did well to abandon the concept.[10] Yet as Bernstein and others have argued, Arendt never uses the term to attribute any demonic dimension to totalitarian perpetrators.[11] In fact, she uses it to name the specific nature of a new kind of crime committed by a new kind of perpetrator, and she remained adamant at this early stage that we could only take these new threats seriously if we learned to face "the music of man's genuine capacity for evil" and see that "the Nazis are men like ourselves" (EU 134).

We gain important insight into the meaning of radical evil by considering where it fits in the broader scheme of *The Origins of Totalitarianism*, the work in which Arendt introduces the term. She discusses it in the penultimate chapter in a section entitled, "Total Domination," which includes her account of the final stages of totalitarianism and her analysis of the concentration camps. That it is only here that she invokes the term is important, as she takes this stage to be different from earlier stages in significant ways.

In its early stages, totalitarianism functions like any of the vicious tyrannies of the past, using terror to accomplish a variety of objectives: to suppress political opposition, detain criminals, make up for labor shortages, and generally solidify its grip on power. But totalitarianism as a unique form of government really only comes into its own when these objectives have been met and there is no longer any strategic use for terror, when "the regime no longer has anything to fear from the opposition" and "everybody who might be described as a child of the revolution ... has long since been devoured" (OT 440). At exactly the point where we would expect the use of terror to stop, it increases. In trying to understand what happens next, she says we are inevitably held back by our liberal habits of thought. "There is a great temptation to explain away the intrinsically incredible by means of liberal rationalizations. In each one of us, there lurks such a liberal, wheedling us with the voice of common sense" (439–40). Thus we point to historical precedents such as expulsion, slavery, and concentration camps and conclude that there is actually nothing new about totalitarian domination. But for Arendt this is to miss the real difference, which is not the techniques themselves, but how they are employed. In past regimes, they were employed under the banner, "everything is permitted," which is to say, as a means to an end; under totalitarianism, however, they effectively become ends in themselves. She observes:

> But wherever these new forms of domination assume their authentically totalitarian structure they transcend this principle, which is still tied to the utilitarian motives and self-interest of the rulers, and try their hand in a realm that up to now has been completely unknown to us: the realm where "everything is possible." And, characteristically enough, this is precisely the realm that cannot be limited by either utilitarian motives or self-interest, regardless of the latter's content. (440)

If we cannot understand totalitarian domination through the lens of utility or self-interest, then how should we understand it?

Here Arendt argues that we must view the final stage of totalitarianism through the lens of the ideologies that inspire it. "An ideology," she writes, "is quite literally what its name indicates: it is the logic of an idea" (469). Ideologies purport to explain everything, all of human history, "the secrets of the past, the intricacies of the present, the uncertainties of the future" (469), by tracing out the logic of a single idea: in the case of Nazi totalitarianism, it is the idea of history as a race struggle; in Stalinist totalitarianism, it is history as a class struggle. "The ideology treats the course of events as though it followed the same 'law' as the logical exposition of its 'idea'" (469). Thus it sees history, no less than nature, as a realm of necessity, following strict laws that operate independent of human agency. Our role is essentially to conform to these laws, which means that expressions of human freedom can only be regarded as "an annoying interference with higher forces" (466). This is where terror assumes its central significance. Human freedom may not ultimately derail the course of history, but it can slow it down, and the role of terror is to speed it back up. "In the iron band of terror," she writes, "a device has been found not only to liberate the historical and natural forces, but to accelerate them to a speed they never would reach if left to themselves" (466). Terror plays another, equally important role, which relates to the fact that totalitarian ideologies do not concern the fate of individual, but instead focus upon the broader fate of the human species. The goal is to achieve a racially purified race or a single, homogenous class, and from this vantage point, individuality is regarded as much of an interference as freedom. Thus terror, in its capacity to compel the many to act as One, is what ensures that this broader collective race or class appears. Through the use of terror, the totalitarian regime "strives to organize the infinite plurality and differentiation of human beings as if all of humanity were just one individual" (438), aiming to "form and maintain a society, whether one dominated by a particular race or one in which classes and nations no longer exist, in which every individual would be nothing other than a specimen of the species" (EU 305–6).

The role of terror in the later stages of totalitarianism is thus not to secure power, guard against internal threats, maximize profits, or some other strategic purpose; it is to bring human society into conformity with higher laws. It is a means of verifying the truth of ideological claims by fabricating the conditions in which these claims can be displayed. The camps emerge as the "central institution" of totalitarianism because they offer the only conditions in which it becomes possible to contemplate the elimination of freedom and individuality as such. In this sense, the point of the camps is not just to destroy human life. The point is to change what human life is. The camps serve as "laboratories" in which the pliability of the human being can be tested and glimpses of the new human species can come into view.

Arendt describes three stages through which this happens. First, there is the destruction of the "juridical person in man" (OT 447). Before detainees are sent to the camps, totalitarian regimes make a point of formally stripping them of their citizenship. This renders them stateless persons without any rights, individuals for whom no other state feels responsible. That such persons are sent to camps without having committing any offense cuts them off from the juridical world where punishments correspond to specific actions, preparing them for a new, arbitrary world where nothing they suffer corresponds to anything they say or do. The second step is the destruction of the "moral person in man," which is twofold: the destruction of the conditions necessary for moral protest or witness (one cannot die a martyr if there are no witnesses), and the creation of impossible moral dilemmas that make "the decisions of conscience absolutely questionable and equivocal" (452). Arendt observes:

> When a man is faced with the alternative of betraying and thus murdering his friends or of sending his wife and children, for whom he is in every sense responsible, to their death; when even suicide would mean the immediate murder of his own family—how is he to decide? The alternative is no longer between good and evil, but between murder and murder. (452)

This is followed by a final step, the destruction of a person's individuality, which is accomplished through uniform codes of dress, diet, labor, and movement, whereby a person's capacity for individual expression is gradually disabled and the individual is absorbed into the mass rhythms of one overall camp personality. "Nothing then remains but ghastly marionettes with human faces, which all behave like the dog in Pavlov's experiments, which all react with perfect reliability even when going to their own death, and which do nothing but react" (455).

Such a process, Arendt argues, can hardly be classified as murder. Murder, she observes, "is only a limited evil. The murderer who kills a man ... still moves within the realm of life and death familiar to us ... The murderer leaves a corpse behind and does not pretend that his victim has never existed ... he destroys a life, but he does not destroy the fact of existence itself" (442). The concentration camps, on the other hand, "treat people as if they had never existed and make them disappear in the literal sense of the word" (442). "The real horror of the concentration and extermination camps," she observes, "lies in the fact that the inmates, even if they happen to keep alive, are more effectively cut off from the world of the living than if they had died, because terror enforces oblivion" (443). It is at this point that we can no longer speak of a "limited" evil but must venture to speak of a "radical" evil. Arendt writes:

> It is the appearance of some radical evil previously unknown to us, that puts an end to the notion of developments and

transformations of qualities ... something seems to be involved in modern politics that actually should never be involved in politics as we used to understand it, namely all or nothing—all, and that is an undetermined infinity of forms of human living-together, or nothing, for a victory of the concentration-camp system would mean the same inexorable doom for human beings as the use of the hydrogen bomb would mean for the human race. (443)

As Arendt introduces the term, we see that radical evil is her way of naming what she takes to be unprecedented about totalitarian domination. It refers to the attempt to make politics a matter of "all or nothing" by eliminating the individuality and spontaneity that have always been thought to be an inalienable feature of human life. Such an evil does not intend to use a human being as a means to an end; it attempts to render the human being useless, not even worth oppressing or enslaving. As she puts it in a letter to Jaspers shortly after the publication of *Origins*:

> What radical evil really is I don't know, but it seems to me it somehow has to do with the following phenomenon: making human beings as human beings superfluous (not using them as means to an end, which leaves their essence as humans untouched and impinges only on their human dignity; rather, making them superfluous as human beings). This happens as soon as all unpredictability—which, in human beings, is the equivalent of spontaneity—is eliminated. (HAKJ 166)

As Dana Villa summarizes, "The whole thrust of Arendt's analysis of totalitarianism ... is that *total* domination is a new aspiration in the history of human power, an aspiration that could arise only when politics entered the hitherto unthinkable realm of 'everything is possible.'"[12]

Notably for Arendt, a system of total domination means that a sense of superfluousness extends to perpetrators as well. Radical evil, she observes:

> emerged in connection with a system in which all men have become equally superfluous. The manipulators of this system believe in their own superfluousness as much as in that of all

others, and the totalitarian murderers are all the more dangerous because they do not care if they themselves are alive or dead, if they ever lived or never were born. (OT 459)

Arendt points out that when the camps were first organized, they were administered by men who exhibited the "deep hatred and resentment" that we would expect from Nazi thugs, guided by motives which, in their very perversity, still kept them in touch with the realm of human feeling.[13] Such men were later replaced by members of the SS, who were selected not on the basis of their convictions but more "objective" racial criteria. She observes:

> The consistent elimination of conviction as a motive for action has become a matter of record since the great purges in Soviet Russia and the satellite countries. The aim of totalitarian education has never been to instill convictions but to destroy the capacity to form any. (467–8)

Anticipating her later account of Eichmann, she makes an important distinction between ideological deduction and thinking. To deduce a conclusion from an ideological premise does not require thinking in Arendt's sense of the word. Thinking for her is the "freest and purest of all human activities" (473), what in the life of the mind corresponds to the faculty for free action in politics. Thinking interrupts ordinary life, problematizes assumptions, and generally follows questions wherever they lead. The deductive process of ideological thinking, however, remains bound to its working premise of race or class. Such deductive reasoning subjects the mind to an inner compulsion, what Arendt calls the "tyranny of logicality," whose never-ending process keeps one permanently alienated from anything that would interrupt it. "As terror is needed lest with the birth of each new human being a new beginning arise and raise its voice in the world, so the self-coercive force of logicality is mobilized lest anybody ever start thinking" (473). This means that the independent process of forming personal motivations or making judgments breaks down, or never really begins. The perpetrator willingly commits his crimes, but the only reasons he can give are ideological ones: "The aggressiveness of totalitarianism springs not from the lust for power, and if it feverishly seeks to expand, it does so neither for expansion's sake nor for profit, but only for ideological reasons: to make the world consistent, to prove that its respective supersense has been right" (458). She adds, "We attempt to understand the behavior of concentration-camp inmates and SS-men psychologically, when the very thing that must be realized is that the psyche *can* be destroyed even without the destruction of the physical man" (441). The ideal perpetrator is the replaceable perpetrator, the perpetrator whose individual traits, like those of his victim, no longer matter. He, like his victims, comes to see himself as superfluous.

Thus traditional categories for evil prove inadequate not only because they fail to anticipate the new kind of crime, but also because the actions of perpetrators cannot be "understood and explained by the evil motives of self-interest, greed, covetousness, resentment, lust for power, and cowardice" (459). She writes:

> It is inherent in our entire philosophical tradition that we cannot conceive of a "radical evil," and this is true both for Christian theology, which conceded even to the Devil himself a celestial origin, as well as for Kant, the only philosopher who, in the word he coined for it, at least must have suspected the existence of this evil even though he immediately rationalized it in the concept of a "perverted ill will" that could be explained by comprehensible motives. (459)

Whether it is the theological claim that the devil is a fallen angel whose priorities are confused or Kant's rendering of radical evil as the mistaken formulation of the wrong maxim, Arendt detects a common tendency to hold evil too close, to see it as something that is ultimately intelligible within a fairly familiar framework of motivations, as something merely disordered rather than something that rejects the established order altogether.

Given the way she believed radical evil broke our usual standards of judgment, Arendt was left deeply skeptical about the possibility of adjudicating such crimes in a court of law. She considered the Nuremberg trials an "abysmal failure" because "the very enormity of the crimes rendered any conceivable punishment ridiculous" (EU 310). No punishment, she argued, "could even be accepted as 'legal' ... since it presupposed ... a possible range of motives ... which quite obviously were completely absent in the accused" (310). As she wrote to Jaspers:

> The Nazi crimes, it seems to me, explode the limits of the law; and that is precisely what constitutes their monstrousness ... We are simply not equipped to deal, on a human, political level, with a guilt that is beyond crime and an innocence that is beyond goodness or virtue. (HAKJ 54)

For his part, Jaspers found Arendt's conclusions too drastic:

> You say that what the Nazis did cannot be comprehended as "crime"—I'm not altogether comfortable with your view, because a guilt that goes beyond all criminal guilt inevitably takes on a streak of "greatness"—of satanic greatness—which is, for me, as inappropriate for the Nazis as all the talk about the "demonic" element in Hitler and so forth. (62)

In response, Arendt confesses that she is still struggling with how to frame these issues, specifically, how to emphasize the monstrousness of the deeds without mythologizing the perpetrators:

> I realize completely that in the way I've expressed this up to now I come dangerously close to that "satanic greatness" that I, like you, totally reject. But still, there is a difference between a man who sets out to murder his old aunt and people who without considering the economic usefulness of their actions at all (the deportations were very damaging to the war effort) built factories to produce corpses. One thing is certain: We have to combat all impulses to mythologize the horrible, and to the extent that I can't avoid such formulations, I haven't understood what actually went on. Perhaps what is behind it all is only that individual human beings did not kill other human beings for human reasons, but that an organized attempt was made to eradicate the concept of the human being. (69)

These would not be Arendt's last words on the subject.

II. The Banality of Evil

When we come to *Eichmann in Jerusalem*, written twelve years later, Arendt is no longer using the language of radical evil, but has adopted a new phrase, "the banality of evil." Most observers take this to mean that she abandoned her former view.[14] They have a good reason for thinking so. In a 1963 letter to Gershom Scholem, Arendt says:

> You are quite right: I changed my mind and do no longer speak of "radical evil" ... It is indeed my opinion now that evil is never "radical," that it is only extreme, and that it possesses neither depth nor any demonic dimension. It can overgrow and lay waste the whole world precisely because it spreads like a fungus on the surface. It is "thought-defying," as I said, because thought tries to reach some depth, to go to the roots, and the moment it concerns itself with evil, it is frustrated because there is nothing. That is its "banality." Only the good has depth and can be radical. (JW 470–1)

These words appear to leave little doubt that she changed her mind. Yet as several Arendt scholars have suggested, we should be careful about weighing them too heavily.[15] For one, Arendt's characterization of radical evil here does not accurately represent her own understanding of the concept.[16] As we have seen, she never attributed a demonic dimension to the Nazis. In her comments to Jaspers above, she clearly rejects any attempt to mythologize them. Moreover, in her account of the "tyranny of logicality," she already drew attention to the breakdown of thought in totalitarian perpetrators, noting that their crimes cannot be understood in terms of the usual catalog of evil motives, and thus lack the kind of motivational depth that we might expect. Thus as we turn to her treatment of the Eichmann trial, we have reason to suspect that there may be more continuity than Arendt herself lets on.

Indeed, Arendt continues to insist upon the unprecedented nature of totalitarian evil and does so with the same twofold focus upon the novelty of the crimes and the "new criminal" who commits them. To begin with the crime, Arendt suggests that one significant advance of the Eichmann trial over the Nuremberg tribunal was that by focusing specifically upon the crimes against the Jews, it helped to clarify how these crimes were different from conventional war crimes.[17] The terms of the difference will sound familiar from our discussion above: if war crimes are committed in the context of pursuing military objectives, the crimes against the Jews "were not committed solely for the purpose of stamping out opposition" but were "part of a plan to get rid of whole native populations" (EJ 275). As such, they "could not be explained by any utilitarian purpose" (275). This same lack of utilitarian purpose distinguishes these crimes from "inhuman acts," which employ expulsion and annihilation in the pursuit of criminal ends such as colonization or expansion. But what the Jerusalem Court did not recognize, Arendt argues, is how Eichmann's crimes were more than crimes against the Jews:

> It was when the Nazi regime declared that the German people not only were unwilling to have any Jews in Germany but wished to make the entire Jewish people disappear from the face of the earth that the new crime, the crime against humanity—in the sense of a crime "against the human status," or against the very nature of mankind—appeared ... [This crime] is an attack upon human diversity as such, that is, upon a characteristic of the "human status" without which the very words "mankind" or "humanity" would be devoid of meaning. (268–9)

If in her writings on radical evil Arendt focused upon the dehumanizing effects of the camps at the level of the individual, here she broadens her focus to the level of whole groups. Recall that in *The Human Condition*, published a few years before the trial, Arendt names "plurality" as one of the basic conditions of human existence. Plurality for Arendt refers to the fact that human existence is not only inherently social, but also inherently diverse. As she puts it, "we are all the same, that is, human, in such a way that nobody is ever the same as anyone else who ever lived, lives, or will live" (HC 8). From this vantage point, to attempt to render human beings superfluous by stripping them of their individuality represents a "crime against humanity" in that it seeks to eliminate the individual differences that make human existence plural. The Eichmann trial now challenged Arendt to extend the point to genocide. To attempt to exterminate the Jews was to attempt to alter humanity itself, as this would diminish the plurality of groups that is constitutive of the human family as a whole. Mankind, she says, "would certainly be destroyed if states were permitted to perpetrate such crimes" (EJ 270). Thus as she sees it, the extermination of the Jewish people is more accurately described as "a crime against humanity, perpetrated upon the body of the Jewish people" (269). Such evil remains "radical," not in the sense that it has ontological depth, which, as mentioned above, was not part of her original concept, but in the sense that its effects are radically destructive, depriving human beings of the plurality that lies at the heart of humanity.

Of course, Arendt recognizes that while the legal term "genocide" is of recent coinage, genocide itself is not new. She notes that in terms of Eichmann's crimes, the term genocide, "introduced explicitly to cover a crime unknown before" is "not fully adequate, for the simple reason that massacres of whole peoples are not unprecedented" (288). One could point to the Armenian genocide as only the most recent example. Thus she suggests that "administrative massacres" (288) may better capture the particular nature of Eichmann's crimes, given the centrality of the concentration camps in the Holocaust and the broader ideological scope of totalitarianism itself, which would eventually expand to include the genocide of many additional groups. In view of the fact that such a crime had implications for every one who is a human being, Arendt, like Jaspers, believed the appropriate venue was an international tribunal. As they saw it, "The very monstrousness of the events is 'minimized' before a tribunal that represents one nation only" (270).

This brings us to the "new criminal," Eichmann. For Arendt, Eichmann only emerges as a problem if we keep the monstrousness of his deeds squarely in view. Our assumption is that only a monster could commit such crimes. This is certainly the assumption that guided the prosecution, who, Arendt notes, portrayed him as a "perverted sadist" and the "most abnormal monster the world had ever seen" (276). Arendt acknowledges that it would be comforting if this were true, but Eichmann provides no such comfort:

> The trouble with Eichmann was precisely that so many were like him, and that the many were neither perverted nor sadistic, that they were, and still are, terribly and terrifyingly normal.

> From the viewpoint of our legal institutions and of our moral standards of judgment, this normality was much more terrifying than all the atrocities put together, for it implied ... that this new type of criminal ... commits his crimes under circumstances that make it well-nigh impossible for him to know or to feel that he is doing wrong. (276)

As is typical of Arendt, here she makes a number of bold claims in the span of a few sentences: first, that Eichmann is "normal" and not "perverted or sadistic"; second, that there are unique "circumstances" under which he commits his crimes; and third, by some confluence of the first and second, that he does not know he is doing wrong. If we are to understand the "new type of criminal," we need to understand all three.

On the first claim, we see Arendt returning to a theme from her earlier discussion of radical evil: namely, the strange absence of the kind of evil motives that we would expect to see in perpetrators who have committed such ghastly crimes. Nothing struck Arendt as more obvious than the fact that Eichmann was not Iago or Macbeth. He manifested no strong hatreds, no burning desire for vengeance, and no love of cruelty. He was not a party fanatic and there were no signs of firm convictions. "Except for the extraordinary diligence in looking out for his personal advancement, he had no motives at all" (287). What Eichmann believed in was success, "the chief standard of 'good society' as he knew it" (126). Hitler was worth following because, in Eichmann's words, "the man was able to work his way up from lance corporal in the German Army to Führer of a people of almost eighty million" (126). Eichmann had had enough of being a traveling salesman of the Vacuum Oil Company:

> From a humdrum life without significance and consequence the wind had blown him into History, as he understood it, namely, into a Movement that always kept moving and in which somebody like him—already a failure in the eyes of his social class, of his family, and hence in his own eyes as well—could start from scratch and still make a career. (33)

Closely tied to this desire to make something of himself was his commitment to duty: "whatever he did, as far as he could see, he did as a law-abiding citizen. He did his *duty*, as he told the police and the court over and over again; he not only obeyed *orders*, he also obeyed *the law*" (135). Arendt takes special note of the fact that during a police examination Eichmann declared that "he had lived his whole life according to Kant's moral precepts, and especially according to a Kantian definition of duty" (135–6). Of course, this is an "outrageous" suggestion because, as Arendt points out, Kant's understanding of judgment rules out blind obedience. But it will be this distorted sense of Kantian duty, combined with Eichmann's desire for success, that will prepare him to commit horrendous evil.

To appreciate how requires talking about the "circumstances" under which he committed his crimes. From the Nuremberg Laws forward, the Third Reich was careful to legalize its crimes, and where it did not, it was understood that "the Führer's words had the force of law" (148). Arendt explains that in a state founded upon "criminal principles," the normal relationship between rule and exception is reversed (291–2). Ordinarily, the exception is what is "manifestly unlawful," what even the lowest subordinate is expected to cite as grounds for disobeying his superior's orders. In the language of the trial judgment, such unlawfulness flies "like a black flag above [him] as a warning reading: 'Prohibited!'" (148). But as Arendt explains, "in a criminal regime this 'black flag' with its 'warning sign' flies as 'manifestly' above what normally is a lawful order—for instance, not to kill innocent people just because they happen to be Jews—as it flies above a criminal order under normal circumstances" (148). This is where Arendt finds it instructive to return to Eichmann's corruption of Kant:

> What he failed to point out in court was that in this "period of crimes legalized by the state," as he himself now called it, he had not simply dismissed the Kantian formula as no longer applicable, he had distorted it to read: Act as if the principle of your actions were the same as that of the legislator or of the law of the land—or, in Hans Frank's formulation of "the categorical imperative in the Third Reich," which Eichmann might have known: "Act in such a way that the Führer, if he knew your action, would approve it." (136)

Here "all that is left of Kant's spirit is the demand that a man do more than obey the law, that he go beyond the mere call of obedience and identify his own will with the principle behind the law—the source from which the law sprang" (136–7). If the source of law in Kant is practical reason, in Eichmann, it became the will of the Führer. In emphasizing this connection between duty, lawfulness, and the will of the Führer, we see Arendt providing a more nuanced version of her earlier account of the tyranny of logicality. In *Origins*, Arendt explains that totalitarianism aspires to the utmost consistency with the laws of history or nature. Totalitarian domination only appears arbitrary if we assume that its sense of lawfulness is limited to positive law. In fact, under the tyranny of ideological thinking, consistency with the source of law is valued above all else. Likewise, Eichmann strives to act in a manner consistent with the source of law, the will of the Führer, which is not arbitrary but the visible sign of the invisible laws. No further thought is necessary. Yet Arendt notes that we should not mistake his absence of thought for the absence of conscience. His conscience still "worked," but it followed the will of the Führer. As she puts it:

> And just as the law in civilized countries assumes that the voice of conscience tells everybody "Thou shall not kill," even though man's natural desires and inclinations may at times be murderous, so the law of Hitler's land demanded that the voice of conscience tell everybody: "Thou shalt kill," although the organizers of the massacres knew full well that murder is against the normal desires and inclinations of most people. (150)

Conflating morality with the source of legality, Eichmann does not have to ask any more questions. He can act with a clear conscience. In Arendt's words, "it was not his fanaticism but his very conscience that prompted him to adopt his uncompromising attitude" (146). Villa summarizes:

> In a regime where the will of the Führer was indeed, both theoretically and practically, the source of law, this "Kantian" reification of duty and law-abidingness was morally fatal. Eichmann was a law-abiding citizen of a regime which had made murder into a law, a legal (and thus "moral") obligation.[18]

Under these circumstances, evil took on a very different face, losing "the quality by which most people recognize it—the quality of temptation" (150). "Many Germans and many Nazis," Arendt concludes, "probably an overwhelming majority of them, must have been tempted *not* to murder, *not* to rob, *not* to let their neighbors go off to their doom ... But, God knows, they had learned how to resist temptation" (150).

Arendt maintains that it is this aspect of the "new criminal" for which our traditional categories fail to prepare us. She notes that most accounts depict the actor as either baldly pursuing evil for evil's sake—out of malice, sadism, etc.—or, as is more typical, especially in moral philosophy and Christian theology, out of weakness.[19] Think of Augustine in the garden: he knows the good and wants to do it, but is held back by his will and the force of habit. What our traditions seem to have failed to anticipate, she contends, is the banal, "thoughtless" evildoer who is not motivated by evil, not tempted by evil, and not even motivated by a mistaken conception of the good, but who suspends all moral deliberation out of a single desire to follow the prevailing conception of what is lawful. Villa again captures the point:

> The "new type of criminal" represented by Eichmann is neither a party fanatic nor an indoctrinated robot. Rather, he is the individual who participates willingly in the activities of a criminal regime, while viewing himself as insulated from any and all responsibility for his actions by both organizational structure and law. Through such self-deception (and the "remoteness from reality" it promotes), an individual can successfully avoid ever confronting the question of the morality of his actions.[20]

From the perspective of our legal systems, this is why Eichmann's banality is so terrifying. He lacks the very thing our legal concept of guilt demands: *mens rea*, or criminal intent. "On nothing, perhaps, has civilized jurisprudence prided itself more than on this taking into account of the subjective factor," Arendt observes. "Where this intent is absent, where, for whatever reasons, even reasons of moral insanity, the ability to distinguish between right and wrong is impaired, we feel no crime has been committed" (277). The crisis is made acute when we consider the defense of superior orders, which under normal circumstances would be dismissed out of hand given crimes as manifestly unlawful as Eichmann's. But when rule and exception have been reversed, what is manifestly unlawful is *not* killing. This temptation presented itself late in the war through Himmler's order to stop the deportations, which Eichmann disobeyed. This did not reveal a cunning malice, but how deep his commitment to lawfulness ran. "If we are to apply this whole reasoning to the Eichmann case in a meaningful way, we are forced to conclude that Eichmann acted fully within the framework of the kind of judgment required of him: he acted in accordance with the rule" (293). We experience this as a crisis because we *know* Eichmann is guilty, but our existing legal framework would appear to demand that we acquit him. Arendt concludes that if the judges were more forthright, they would have simply admitted they "judged freely," declaring him guilty not on the basis of a guilty mind, but solely on the basis of his willful participation in the crimes.[21] That, and that alone, is a sufficient basis of culpability.

Below we will have the opportunity to assess Arendt's claims about the limits of traditional approaches to such evil. But for now, it is helpful to consider the picture that emerges from her writings on evil as a whole. Despite her own statements to the contrary, we can see that there is fairly broad continuity between her early writings on radical evil and her later account of the banality of evil. She consistently frames totalitarian evil in terms of a new kind of crime and a new kind of criminal. In her early writings she focuses upon the organized attempt to render human beings superfluous; she extends this in her later writings to account for the way administrative massacres attempt to alter the nature of humanity by eliminating whole groups. She also consistently draws our attention to important attributes of what she regards as a new kind of criminal. In her early writings, she focuses upon perpetrators who do not manifest conventional evil motives but whose capacity to think is crippled under the "tyranny of logicality"; in her account of Eichmann, she continues to emphasize the lack of evil motives through the language of "thoughtlessness," and extends this account by describing in greater detail the relationship between criminal states and the perversion of duty. Put together, Arendt's writings on evil offer an approach that neither mythologizes perpetrators nor minimizes evil's destructive impact upon victims, challenging us to consider that the greatest threat in our age may not be the criminal mastermind but the thoughtless, law-abiding citizen.

This picture of broad continuity should not cause us to lose sight of the important ways that Arendt's thinking does change.

Remember that for Arendt, events are always "guideposts for thought," occasions to reconsider, revise, and begin again. Within the picture of continuity I have sketched we have already noted important changes and innovations in her accounts of both the crime and the criminal, which were prompted no doubt by the concrete discipline of sitting in a courtroom and dwelling for an extended period of time upon one particular case. This discipline seems to have brought about another, much more dramatic change, one that has probably been too obvious to notice: namely, that Arendt now accepts the basic premise of a judicial response to such crimes.[22] Recall that Arendt had regarded the Nuremberg Trials as an "abysmal failure" and considered the idea of punishing Nazi perpetrators "ridiculous." Even if such punishment were possible, she believed there was no category of crime and no definition of guilt and that could legitimate it. Arendt has now reversed course. While she would have preferred to see Eichmann tried before an international tribunal, she defends the Jerusalem Court's jurisdiction as the last of the Successor trials. She believes that international law now provides the appropriate legal categories for judging Eichmann's crimes (genocide and crimes against humanity), even though she continues to believe the court failed to understand their meaning. While she thought the court also failed to provide an adequate account of Eichmann's guilt, she is now prepared to present her own, and in her most dramatic reversal, she now accepts the idea of punishment so wholeheartedly she closes the book with a defense of his execution, spoken in the voice of the court and addressed to Eichmann himself.[23]

None of this should be entirely surprising, for if the Nazis really are "men like ourselves," as Arendt affirmed all along, then nothing could be more appropriate than to subject them to the ordinary machinations of a criminal trial. All illusions that individuals such as Eichmann acted as mere functionaries must cease in such a setting, where "all cogs in the machinery" are "forthwith transformed back into perpetrators, that is to say, into human beings" (289). Some years later, Arendt reflects:

> It is the undeniable greatness of the judiciary that it must focus its attention on the individual person ... The almost automatic shifting of responsibility that habitually takes place in modern society comes to a sudden halt the moment you

enter a courtroom. All justifications of a nonspecific abstract nature—everything from the Zeitgeist down to the Oedipus complex that indicates that you are not a man but a function of something and hence yourself an exchangeable thing rather than a somebody—break down ... And the moment you come to the individual person, the question to be raised is no longer, How did this system function? but, Why did the defendant become a functionary in this organization? (RJ 57–8)

In her earlier writing, Arendt believed that the radical consequences of evil not only shattered traditional legal categories, but the very possibility of any legal response. Arendt's coverage of the Eichmann trial did not change her view about the inadequacy of traditional legal categories, but it did open her to the possibility of developing new ones. This was not because she had come to see the effects of evil as any less radical, but because she had come to appreciate that in a courtroom, it is not the entire historical legacy of evil that is on trial, but specific crimes and particular individuals.

III. The Ironies of Thinking without Bannisters

Having traced the progression of Arendt's thought from radical evil to the banality of evil, I now want to return to the question of her relationship to tradition. As we have seen, Arendt consistently maintains throughout her writings that the specific character of totalitarian evil breaks the thread of tradition and must be understood on its own terms. Such evil demands that both judges and individual citizens "judge freely" so that new idioms of judgment (radical evil, the banality of evil, crimes against humanity, genocide, etc.) can help us understand the challenge and prevent its occurrence in the future. Elsewhere Arendt calls this task "thinking without a bannister," which demands letting go of our reliance upon existing precedents and attempting to come to terms with political phenomena in their novelty.[24] At the same time, we have observed that Arendt's self-understanding is not always the most reliable guide to her thought. She overplays the differences between her accounts of radical evil and the banality of evil, and may be doing something similar with her various disavowals of tradition. Several issues require further exploration. First, does Arendt's thinking on evil really leave tradition behind? Or is she more indebted to tradition than she is aware? Second, what specific conception of tradition informs her various disavowals? Are there other ways of conceiving tradition that are not as vulnerable to her criticisms, ways that present tradition as more open to innovation than she assumes? I want to suggest that there are, and that it is Arendt's own thinking that can help us see how.

Let's return for a moment to Arendt's shift on the question of a legal response to totalitarian crimes. In *Eichmann in Jerusalem*, she argues that our existing conception of guilt presumes that criminals must know at some basic level that what they are doing is wrong or unlawful. Eichmann represents a new kind of criminal because he acted in a context in which all normal legal and moral assumptions had been turned upside down, where manifestly unlawful crimes became morally sanctioned and licit, thus leaving him without the requisite guilty mind. Arendt believes the court was right to find Eichmann guilty, but that it could not rely upon existing legal precedents to do so. If the court had articulated the basis of guilt upon which it actually reached its judgment, it would have made plain that it "really passed judgment solely on the basis of the monstrous deeds" (294) and that Eichmann's state of mind—whether he thought his actions were right or wrong, legal or illegal—was irrelevant. Guilt should have nothing to do with one's beliefs, convictions, or motives. Speaking in the imagined voice of the court, she puts it this way:

> Let us assume, for the sake of argument, that it was nothing more than misfortune that made you a willing instrument in the organization of mass murder; there still remains the fact that you have carried out, and therefore supported, a policy of mass murder. For politics is not like the nursery; in politics obedience and support are the same. (279)

In an age of bureaucratic murder, this is the new definition of guilt that Arendt believes we must insist upon.

Two things are worth highlighting here. First, as David Luban points out, Arendt mischaracterizes the traditional legal requirement for *mens rea*.²⁵ He clarifies: "*Mens rea* deals with intent and knowledge, not motive, and nobody suggested that Eichmann acted unintentionally or lacked knowledge of what he was doing or the consequences to his victims."²⁶ Uncharacteristically for a thinker usually insistent upon the importance of distinctions, Arendt seems to have conflated motive and intention. As she herself points out, Eichmann was well aware of the nature of the crimes he was committing. He fully *intended* to eliminate the Jews and "knew what it was all about." Legally speaking, that is all that is required for the *mens rea* of genocide. That he may have done so without feeling hatred, pride, or envy is irrelevant. "As for intent to do moral wrong or knowledge that one's act is morally wrong," Luban adds, "neither are legal requirements for criminal conviction, and neither belongs to the legal concept of *mens rea*."²⁷ Even knowledge that an act is unlawful is only required for a special "subset of crimes—generally either purely regulatory (*mala prohibita*) offenses, or those specific intent (*dolus specialis*) crimes whose statutes specify knowledge of the act's illegality as an element."²⁸ Thus the irony of Arendt's revised definition of guilt, which marginalizes considerations of motive and knowledge of an act's immorality and/or unlawfulness, is that it confirms the ongoing relevance of the traditional definition.

Where Arendt does identify a genuine problem, Luban suggests, is the case of superior orders in the kind of inverted legal context she describes. He observes: "This is the biggest challenge that Arendt poses to international criminal law. When faced with a criminal state, and 'banal' perpetrators who recognize evil only when it deviates from prevailing norms, the basis for criminal punishment must somehow be severed from *mens rea*."²⁹ Both Arendt and Luban believe it can, and it has been severed in the case of genocide and crimes against humanity at the recent ad-hoc tribunals in Rwanda and the ex-Yugoslavia.³⁰ The possibility of such legal innovation brings us to a second point on Arendt's relationship to tradition. As mentioned above, at the time of Arendt's writing on radical evil, she believed that no legal response to the Holocaust could be made, and in this sense, she held that such crimes not only broke the thread of tradition, but effectively *ended* tradition. When we come to the Eichmann trial, she now believes new idioms of judgment can be devised, but implies that this still represents a kind of thinking beyond tradition. Yet in accepting the basic framework of a criminal trial, proposing an amendment to the existing legal definition of criminal guilt, and appropriating categories devised in recent international criminal law, Arendt is not so much modeling thinking beyond tradition as showing what innovation within a tradition looks like. As the legal scholar Lawrence Douglas suggests, the Holocaust trials of the twentieth century show us a legal tradition in crisis, but they also show us how this same tradition attempted to meet that crisis by devising new standards of judgment.[31] Devising such new standards represents not the end of a legal tradition, but the process by which traditions remain responsive to the world around us. When Arendt herself appropriates these new idioms, she lends her voice in support of the capacity of traditions to do just this.

One can observe a similar pattern when we turn to her criticisms of theological approaches to evil. As mentioned above, Arendt argues that while theological approaches offer an extensive catalog of motives that may account for why most people commit evil, they do not anticipate the possibility of a "thoughtless" criminal who has no motives at all, whose capacity to form motivations and reflect morally and critically upon his actions has been eroded under the "consistency" of ideological thinking and the routine of state-sanctioned murder. Certainly one can concede her point that something other than the *libido dominandi* is at work in the camps. And it is quite true that Eichmann does not struggle like Augustine in the garden. Yet there do appear to be resources within the Christian tradition for accounting for the specific kind of psychology that Eichmann presents. To stick with Augustine for a moment, his own life shows us various stages of moral awareness, including a rather long period where he is oblivious to the moral status of his actions. James Wetzel notes that this part of his journey roughly corresponds to what Augustine elsewhere calls "the stage prior to the law," a condition in which "we do not fight ourselves, since not only do we covet and sin, but even look favorably upon our sins."[32] It is only when we receive knowledge of the law, in what Augustine calls "the stage under the law," that we experience inner conflict, which is what we see dramatized in the garden scene. Stephan Kampowski notes that we find something similar expressed in Aquinas' distinction between incontinence and intemperance.[33] The incontinent person has knowledge that a particular act is wrong but finds the pleasure of the act too much to resist; a person who is intemperate, on the other hand, has no such knowledge and experiences no such struggle. Such a person indulges the pleasure thoughtlessly, without any deliberation at all. As Kampowski puts it:

> When confronted with a particular dishonorable pleasure, he will not even consider it under the aspect of dishonorableness. All that matters to him is the pleasure ... Having decided that every pleasure is to be pursued, he does not even have to "think" twice ... He is a "thoughtless" man.[34]

Kampowski suggests that Eichmann's thoughtlessness could also be described as a kind of sloth, "the tendency to avoid all personal inconvenience or trouble at any cost," which "can lead people to close their eyes and not 'think' of the fate of their disappearing neighbors or to question the orders they are given."[35] The point is not to deny the new circumstances exacerbating Eichmann's thoughtlessness, but to suggest that traditional theological resources can help illumine some of the psychological factors at play. In emphasizing the particular role that thoughtlessness plays in Eichmann's involvement in horrendous evil, Arendt is not so much breaking new ground as showing how traditional resources can be applied and adapted to illumine a genuinely novel problem.

As mentioned in the introduction, a number of Augustinian readers point to another area of overlap, and this concerns some of the deeper ontological issues surrounding evil. Elshtain draws attention to the specific language Arendt uses in her letter to Scholem above, where she says evil "possesses neither depth nor any demonic dimension," and "can overgrow and lay waste to the whole world," spreading "like a fungus on the surface." For Elshtain, these are the classic watchwords of Augustine's privation account of evil. As she explains, for Augustine, all creation is good in virtue of the fact that the God who created it is good:

> Goodness cannot generate evil, for that would mean that goodness somehow partakes of evil. It follows that evil does not emerge through an act of generation. It is not created. Rather, evil is a kind of noncreation, a draining away from that which is.[36]

Elshtain argues that such an understanding, which Arendt knew well from her dissertation on Augustine, offers "one compelling way to account for Arendt's choice of the banality of evil to name Nazism."[37] Arendt does not mention Augustine in *Eichmann in Jerusalem*, as is her practice in other parts of her work where she is influenced by his thought, so it is difficult to say.[38] As mentioned in the introduction, there is the added difficulty of her explicit criticisms of the privation account elsewhere in her work. Yet, as in the case of her discussion of *mens rea*, it is not clear the version of privation Arendt rejects is the version to which Augustine subscribes, the version that Elshtain sees as paralleled in Arendt's account.[39] Thus once again we need to balance Arendt's own words with the substance of her account. As Charles Mathewes puts it, "What is perhaps most surprising about Arendt's attempt to create a new political vocabulary for our new situation is how very Augustinian (albeit, only partially so) her resulting position turns out to be."[40] Mathewes draws our attention to two specific points of overlap: both thinkers share the same basic ontological framework, one which prioritizes the goodness of the created order (Augustine) or man-made world (Arendt) over evil; which, in turn, leads both to theorize evil in terms of its nihilating effects upon what exists, rather than something that has existence itself. Mathewes writes:

> Just as, for Augustine, goodness is a matter of participation in God's creation through the (intelligible) Word, and evil is a measure of non-participation in the Word—a lack of reality and a mute unintelligibility—so for Arendt evil is ontologically describable only negatively, in terms of what it destroys, what it lacks. Evil is empty, shallow, banal; it destroys the possibility of real human community, community manifest through action in speech and creative of a common world in terms of which we find our meaning and our flourishing.[41]

Thus whether intended or not, Arendt's account suggests that one of the most ancient ways of conceiving evil continues to apply in the modern age. Again, this does not require denying what is unique about either Eichmann as a perpetrator or genocide as a crime. Instead, it is to appreciate how Arendt's work can teach us how the resources of the Augustinian tradition can be fruitfully developed and extended to meet these new challenges.

Pulling back a bit, how should we account for the fact that

Arendt remains so skeptical in her rhetoric about the capacity of traditions to address unprecedented events while the practical effect of her conclusions testifies to the capacity of traditions to do exactly this? The deeper issue, I think, is the conception of tradition upon which Arendt's various disavowals are based. In *Between Past and Future,* she likens tradition to "the thread which safely guided us through the vast realms of the past" (BPF 94). She suggests that it is the role of traditions to help "select and name," to "hand down and preserve" (5). Arendt's favorite metaphor for tradition is that of a testament, a set of directions that "indicates where the treasures are and what their worth is" (5). The metaphor is telling: it suggests that a tradition remains essentially the same through time, and that it is our predecessors who specify how the treasures should be used. On this view, it is not altogether surprising that Arendt would be so doubtful about the possibility of tradition illuminating the challenges of our age, given how few of them our predecessors were able to foresee. Thus, drawing from René Char, she likens our position to that of receiving an inheritance without a testament. What is required of us now, to echo what was said above, is that we do the thinking that our predecessors cannot do for us, to think "between past and future" and "without bannisters."

But must we conceive tradition this way? Take Alasdair MacIntyre's well-known definition of tradition as "an argument extended through time."[42] On MacIntyre's account, tradition is hardly a seamless bequeathing of treasures from one generation to the next. Instead, its history is marked by rupture, discontinuity, and crisis. For MacIntyre, there is no tradition—no living tradition at least—that has not experienced multiple and repeated crises. Tradition on this account just is the ongoing task of meeting such crises: of registering their full impact, of discerning the questions they raise and the answers that are no longer adequate, and applying all one's creative energy in community with others to try to put the pieces back together. This is not an exceptional task, but the normal condition of tradition. On this view, we are always in some sense left in the gap between past and future, always picking up the pieces and trying to figure out how traditional categories apply or need to be re-imagined. One can hear a similar sentiment animating many other visions of tradition, some very different from MacIntyre's.[43] The point is that thinking within a tradition and making judgments about new challenges is a necessary opposition only on one account of tradition. On a revised definition of tradition, "thinking without bannisters" appears less an alternative to tradition than one form that tradition-based reasoning can take. Indeed, one is tempted to say that there is a kind of "thinking without bannisters" inherent in all tradition-based reasoning, just to the extent that the question of how a tradition applies is never certain and always demands the kind of responsive, creative thinking that Arendt models.

In trying to account for the overlap between some of Arendt's conclusions and those of traditional approaches, one should also keep in mind that despite her explicit criticisms of tradition, she remained the consummate pearl diver. She describes her own practice of thinking without bannisters this way: "I always thought that one has got to start thinking as though nobody had thought before, and then start learning from everybody else."[44] As we saw in the last chapter, Arendt's conviction about the "break in tradition" did not mean she thought we should abandon the past. Instead, she thought it demanded that we should look upon the past with new eyes. Her creative appropriation of Kant's concept of radical evil is one example of this sensibility. If her use of some of the classical images and metaphors of the privation account is intentional, this represents another. Thus Arendt continues to draw upon traditional sources, even as she criticizes the traditions which carry them down to us, reflecting the strategy of "reliance" and "renunciation" that Mara Willard argues characterizes her approach to theological sources more generally.[45] The question, again, is whether pearl diving needs to be conceived as an alternative to tradition, or if in fact it represents another fruitful way of conceiving tradition-based reasoning.[46] Here one thinks of the twentieth-century *ressourcement* movement in Catholic theology, which attempted to breathe new life into the Catholic tradition by going "back to the sources" and listening for the ways that neglected voices might speak in new ways. The idea was not to present these voices as alternatives to tradition, but as resources that might help revive a tradition and enable it to become more responsive to contemporary challenges. As we will explore in greater detail in Chapter 5, this offers one way to think about how Arendt's notions of "thinking between past and future" and "pearl diving" might be fruitfully appropriated within Christian theology.

To summarize, Arendt's writings on evil were shaped by tradition in more ways than she knew, and inadvertently testify to the ongoing relevance of a number of legal and theological approaches to evil. At the same time, she helped to name a number of the genuinely unprecedented features of political evil in the twentieth century, from the new kind of crime (the attempt to render human beings superfluous; the attack on human plurality as such) to the new circumstances under which criminals such as Eichmann act. In doing so, her thought invites those working within theological traditions to remain responsive to the specific challenges she raised and consider how these challenges have evolved or taken new shape today. That is what I want to consider in closing.

IV. The Fearful Imagination

Arendt concluded *The Origins of Totalitarianism* with this haunting warning: "Totalitarian solutions may well survive the fall of totalitarian regimes in the form of strong temptations which will come up whenever it seems impossible to alleviate political, social, or economic misery in a manner worthy of man" (459).[47] In the past half-century, Arendt's words have proven all too true. We need no reminding of how much of a temptation genocide has remained for governments in Cambodia, Rwanda, and the former Yugoslavia, which not only used the bureaucratic machinery of the state to organize mass murder, but enlisted ordinary citizens to do much of the killing for them. We have seen states resort to ethnic cleansing in Kosovo, East Timor, and Darfur, and systematic and widespread atrocities in Congo, Lebanon, Syria, and too many other places to name. Moreover, we have learned that the use of such solutions is hardly limited to states or their bureaucracies. Non-state actors from the Lord's Resistance Army to al-Qaeda and the Islamic State have proven just as effective in leveraging terror and ideology to eliminate freedom, arrest thinking, and attack plurality.

Arendt presciently sensed that a day would come when it would not take a totalitarian regime to impose totalitarian solutions, and the fact that totalitarianism as a form of government has proven a relatively rare phenomenon provides us with little comfort. Instead of total domination, we have inherited a proliferation of innumerable forms of partial domination, and thus it seems that our inheritance too has been left to us without a testament. Arendt has, however, provided us with some guideposts. I want to consider three.

In trying to understand the unique character of political evil in her own day, Arendt spoke of the importance of what she called the "fearful imagination." In a central passage from *Origins*, she writes:

> If it is true that the concentration camps are the most consequential institution of totalitarian rule, "dwelling on horrors" would seem to be indispensible for the understanding of totalitarianism ... Only the fearful imagination of those who have been aroused by such reports but have not actually been smitten in their own flesh, of those who are consequently free from the bestial, desperate terror which, when confronted by real, present horror, inexorably paralyzes everything that is not mere reaction, can afford to keep thinking about horrors. Such thoughts are useful only for the perception of political contexts and the mobilization of political passions. (441)

Here Arendt envisions a role for those who have not endured horrors themselves but who have been "aroused" by reports of them. This seems especially relevant for us, who live in an age where we are not simply aroused but bombarded with images of horrendous evil.[48] This bombardment can prompt many responses: a sentimental gesture, a check to a humanitarian organization, voyeuristic curiosity, or in most cases, indifference. The point is that in a situation of constant bombardment, we are more likely than ever *not* to be aroused, never to admit the claim that such reports make upon our thinking, and thus never actually think about them. For as we saw in the last chapter, one of Arendt's core methodological claims is that our ability to think is intimately caught up with our ability to feel horror, the unspeakability of which generates the questions that lead to understanding and judgment. The particular challenge that Arendt names so powerfully, one that goes beyond the familiar problem of media saturation, is that the greatest horrors happen to those whose lives have been rendered superfluous, who appear useless to us, whose claim we no longer feel, and thus whose plight is least likely to arouse our horror. Both

Talal Asad and Judith Butler, each influenced by Arendt in their own ways, have drawn attention to the disciplinary frames that regulate our horror—how, for example, we feel horror at suicide bombing but not at the torture applied to their conspirators, or horror at another government's genocide but not at our own government's bombing of innocent civilians.[49] This in turn shapes our understanding of what constitutes evil and the nature of those who commit it. As Butler suggests, we end up judging a world we do not know.

Thus our ability to think about contemporary forms of evil is hindered by the very form this evil takes. Here it is essential to recall Arendt's analysis of the process by which those in the camps were rendered superfluous, as certain features of this process continue to enable the use of totalitarian solutions today. The first step of that process was the destruction of the "juridical person" in man, which entailed formally stripping the person of his or her rights. This was done with the knowledge that once stripped of such rights, the correlative duties they entail would no longer apply and the claim of the person's life would no longer be felt, at home or abroad:

> Even the Nazis started their extermination of Jews by first depriving them of all legal status (the status of second-class citizenship) and cutting them off from the world of the living by herding them into ghettos and concentration camps; and before they set the gas chambers into motion they had carefully tested the ground and found out to their satisfaction that no country would claim these people. The point is that a condition of complete rightlessness was created before the right to live was challenged. (296)

Giorgio Agamben is one of many thinkers who have drawn upon this aspect of Arendt's work to show how such a dynamic continues to be exploited today.[50] The difference between Arendt's day and our own is that there are now humanitarian organizations who exist to fill in the gap, setting up refugee camps to care for displaced peoples to whom no state is willing to offer a home. The problem, as Agamben sees it, is that this normalizes the refugee's vulnerable position, as humanitarian camps become semi-permanent zones of exception where refugees subsist in limbo between asylum and repatriation.[51] In Agamben's view, it is as if the first stage of totalitarian domination has been extracted and made to exist as a separate, self-sustaining form of life, what he famously calls "bare life." Such life is, in the eyes of oppressive governments and, sadly, the rest of the world, regarded as superfluous. In Agamben's terms, such persons can be "killed but not sacrificed," meaning they can be killed with impunity, without anyone perceiving their loss as a human loss, as something horrible or grievable.[52] Invariably it is the populations who are reduced to bare life that tend to be most vulnerable to genocide, ethnic cleansing, and other forms of political evil. Butler notes how a similar pattern increasingly characterizes the position of perpetrators themselves, who now exist in the limbo status of "unlawful combatants," denied both the rights of citizens and combatants.[53] Without such rights, they too can be tortured and killed with impunity. In a rather startling way, Arendt's picture of a world in which perpetrators are convinced of their superfluousness no less than their victims continues to apply, and yet we remain numb to it because this superfluousness fails to break through the frames that regulate our moral senses. Thus if we are even to arrive at a point where thinking about evil can be initiated, we have to address the underlying disciplinary mechanisms that regulate our horror and find ways to re-open our affections and minds to the claims of others.

This is why Arendt speaks the fearful *imagination*. In "Understanding and Politics," she writes:

> Imagination alone enables us to see things in their proper perspective, to be strong enough to put that which is too close at a certain distance so that we can see and understand it without bias and prejudice, to be generous enough to bridge abysses of remoteness until we can see and understand everything that is too far away from us as though it were our own affair. This distancing of some things and bridging the abysses to others is part of the dialogue of understanding, for whose purposes direct experience establishes too close a contact and mere knowledge erects artificial barriers. (EU 323)

For Arendt, it is the imagination that allows us to entertain new solidarities beyond the boundaries that regulate our affections, and the fearful imagination that enables us to do so beyond the specific disciplines that regulate our horror. Such an imagination is generous enough to consider the pain of the stateless as our pain, yet distant enough to be able to keep thinking about it, which the intensity of the direct experience of horror would disable. This is one modest way we can begin to register the worst forms of evil as evil, which has the potential to awaken our affections and in turn generate understanding and judgment.[54]

The unsettling part of Arendt's fearful imagination, and part of what accounts for its great power, is that she extends it to perpetrators as well.[55] Arendt's fame on the problem of evil in large part derives from her willingness to step inside the mind of perpetrators, whether it was those whose thinking has been crippled under the tyranny of logicality or Eichmann's banal careerism and love of duty. Certainly we can imagine Arendt challenging us to imagine how perpetrators "think" (or don't think) today, but she would have likely urged two cautions. Take these as two additional guideposts for responding to political evil today. First, she would urge that our investigations into the moral psychology of evil not be detached from either the circumstances in which evil acts are committed or the evil acts themselves. Eichmann was not simply a banal bureaucrat; he was a banal bureaucrat operating in an extraordinary legal culture that transformed ordinary weaknesses into murderous weapons. That is part of understanding who he was and what it means to come to terms with his responsibility as a political actor. Thus in addition to peering into the mind of a Milosevic or a bin Laden, we can imagine her analyzing pan-nationalistic ideologies of Serbian identity, mapping the cell structure of al-Qaeda terrorist networks, exploring how resource exploitation is used to fund rebel movements in East Africa, or examining how the Islamic State exploits new social media in its recruitment strategies. What all of this might reveal about the motivation of perpetrators would likely not have interested Arendt, but she would have been determined to understand how such circumstances illumine the nature of the acts themselves and what enables them to occur—why *this* group has become the target of genocide, or how *that* individual's actions fit within a systematic attack. It is where psychology meets act and circumstance that Arendt would focus our attention today.

Second, she would have insisted that the task of understanding not become a substitute for judgment. We have certainly heard many appeals to understand evildoers today. But for Arendt, understanding was always tied to the correlative task of judgment. As we saw above, Arendt's thinking underwent a dramatic shift on the question of the legal response to Nazi perpetrators, and paradoxically, it was her sense of both the banal nature of the perpetrators and the gravity of their crimes that ultimately convinced her that court trials were not only possible but also necessary. One can hear an echo of Arendt's early, dismissive attitude towards the idea of putting perpetrators on trial in the exasperation that often greets criminal justice approaches to terrorists and other unlawful combatants today. Arendt's own exasperation dissipated when she saw how trials facilitated the necessary judgment that evil requires. At one level, they apportion guilt and innocence, transforming supposed monsters and cogs back into perpetrators responsible for the evil they have done. The great challenge, as Arendt saw it, was how to insist upon such accountability in an age where the systematic character of much political evil mitigates against this very thing. A court trial was one tangible way to restore it, if only after the fact. One modest fruit of the expansion of international law and increase in post-conflict tribunals over the past fifty years is that it has become much harder for criminals to claim they did not know the atrocities they committed were manifestly unlawful. The Rome Statute of the International Criminal Court, for example, stipulates that the defense of superior orders is no longer a permissible excuse for either genocide or crimes against humanity.[56] Thus in one important way, Arendt's hopes have been borne out, even if they are still honored more often in the breach than in the observance. The denial of court trials to terrorists and other unlawful combatants does not allow such individual responsibility to be apportioned, leaving responsibility hovering somewhere in the nefarious region of such abstract forces as "terrorism" and "radical Islam." In the process, not only are functionaries in these movements not turned back into perpetrators, they are transformed into something else entirely: superfluous detainees whose existence threatens not only their humanity, but our own. From Arendt's perspective, perhaps the greatest loss for justice is the fact that a clear judgment about the gravity of the crime and the community that has been injured is never delivered. She believed the monstrousness of Eichmann's crimes were minimized before a tribunal that represented one nation only, as this failed to acknowledge how such crimes injured mankind as a whole. Surely she would have considered the monstrousness of today's crimes only further minimized in light of the fact that few of these crimes reach a court at all. With Jaspers, Arendt anticipated the day when crimes against humanity would be tried before a permanent court representing the international community as a whole. In the 1960s, this must have sounded like a cosmopolitan philosopher's idle dream. Yet such a court now exists in the Hague. And in the years to come, it will be one place where we take the measure of our convictions about both the nature of perpetrators and the monstrousness of their deeds.

Of course, Arendt believed court trials represented only one small part of the much broader response that evil in the twentieth century required. The notion of a crime against humanity only became conceivable when totalitarian regimes began to alter living conditions so radically as to deprive human beings of some of their most basic capacities. Responding to evil required nothing less than a recovery of these conditions. What these conditions are, and the deeper practices and habits that are necessary to sustain them, is our subject for the next chapter.

Notes

1. See Richard Bernstein, "Did Hannah Arendt Change Her Mind? From Radical Evil to the Banality of Evil," in *Hannah Arendt: Twenty Years Later*, eds. Larry May and Jerome Kohn (Cambridge: MIT Press, 1996), 127.
2. See Jean Bethke Elshtain, "Augustine's Evil, Arendt's Eichmann," in *Augustine and the Limits of Politics*, 69–87; Charles Mathewes, *Evil and the Augustinian Tradition*; David Grumet, "Arendt, Augustine and Evil," *Heythrop Journal* 61 (2000): 154–69; and Eric Gregory, *Politics and the Order of Love*, 199–201.
3. Elshtain, "Augustine's Evil, Arendt's Eichmann," 77, 81.
4. Elshtain, "Augustine's Evil, Arendt's Eichmann," 74. The original source for the Arendt quote is Roger Errera, "Hannah Arendt: From an Interview," *The New York Review of Books*, October 26, 1978, 18.
5. Elshtain, "Augustine's Evil, Arendt's Eichmann," 76–7. In his own comparison of the two views, David Grumet goes as far as to say: "Her concept of the banality of evil could rightly be called 'theological' ... The unusual power of Arendt's analysis suggests

a need for the greater diffusion of theological concepts in current 'secular' political thought" ("Arendt, Augustine, and Evil," 167).
6 Mathewes, *Evil and the Augustinian Tradition*, 6, 150.
7 Mathewes, *Evil and the Augustinian Tradition*, 66.
8 Alan Wolfe, *Political Evil* (New York: Knopf, 2011), 63.
9 These comments come in the course of a broader discussion of the philosophy of history, an early clue that what she understands by the privation account and what Augustinians mean by it may not be the same thing: "Hegel's and Marx's great trust in the dialectical 'power of negation,' by virtue of which opposites do not destroy but smoothly develop into each other because contradictions promote and do not paralyze development, rests on a much older philosophical prejudice: that evil is no more than a privative *modus* of the good, that good can come out of evil; that, in short, evil is but a temporary manifestation of a still-hidden good. Such time-honored opinions have become dangerous. They are shared by many who have never heard of Hegel or Marx, for the simple reason that they inspire hope and dispel fear—a treacherous hope used to dispel legitimate fear" (OV 56). Defenders of the privation account of evil (at least Augustine's version of it) would hasten to say that no good can come from evil because evil is quite simply nothing. It is not generative or creative; it can only diminish the good. On this point, see Elshtain, "Augustine's Evil, Arendt's Eichmann," 85–6. I return to the issue of how to reconcile the substance of Arendt's account of evil with her explicit rejections of the privation account in the third section of this chapter.
10 Elshtain observes that Arendt's "earlier use of the category—radical evil—had missed the boat in critical ways," attributing to the Nazis a "demiurgic standing," as if they "had poured forth from the portals of hell itself" ("Augustine's Evil, Arendt's Eichmann," 75). Young-Bruehl provides a similar reading, dismissing the concept as little more than "the idea that monsters and demons had engineered the murder of millions" (*Hannah Arendt*, 367).
11 Bernstein, "Did Hannah Arendt Change Her Mind?", 132.
12 Villa, *Politics, Philosophy, Terror: Essays on the Thought of Hannah Arendt* (Princeton: Princeton University Press, 1999), 20.
13 Arendt, "The Concentration Camps," *Partisan Review* 15:7 (July 1948), 758; cited in Bernstein, "Did Hannah Arendt Change Her Mind?", 132.
14 In addition to those authors mentioned in note 10, see Villa, *Politics, Philosophy, Terror*, 54–8.

15 See Bernstein, "Did Hannah Arendt Change Her Mind?" and Peg Birmingham, "Holes in Oblivion: The Banality of Radical Evil," *Hypatia* 18:1 (Winter 2003): 80–103. Mathewes also makes a case for continuity in *Evil and the Augustinian Tradition*, 165–70.

16 Bernstein is especially clear on this point. See "Did Hannah Arendt Change Her Mind?", 142.

17 While the Nuremberg Charter introduced the category of "crimes against humanity," Arendt argues that it blurred the meaning of the concept by stipulating a nexus requirement between the crime and the broader war. See EJ 256–8.

18 Villa, *Politics, Philosophy, Terror*, 51.

19 In *The Life of the Mind*, she provides a catalog of perspectives and assumptions that she thinks fail to anticipate a criminal like Eichmann. She writes: "Evil, we have learned, is something demonic; its incarnation is Satan, a 'lighting fall from heaven' (Luke 10:18), or Lucifer, the fallen angel ('The devil is an angel too'—Unamuno) whose sin is pride ('proud as Lucifer'), namely, that *superbia* of which only the best are capable: they don't want to serve God but to be like Him. Evil men, we are told, act out of envy; this may be resentment at not having turned out well through no fault of their own (Richard III) or the envy of Cain, who slew Abel because 'the Lord had regard for Abel and his offering, but for Cain and his offering he had no regard.' Or they may be prompted by weakness (Macbeth). Or, on the contrary, by the powerful hatred wickedness feels for sheer goodness (Iago's 'I hate the Moor: my cause is hearted'; Claggart's hatred of Billy Budd's 'barbarian' innocence (a hatred considered by Melville a 'depravity according to nature'), or by covetousness, 'the root of all evil'" (LMT 4). In Eichmann, she says, "what I was confronted with was utterly different and still undeniably factual" (3–4).

20 Villa, *Politics, Philosophy, Terror*, 52.

21 Arendt writes: "This is only one example among many to demonstrate the inadequacy of the prevailing legal system and of current juridical concepts to deal with the facts of administrative massacres organized by the state apparatus. If we look more closely into the matter we will observe without much difficulty that the judges in all these trials really passed judgment solely on the basis of the monstrous deeds. In other words, they judged freely, as it were, and did not really lean on the standards and legal precedents with which they more or less convincingly sought to justify their decisions" (EJ 294).

22 For more on this shift, see Robert Fine, "Crimes Against Humanity: Hannah Arendt and the Nuremberg Debates," *European Journal of Social Theory* 3:3 (2000): 297–9.

23 At the end of the Epilogue, she writes: "And just as you supported and carried out a policy of not wanting to share the earth with the Jewish people and the people of a number of other nations—as though you and your superiors had any right to determine who should and who should not inhabit the world—we find that no one, that is, no member of the human race, can be expected to want to share the earth with you. This is the reason, and the only reason, you must hang" (EJ 279).

24 At a symposium on her work in November 1972 at York University, Toronto, Arendt responded to a participant's reference to "groundless thinking" by saying: "I have a metaphor which is not quite that cruel, and which I have never published but kept for myself. I call it thinking without a bannister. In German, *Denken ohne Geländer*. That is, as you go up and down the stairs you can always hold onto the bannister so that you don't fall down. But we have lost this bannister. That is the way I tell it to myself. And this is indeed what I try to do." See "Hannah Arendt on Hannah Arendt,' in Melvyn A. Hill, ed. *Hannah Arendt: The Recovery of the Public World* (New York: St. Martin's Press, 1979), 336–7.

25 David Luban, "Hannah Arendt as a Theorist of International Criminal Law," Georgetown Public Law and Legal Theory Research Paper No. 11–30 (2011): 1–30.

26 Luban, "Hannah Arendt," 26.

27 Luban, "Hannah Arendt," 27.

28 Luban, "Hannah Arendt," 27.

29 Luban, "Hannah Arendt," 28.

30 William Schabas discusses this point in *The International Criminal Court: A Commentary on the Rome Statute* (Oxford: Oxford University Press, 2010), 509. While Article 33 of the Rome Statute of the International Criminal Court appears to open the door for the defense of superior orders when the subordinate is under legal obligation to obey orders, did not know the order was unlawful, or the order was not manifestly unlawful, it states that "orders to commit genocide or crimes against humanity are manifestly unlawful" (33.2), thus ruling out the defense of superior orders in such cases.

31 Lawrence Douglas, *The Memory of Judgment: Making Law and History in the Trials of the Holocaust* (New Haven: Yale University Press, 2001). See especially his response to Arendt in Chapter 2, "The Idiom of Judgment: Crimes Against Humanity," 38–64.

32 James Wetzel, *Augustine and the Limits of Virtue* (Cambridge: Cambridge University Press), 146. Arendt appears to have been

aware of the point. See her discussion of Augustine's account of the sinner "under the law" (*sub lege*) in LSA, 87–9.

33 See Kampowski, *Arendt, Augustine, and the New Beginning*, 113–19. For Aquinas' views on the difference between incontinence and intemperance, see *Summa theologiae* II.II 156.3.

34 Kampowski, *Arendt, Augustine, and the New Beginning*, 116.

35 Kampowski, *Arendt, Augustine, and the New Beginning*, 116.

36 Elshtain, "Augustine's Evil, Arendt's Eichmann," 81.

37 Elshtain, "Augustine's Evil, Arendt's Eichmann," 81.

38 It is more likely that she is borrowing language from Karl Jaspers. Richard Bernstein points to Jaspers' comments in a letter he wrote to Arendt on October 19, 1946: "It seems to me that we have to see those things in their total banality, in their prosaic triviality, because that's what truly characterizes them. Bacteria can cause epidemics that wipe out nations, but they remain merely bacteria" (Bernstein, "Did Hannah Arendt Change Her Mind?", 139).

39 See note 9 above. In her doctoral dissertation, Arendt explains that for Augustine, sin manifests itself in human beings as pride, that is, as perversion. "Such perversion may arise out of the nothing from which man was made. However, for Augustine it is a perversion of being, and not a falling into nothingness, that is constitutive of vice and sin, although he occasionally calls these evil acts those that approach nothingness" (LSA 54). She later notes the influence of Plotinus: "Plotinus's notion of evil, that one should 'not think it to be anything but ... a lesser good and a continuous diminution,' echoes through most of Augustine's discussions of this question" (65). This seems a fairly accurate rendering of the privation account. Where Arendt appears to differ from her Augustinian readers is her sense of what such a view entails. In OV, she thinks it entails the belief that goodness can come from evil (56). In LMW, her criticism focuses more on the intellectualism of the view, suggesting that adherents of privation "evade" evil by attributing its appearance to a "fault" in our "limited intellect, which fails to fit some particular properly into the encompassing whole that would justify it ... Evil, not unlike freedom, seems to belong to those 'things about which the most learned and ingenious men can know almost nothing' [Duns Scotus]" (34; see also 118, LMT 178–9). As her Augustinian readers see it, however, her account offers compelling responses to these objections, while carrying forward much of the substance of the privation view.

40 Mathewes, *Evil and the Augustinian Tradition*, 194.

41 Mathewes, *Evil and the Augustinian Tradition*, 195.

42 MacIntyre provides this definition of tradition in *Whose Justice? Which Rationality?* (South Bend, IN: University of Notre Dame Press, 1988). He writes: "A tradition is an argument extended through time in which certain fundamental agreements are defined and refined in terms of two kinds of conflict: those with critics and enemies external to the tradition who reject all or at least key parts of those fundamental agreements, and those internal, interpretative debates through which the meaning and rationale of the fundamental agreements come to be expressed and by whose progress a tradition is constituted" (12). See also "Epistemological Crises, Dramatic Narrative, and the Philosophy of Science," in *The Tasks of Philosophy: Selected Essays, Volume I* (Cambridge: Cambridge University Press, 2006), 3–23.

43 See, for example, Kathryn Tanner's conception of tradition in *Theories of Culture: A New Agenda for Theology* (Minneapolis: Fortress Press, 1997). She writes: "There is consistency [in such a vision of tradition] here—the consistency of a God of free grace—but it is a consistency that, because it could not have been predicted in advance, appears to be such only in retrospect. Ever beyond the control of human expectation, it is a consistency, moreover, that cannot rule out rather outrageous novelty to come, novelty that breaks previous human assumptions about the way it all hangs together" (136). Thus, "one stands at a particular place in the ongoing course of that history and, looking back and across to what others have understood by Christian discipleship, one forms judgments about the consistency of it all so far, to use in assessing the appropriate shape of Christian discipleship now" (137).

44 "Hannah Arendt on Hannah Arendt," 337.

45 Mara Willard, "'Recasting the Old Questions': Theological Reliance and Renunciation in the Political Thought of Hannah Arendt" (Ph.D. diss., Harvard University, 2011).

46 On this possibility, see Jeffrey Stout's notion of "bricolage" in *Ethics After Babel: The Languages of Morals and Their Discontents* (Princeton: Princeton University Press, 1988), 74–7. Interestingly, while his account of tradition differs from MacIntyre's in significant ways (and may be said to be closer to the spirit of Arendt's more ad hoc, "pearl diving" sensibility), he points to the same exemplar: Aquinas. Aquinas' achievement, Stout argues, "was to bring together into a single whole a wide assortment of fragments—Platonic, Stoic, Pauline, Jewish, Islamic, Augustinian, and Aristotelian ... [V]iewing Aquinas as a sort of bricoleur, a strong moralist engaging in a kind of selective retrieval and reconfiguration of available moral languages

for his own use, helps to make sense of what he was doing" (76). For a helpful illustration of what bricolage might look like at the intersection of theology, history, and culture, see Ted Smith, *The New Measures: A Theological History of Democratic Practice* (Cambridge: Cambridge University Press, 2007), 26–30.

47 Arendt makes a similarly haunting warning at the end of EJ: "once a specific crime has appeared for the first time, its reappearance is more likely than its initial emergence could ever have been. The particular reasons that speak for the possibility of a repetition of the crimes committed by the Nazis are even more plausible. The frightening coincidence of the modern population explosion with the discovery of technical devices that, through automation, will make large sections of the population 'superfluous' even in terms of labor, and that, through nuclear energy, make it possible to deal with this twofold threat by the use of instruments beside which Hitler's gassing installations look like an evil child's fumbling toys, should be enough to make us tremble" (EJ 273).

48 On this point, see Michael Ignatieff, *The Warrior's Honor* (New York: Henry Holt, 1997), 9–33 and David Rieff, *A Bed for the Night: Humanitarianism in Crisis* (New York: Simon and Schuster, 2003).

49 Talal Asad, *On Suicide Bombing* (New York: Columbia University Press, 2007), esp. Ch. 3, "Horror at Suicide Terrorism"; Judith Butler, *Precarious Life: The Powers of Mourning and Violence* (London: Verso, 2004) and *Frames of War: When is Life Grievable?* (London: Verso, 2010), esp. Ch. 1, "Survivability, Vulnerability, Affect."

50 Giorgio Agamben, *Homo Sacer: Sovereign Power and Bare Life* (Stanford: Stanford University Press, 1998), esp. 126–35.

51 In *Homo Sacer*, Agamben writes: "The separation between humanitarianism and politics that we are experiencing today is the extreme phase of the separation of the rights of man from the rights of the citizen ... A humanitarianism separated from politics cannot fail to reproduce the isolation of sacred life at the basis of sovereignty, and the camp—which is to say, the pure space of exception—is the biopolitical paradigm that it cannot master" (133–4). For a theological treatment of these issues, see Luke Bretherton, "National: Christian Cosmopolitanism, Refugees, and the Politics of Proximity," in *Christianity and Contemporary Politics* (Oxford: Blackwell, 2010), 126–74.

52 Agamben, *Homo Sacer*, 83.

53 See "Indefinite Detention," in Butler, *Precarious Life*, 50–100.

54 Strikingly, it is imagination that Arendt thinks Eichmann lacks the most: "It was precisely this lack of imagination which enabled him to sit for months on end facing a German Jew who was conducting the police interrogation, pouring out his heart to the man and explaining again and again how it was that he reached only the rank of lieutenant colonel in the S.S. and that it had not been his fault that he was not promoted" (EJ 287).

55 See George Kateb's discussion of the role of imagination in Arendt's writings on evil in *Hannah Arendt: Politics, Conscience, Evil* (Totowa, NJ: Rowman & Allanheld, 1984), 52–84. On the role of the imagination in her work more generally, see his "Arendt and Individualism," *Social Research* 61:4 (Winter 1994), 779–84.

56 See Rome Statue Article 33, "Superior Orders and Prescription of Law."

3

Amor Mundi: Worldliness, Love, and Citizenship

Arendt's investigations into the problem of evil left her with a profound sense of the fragility of some of the most basic features and capacities that define us as human beings. Our uniqueness as individuals, the plurality of our communities, our ability to speak with meaning, our capacity to act freely and with consequence—the experience of totalitarianism represented a fundamental challenge to each of these. It revealed that our being human is caught up in certain conditions, and that these conditions are themselves fragile and must be cared for if they are to endure. The fact that so many of the indignities that befell Jews and other groups could be traced back to their statelessness suggested that citizenship was one of these conditions. Citizenship guaranteed what Arendt called the "right to have rights," the right to "a community willing and able to guarantee any rights whatsoever" (OT 297). It offered the deeper framework that "makes opinions significant and actions effective," that ensures we will be judged by our actual words and deeds (296–7). Despite our rhetoric about human rights transcending national belonging, Arendt believed that the experience of the stateless in the twentieth century clearly demonstrated that in a world of nation-states, citizenship remains the surest way to guarantee them.

Yet as early as *The Origins of Totalitarianism*, Arendt began to question whether citizenship alone was enough. Her review of the events leading up to totalitarianism revealed that a certain kind of rootlessness characterized the life of citizens as well. She pointed to growing numbers of workers uprooted by new modes of production, familial and other bonds dissolving into impersonal, mass forms of identity, and a widening sense of loneliness and anomie. In her next work, *The Human Condition*, she provides a more comprehensive survey of the modern age, and her suspicions only deepen. She describes the rise of a consumer economy in which durable goods and tangible property are replaced by fleeting objects of consumption and abstract forms of wealth, leaving citizens with less of a solid world to hang on to. She points to the emergence of the "no-man rule" of bureaucracy and the increasing dominance of politics by managers and experts, leaving ordinary citizens with fewer opportunities to participate directly in government. And she notes the appearance of new forms of social organization such as the division of labor, urban planning, and population control, which, while promising greater efficiency and improved social welfare, tend to approach citizens in the aggregate and elevate statistical consistency and normative behavior over individual expression and creativity. The result, Arendt argues, is that we increasingly lack public space in which to appear to one another. We are deprived of concrete locations where we can affirm one another's identities, deliberate over common concerns, and participate in collective action. In short, we lack the actual *practice* of citizenship: the sense of being part of an enterprise that transcends our own private interests and fosters genuinely public goods.

Thus Arendt sought to broaden the discussion by shifting her attention to those deeper conditions that enable us to realize our full capacities as citizens. She turned to an exploration of what she called "worldliness," the range of factors that inform a citizen's sense of place in the world. To talk of worldliness was to talk about the role of property and the household in giving us a stable location in which to meet our basic needs, as well as the role of work in producing tangible things that mediate our relationships with others. It was to explore the role of culture in providing lasting treasures that transcend the lifespan of those who inhabit the world, and the role of education in preserving and transmitting this world to future generations. It entailed identifying the deeper habits and attitudes necessary to motivate this commitment to the world, which Arendt captured through her notion of *amor mundi*, or love for the world, a civic virtue invested in providing the ongoing care that the world requires if it is to last. These were the more fundamental conditions and attitudes that she believed enabled us to act politically, and it was these that Arendt sought to recover in her political theory.

In exploring Arendt's vision of politics, most readers turn directly to her writings on political action, understood as those words and deeds that are exchanged within the public realm. As we will explore in further detail in the next chapter, this is the part of Arendt's work in which she discusses our capacity for "new beginnings" and offers her praise of revolutions, resistance efforts, and other democratic movements for change. Action in this special sense deserves its own discussion, yet it seems we miss something vital to Arendt's vision of citizenship if we move too quickly over the world-building practices that sustain the space in which such action happens, for there could be no such action if such spaces did not exist. This chapter focuses on these practices. It considers how Arendt's vision of *amor mundi* offers an alternative way into debates about democratic citizenship by drawing our attention to the ordinary practices that sustain our common life together. For readers in Christian theology, this area of Arendt's work offers particularly rich resources for extending recent investigations at the intersection of ecclesiology, radical democracy, and civic virtue. It does so by highlighting the role that place, materiality, and culture play in cultivating the kind of worldly conditions necessary for democratic life. This suggests a particular significance for the church, as both a worldly institution in its own right, whose very existence helps to constitute the broader common world, and as an alternative space that challenges wider exclusions and displays possible futures at the local, national, and international level.

Of course, this is to appropriate Arendt's work in a way that runs against the grain of her own understanding of Christianity, which she believed tended in an inherently otherworldly direction and played no small part in laying the foundation for the worldlessness of the modern age. Arendt reserved special criticism for Augustine, whose commitment to the love of God she took to enjoin an instrumental outlook on the world, and whose attempt to introduce charity as a principle of politics she thought threatened to become a substitute for the world and drown politics in necessity. We will take some time to review these criticisms, as Arendt explicitly frames certain core features of her vision of *amor mundi* in opposition to Augustine's outlook, suggesting a fundamental incompatibility between the two views. Drawing upon the work of Rowan Williams and Eric Gregory, I argue that this incompatibility is only an apparent one, as Augustine's understanding of the love of God and neighbor can be read in a way that promotes exactly the kind of non-instrumental relationship to the world that she finds so crucial for its endurance. Arendt's misjudgments on these matters are not without their costs. As Gregory points out, they lead her to extend a suspicion of Christian forms of love to a variety of other forms of love, leaving her inadequately attentive to questions of need and undermining some of the most suggestive possibilities of her own vision of *amor mundi*. With this said, I argue that we should not overlook the important ways in which her vision of *amor mundi* remains indebted to Augustine's thought, most notably in her core assumption that the world is constituted by our love, which she never abandons. Indeed, for all of her anti-love rhetoric, when we look at the actual substance of her vision of *amor mundi*, we find that it continues to rely upon the very characteristics of love that she elsewhere judges unworldly. Crucially, Arendt also carries forward Augustine's concerns about inordinate self-love, critiquing the modern consumer mentality that regards the world as another object to be consumed. Appreciating this is important because, as Shin Chiba argues, it clarifies that while *amor mundi* may fall short of the love of God or neighbor, it is not to be confused with the love of self that characterizes the earthly city. In this way, Arendt conceives a possibility that Augustine seems to have overlooked: that of a civic virtue that seeks the common good without necessarily implying a love of glory. Such a virtue, I conclude, is one we will need to cultivate if we are to take up Arendt's challenge to recover the common world and abide in it in a manner consistent with its fragility.

The chapter proceeds in five parts. It begins with a broad overview of Arendt's views on worldliness, before turning to her criticisms of early Christianity and Augustine. A review of theological responses to these critiques in the third section will prepare us to re-assess Arendt's understanding of *amor mundi* in the fourth section, setting up a conclusion on the import of Arendt's proposal for theology today.

I. The Human Condition of Worldliness

As with most of the terms that one finds in her work, Arendt's concept of the "world" carries a distinctive meaning.[1] Most broadly, it refers to the man-made world, what she sometimes calls the "human artifice," as distinct from nature or the earth. It encompasses both the private realm, "the houses and gardens of citizens" (HC 72), and the "common world," that part of the world that is shared and accessible to all, what "we have in common without owning."[2] This common world is the focus of most of Arendt's attention and includes a variety of phenomena: the built environment of cities and towns, monuments and parks, roads and bridges; cultural artifacts such as works of art and literature; and more intangible but no less enduring frameworks such as constitutions and laws.[3] Most important for Arendt's purposes, the common world houses the "public realm," which she identifies as the location for political action, the "space for appearing" where citizens gather and everything "can be seen and heard by everybody" (50).

In distinguishing the man-made world from nature more generally, Arendt does not mean to imply that the two exist independently of one another. Those who inhabit the world are living beings, subject to the natural life cycle of growth and decay as much as any other being. Moreover, the material with which the world is constructed is borrowed from nature, and everything human beings do in the world impacts their natural surroundings. In her later work, Arendt draws considerable attention to the ways in which human beings increasingly "act into" nature (231) through biomedical engineering, nuclear energy, and other technological innovations, which for her makes any strict distinction between nature and world not only hard to sustain, but naïve and potentially dangerous.[4] Yet Arendt still finds the distinction helpful at a conceptual level for what it helps to reveal about some of the distinctive ways that human beings experience life. Most basically, life in the world offers a shelter against the elements of nature and helps to ease the burdens of meeting life's necessities. More deeply, the world offers an enduring context that outlasts the lifespan of those who inhabit it and has the potential to be shared across the generations. This is the case in a limited sense with our homes and possessions, but all the more so with the common world. As Arendt memorably puts it:

> the common world is what we enter when we are born and what we leave behind when we die. It transcends our lifespan into past and future alike; it was there before we came and will outlast our brief sojourn in it. It is what we have in common not only with those who live with us, but also with those who were here before and with those who will come after us. (55)

For Arendt, the world's capacity to endure is tied to several factors. First, it is related to the specific activity that produces it. Arendt calls this activity "work," which she distinguishes from labor. On her account, labor is the activity through which we sustain the biological process of the human body. Through labor, we produce goods that are meant for immediate consumption, which makes them among the least durable that human beings produce: "It is indeed the mark of all laboring that it leaves nothing behind, that the result of its effort is almost as quickly consumed as the effort is spent" (87). Work, on the other hand, produces objects that exist independently of those who make them; strictly speaking, they are not meant for our consumption at all. They last not only because they have a reified, material character, but also because their use does not, in Arendt's words, "use them up." While food set upon the table is quickly consumed, the table itself has the potential to bring a family together over many meals, over many years, and potentially over many decades.

Of course, Arendt acknowledges that the table and all other use-objects will eventually wear out. "A true reification in which the produced thing in its existence is secured once and for all, has never come to pass" (139). For Arendt, this connects to another essential characteristic of the world: as the product of mortal makers, its durability is not absolute: "Because the world is made by mortals it wears out; and because it continuously changes its inhabitants it runs the risk of becoming as mortal as they" (BPF 192). Nonetheless, while ruin is the certain fate of all man-made things, "it is not so certainly the eventual fate of the human artifice itself, where all single things can be constantly replaced with the change of generations which come and inhabit the man-made world and go away" (HC 137). Thus the world endures not through the durability of the objects alone, but through the willingness of citizens to care for them: to repair those that have been broken and replace those that have worn out. Such care also entails knowing which objects to remove from the realm of use altogether. This is where culture plays an important role. As "the only things without any function in the life process of society," works of art are the most worldly objects, "fabricated not for men, but for the world which is meant to outlast the life-span of mortals, the coming and going of the generations" (BPF 209). The world only becomes a home, Arendt suggests, when citizens can recognize certain objects as valuable and beautiful enough to preserve as the shared backdrop against which all other activity takes place. It endures "only insomuch as it transcends both the sheer functionalism of things produced for consumption and the sheer utility of objects produced for use" (HC 173).

That the world endures has a number of implications for how we perceive and experience human life. For Arendt, it means that life for human beings is defined not by the circular movement of nature, but the rectilinear course of a life story that begins with one's entrance into the world and ends with one's departure. One of Arendt's most original insights concerns the way in which the world shapes the specifically human meaning of birth and death:

> The birth and death of human beings are not simple natural occurrences, but are related to a world into which single individuals, unique, unexchangeable, and unrepeatable entities, appear and from which they depart. Birth and death presuppose a world which is not in constant movement, but whose durability and relative permanence makes appearance and disappearance possible, which existed before any one individual appeared into it and will survive his eventual departure. Without a world into which men are born and from which they die, there would be nothing but changeless eternal recurrence, the deathless everlastingness of the human as of all other animal species. (96–7)

Here Arendt is directing our attention to the underlying conditions that are necessary to perceive individuality as such. A variety of forms of non-human life begin with birth as much as human life, but without a world in which to appear, the discrete character of such life blends in with the rest of nature. The creature appears as a member of a species, but not as an individual. For Arendt, human beings are born "into" a world, a world whose pre-existence is what allows us to become conscious of each person's arrival as a beginning and his or her departure as an ending. In the background here are some of the haunting lessons that Arendt took away from her analysis of the concentration camps. By removing Jews and other groups from the world, administrators were effectively cutting them off from any space in which their discrete identities could become perceptible. From this Arendt learned that human plurality demands a space to appear if the basic features of each individual life are to be recognized and affirmed.

While Arendt believed the world in general provides such a space, she came to appreciate the particular role the public realm plays in facilitating a deeper recognition of our identities. Arendt speaks of our appearance in public as kind of second birth, where we actualize our gifts and talents in word and deed. The public realm offers not only a space for such actions, but a plurality of viewpoints that assures us of their reality. As Arendt puts it, "The presence of others who see what we see and hear what we hear assures us of the reality of the world and ourselves" (50). These viewpoints also help to confirm or challenge our judgments, which bring us to a deeper understanding of ourselves and the wider world through the "enlarged mentality" that comes when we inhabit the perspectives of others.[5] The same public realm that allows us to appear before others in turn mediates our relationship with one another: "To live together in the world means essentially that a world of things is between those who have it in common, as a table is located between those who sit around it; the world, like every in-between, relates and separates men at the same time" (52). The common world provides a shared interest, literally, an *inter-est* or in-between that "gathers us together and yet prevents our falling over each other" (52).

The world's objective quality not only helps to mediate our relationships with others, but also to stabilize our identities in time. Unlike the Heraclitean stream into which no one can step twice, the world's objects remain relatively constant, which means that human beings, "their ever-changing nature notwithstanding, can retrieve their sameness, that is, their identity, by being related to the same chair and the same table" (137). For Arendt, the boundaries of the self go beyond the physical limits of our bodies; they extend outward into the objects we love and the relationships these objects mediate. These objects in turn mediate our experience of time. Arendt places particular emphasis upon the role that material culture plays in the operation of our memory: "remembrance and the gift of recollection ... need tangible things to remind them, lest they perish themselves" (170). Here Arendt is pointing to the fact that it sometimes takes an actual object—Proust's madeleine cake—to activate our memory and re-establish our connection to the past. Related to this, the tangibility of the world helps to transform the most ephemeral dimensions of our lives into something more lasting, allowing us to stay connected to these experiences long after they have ended. As we will explore in greater detail over the next two chapters, Arendt considers action and thought unique in that, unlike labor and work, they do not result in tangible goods or products. Action results in a spoken word or a deed done, but unless these are written down or commemorated in some other way, they effectively disappear as soon they are uttered or performed. The thoughts produced by our mind are even more fleeting, invisible to the world and easily forgotten. "Without remembrance and without the reification which remembrance needs for its own fulfillment," Arendt observes, "the living activities of action, speech, and thought would lose their reality at the end of each process and disappear as though they never had been" (95). As she puts it later, "acting and speaking men need the help of *homo faber* in his highest capacity, that is, the help of the artist, of poets and historiographers, of monument-builders or writers, because without them the only product of their activity, the story they enact and tell, would not survive at all" (173). Through the transformation of our thoughts, words, and deeds into worldly artifacts, what goes on in the world becomes a part of the world, and the world itself lives on as a space for human activity. This, to return to Arendt's point of departure, is what opens up the possibility of a relationship not only with our contemporaries, but with our predecessors and descendants as well.

All of this is contingent upon the notion that the world endures, yet nothing in the modern age is regarded with more suspicion, Arendt contends, than the notion of worldly permanence. She observes that we live in a consumer society that approaches all things as potential goods to be consumed. She describes the economic imperative of limitless growth whose engine is not conservation but destruction, pointing to the "economic miracle" of postwar Germany as one of many examples:

> The result is almost the same: a booming prosperity which, as postwar Germany illustrates, feeds not on the abundance of material goods or on anything stable and given but on the process of production and consumption itself. Under modern conditions, not destruction but conservation spells ruin because the very durability of conserved objects is the greatest impediment to the turnover process, whose constant gain in speed is the only constancy left wherever it has taken hold. (253)

These trends carry over into the realm of culture. Culture becomes entertainment, to be devoured or quickly abandoned; or it comes to be regarded as useful merely for realizing various external goods, such as self-improvement or social status: "The point is that a consumers' society cannot possibly know how to take care of a world and the things which belong exclusively to the space of worldly appearances, because its central attitude toward all objects, the attitude of consumption, spells ruin to everything it touches" (BPF 211).

The result, Arendt argues, is that we have little left of that worldly in-between that mediates our relations with one another. As she puts it:

> What makes mass society so difficult to bear is not the number of people involved, or at least not primarily, but the fact that the world between them has lost its power to gather them together, to relate and to separate them. The weirdness of this situation resembles a spiritualistic séance where a number of people gathered around a table might suddenly, through some magic trick, see the table vanish from their midst, so that the two persons sitting opposite each other were no longer separated but also would be entirely unrelated to each other by anything tangible. (HC 52–3)

Deprived of both a place of one's own and a space in which to appear, we are pressed in upon one another. This leads not to more connections, but loneliness, the feeling of being abandoned not only by others, but by the world of things as well. Without objects to connect us to the past, we also feel abandoned by our predecessors. Our loneliness is compounded by our amnesia. "World alienation, and not self-alienation," Arendt concludes, "has been the hallmark of the modern age" (254). She borrows Bertolt Brecht's phrase "dark times" to summarize our predicament, one in which the light of the public casts but a small flicker of illumination upon the realm of human affairs, enough to measure how much of it has fallen under shadow.

As a mass phenomenon, Arendt considered world-alienation a modern problem, the roots of which could be traced to events such as the expropriation of the peasantry during the Reformation, the rise of the nation-state, and the spread of global capitalism. But she did not think there was anything modern about world-alienation itself. In fact, she believed it was an ancient phenomenon, traceable as far back as the demise of the Greek *polis*, which first led philosophers to despair over the political realm and look for more reliable sources of stability elsewhere. In Plato's philosophy, she suggests, world-alienation took the specific form of an otherworldly flight from the temporal to the eternal, where one could find a template for the more limited stability that is possible for the realm of human affairs; for the Stoics, it took the form of emotional detachment from the world, promising at least the stability of self against the world's various fluctuations and contingencies. Yet Arendt contends that world-alienation would have remained something of an exotic philosophical orientation if it were not for two historical developments: the fall of Rome, "after which no age ever again believed that any human product, least of all a political structure, could endure forever" (BPF 72), and the rise of Christianity, which she argues essentially democratized the otherworldliness of Platonic philosophy and made doubt about the world's capacity to endure a general working assumption for all. These claims will be of obvious concern for any theological reader of her work, as they suggest that Christianity not only played a role in the formation of modern worldlessness, but also continues to loom as an obstacle standing in the way of the kind of worldly existence that Arendt seeks to recover. They warrant our closer attention.

II. Christian Worldlessness? Arendt's Assessment of the Christian Legacy

Arendt suggests that the novelty of Christian views on the world can best be understood by contrasting them to the outlook of the ancient Greeks. Fundamental for the Greek outlook was the belief that although human life is mortal, the *polis* was potentially immortal. Athenians "entered the public realm because they wanted something of their own or something they had in common with others to be more permanent than their earthly lives" (HC 55); the *polis* offered, in the words of Pericles, the guarantee "that those who forced every sea and land to become the scene of their daring [would] not remain without witness" (197). The Christian glad tidings of eternal life, however, promoted life to the position of immortality and its eschatological beliefs relegated the world to the realm of the fleeting, effectively rendering the striving for immortality both "futile and unnecessary" (21). Arendt states the political implications of this reversal in no uncertain terms:

> Political activity, which up to then had derived its greatest inspiration from the aspiration toward worldly immortality, now sank to the low level of an activity subject to necessity, destined to remedy the consequences of human sinfulness on one hand and to cater to the legitimate wants and interests of earthly life on the other. Aspiration toward immortality could now only be equated with vainglory; such fame as the world could bestow upon man was an illusion, since the world was even more perishable than man. (314)

If life for the Greeks only became "good" when one transcended the activities associated with mere subsistence, Christians now saw human life as inherently good, independent of anything they did. As Roxanne Euben explains, "once immortality is a potential associated with individual life rather than the world, human existence becomes the highest good. This is so not because of any lasting significance to worldly events and human actions, but because simple existence is the penultimate step to eternal life."[6] This in turn introduced a new way of thinking about freedom. Freedom for the Athenian citizen meant freedom from the necessity of laboring, freedom to fulfill one's fullest capacities in the *polis*; freedom for the Christian, Arendt argues, now means freedom *from* politics, the freedom to make a living and practice one's religion in peace. She offers Tertullian's declaration, "no matter is more alien to us than what matters publicly" (74), as evidence of this new attitude.[7]

Arendt suggests the very notion of a Christian politics would have remained a contradiction in terms were it not for Augustine, "the last to know at least what it once meant to be a citizen" (14). As we will see in the next chapter, Arendt credits Augustine with introducing an alternative conception of freedom, one that emphasizes the human capacity for new beginnings, which Arendt appropriates for her own action theory. But Arendt thinks Augustine also knew what it meant to be a citizen because he was able to reconceive eternal life in social and political terms:

> What was decisive in this respect was that he, still firmly rooted in the Roman tradition, could add to the Christian notion of an everlasting life the idea of a future *civitas*, a *Civitas Dei*, where men even in the hereafter would continue to live in a community ... Augustine's conviction that some kind of political life must exist even under conditions of sinlessness, and indeed sanctity, he summed up in one sentence: *Socialis est vita sanctorum*, even the life of the saints is a life together with other men. (BPF 73)

Amidst a world that is passing away, Augustine believed there was one institution that could last, "the Church, the *Civitas Dei* on earth, to which had fallen the burden of political responsibility and into which all genuinely political impulses could be drawn" (72–3). The basis of the church's endurance was not the striving for immortality but the trinity of religion, tradition, and authority. Under Augustine's influence, Arendt suggests, the Church could now make "the death and resurrection of Christ the cornerstone of a new foundation, erecting on it a new human institution of tremendous durability" (125); Christians "discovered in their own faith something which could be understood as a worldly event as well and could be transformed into a new mundane beginning to which the world was bound back once more (*religare*) in a curious mixture of new and old religious awe" (126). Thus "Rome's political and spiritual heritage passed to the Christian Church" and enabled it "to offer men in the membership of the Church the sense of citizenship which neither Rome nor municipality could any longer offer them" (125).

Augustine may have salvaged the notion of permanence and the experience of citizenship through the Church, but Arendt argues that his commitment to the love of God and neighbor undermines any meaningful commitment to the world itself, which he, like his predecessors, continued to believe was passing away. The world-denying character of the love of God was, as readers will recall from Chapter 1, Arendt's central preoccupation in her doctoral dissertation. On Arendt's reading, when Augustine conceives love as *appetitus*, as craving, the lover is constantly haunted by the fear of losing what he or she possesses. For this mode of love, there is a certain futility to the love of all mortal things, as these things will eventually be lost, if not while we are alive, then when we die. The world is no exception. To love the world is already a confusion of the proper object of our love. "Augustine's term for this wrong, mundane love that clings to, and thus at the same time constitutes, the world is *cupiditas*. In contrast, the right love seeks eternity and the absolute future. Augustine calls this right love *caritas*" (LSA 17). Love for the eternal in turn orders all our other loves, teaching us to use the things that are ephemeral and to find our rest and enjoyment in the eternal alone. Observing how his famous use/enjoyment distinction shapes his outlook on the world, Arendt observes:

> The fulfillment and end of desire is "enjoyment" (*frui*). This is the goal toward which love aims and which constitutes "happiness" ... Love exists only for the sake of this "enjoyment" and then it ceases ... All desire is harnessed to this "for the sake of," that is, it loves "the highest good for its own sake" and all other "goods" insofar as they may lead to the highest ... Hence, if the object of desire is God, the world is related to God by using it. Since it is used, the world loses its independent meaningfulness and thus ceases to tempt man. The right attitude to the world is to use it: "the world is there for usage, not for enjoyment." (32–3)

As Arendt sees it, this is a kind of Christian precursor to the consumptive attitude of modern man: instead of seeing the world as something to be enjoyed and preserved, we approach it instrumentally, as a stepping stone to something else. Arendt sees the same instrumental outlook at play in those areas of Augustine's work that are more directly shaped by Christian categories, such as when he speaks of the creature's love for the Creator. One would think that such a love would approach the world in an attitude of reverence and care, but as Arendt sees it, this love demands that we reach beyond the world to our true Source, with the same relativizing effects.

Arendt repeatedly comes back to the fact that for Augustine, our loves determine our home, our ultimate place of belonging: "in *cupiditas* or in *caritas*, we decide about our abode, whether we wish to belong to this world or to the world to come" (18). In loving God, we make the next world our home, which renders us strangers in this world. She observes: "Since only love can constitute either world as man's home, 'this world is for the faithful ... what the desert was for the people of Israel'—they live not in houses but in tents" (19). This leaves Arendt wondering, "Would it not then be better to love the world in *cupiditas* and be at home? Why should we make a desert out of this world?" (19). Arendt's own vision of worldliness, Ronald Beiner suggests, can be read as an elaboration upon this basic question, a point to which I will return below.[8]

In her dissertation, Arendt views neighbor-love in a mostly favorable light, as that which establishes a relationship of proximity with others and keeps us attentive to their worldly particularity. The problem was that Augustine's overriding priority for the eternal made it difficult for her to see how the neighbor could retain any genuine relevance. In her later work, Arendt becomes more suspicious of neighbor-love itself, now seeing it as a rival to the worldly ties that bind us to others. She writes:

> Historically, we know of only one principle that was ever devised to keep a community of people together who had lost their interest in the common world and felt themselves no longer related and separated by it. To find a bond between people strong enough to replace the world was the main political task of early Christian philosophy, and it was Augustine who proposed to found not only the Christian "brotherhood" but all human relationships on charity. (HC 53)

Charity loomed as an ideal substitute for the world because unlike other forms of love, it could serve as an "in-between" joining a group of people together without collapsing the distance between them. Arendt quotes from Augustine's *Contra Faustum Manichaeum*: "Even robbers have between them [*inter se*] what they call charity" (53). Given that charity tends to focus upon the alleviation of human need, it was particularly well suited for a politics with the more limited mandate of sustaining life rather than the world. Augustine could plausibly propose it as a basis for all political communities only when general confidence in the world's capacity to endure had collapsed, as it had after the sack of Rome.

While Arendt concedes that charity may be sufficient to carry people through a world that is passing away, she argues that it is "incapable of founding a public realm of its own" (53). This is because genuinely selfless charity must, on Arendt's reading, shun public appearance. Arendt cites Jesus' sayings from the Sermon on the Mount: "Take heed that ye do not your alms before men, to be seen of them" and "Let not thy left hand know what thy right hand doeth." She comments: "it is manifest that the moment a good work becomes known and public, it loses its specific character of goodness, of being done for nothing but goodness' sake" (74). Not even the author of such acts can perceive what he or she is doing because the moment one draws attention to oneself, one is no longer acting selflessly. The actions of the lover of charity "must remain essentially without testimony" (76), forgotten as soon as they are performed. This means that they "can never become part of the world" (76), never transformed into something more lasting. Such deeds "come and go, leaving no trace. They truly are not of this world" (76). Thus while good works are necessarily performed in the world and among others, they are performed as if fleeing from it, "negat[ing] the space the world offers to men, and most of all that public part of it where everything and everybody are seen and heard by others" (77). In the end, Arendt thinks it fitting that Augustine would regard charity a sufficient basis for uniting thieves and Christians alike because neither can afford to come out of hiding and be seen and heard by others (77).[9]

To summarize, on Arendt's account, Augustinian Christianity bestows something of a mixed legacy. On the one hand, it weakens commitment to the world through its teleological prioritization of the love of God and its attempt to replace the world with charity. On the other, she credits Augustine with saving the ancient experience of citizenship through the church and developing an alternative notion of worldly stability rooted in tradition and authority.[10] Arendt goes on to argue that under Augustine's influence, medieval Christian thinkers came to understand the church in the image of the public realm and the "secular" in the image of the household. The secular realm became "what the private realm had been in antiquity. Its hallmark was the absorption of all activities into the household sphere, where they had only private significance, and consequently the very absence of a public realm" (HC 34). In the modern age, the public and private realms blur and "the secular" becomes the primary focus of political activity, hence Arendt's description of modern politics as "nation-wide housekeeping." Christianity's basic affirmation of the sacredness of life continues unchallenged, she notes, but no longer subordinate to God, life now truly becomes the unrivaled, highest human good. "No matter how articulate and how conscious the thinkers of modernity were in their attacks on tradition, the priority of life over everything else had acquired for them the status of a 'self-evident truth,' and as such it has survived even in our present world" (319). It is no small irony, Arendt observes, that Nietzsche and Marx, in their very attempts to reject Christianity, advanced philosophies of life and labor that are completely consistent with its basic affirmation of life. It is no less ironic, she says, that modern revolutionaries have attempted to throw off the chains of religion and authority by appealing to such ideals as fraternity and compassion, which themselves contain not an indistinct echo of Christianity's emphasis upon charity.

For Arendt, the secularity of such appeals does not represent any gain in worldliness. She extends to these appeals the same suspicion she extends to charity, developing a critique of the political uses of love more generally. Haunted by the experience of the French Revolution, she observes that love that "goes public" too often degenerates into pity, which in the name of an abstract humanity and the goal of eliminating human misery, ends up justifying all manner of violence, eliminating the worldly fences between individuals and proving "to possess a greater capacity for cruelty than cruelty itself" (OR 89). Her studies of pan-nationalism made her just as wary of appeals to the love of a "people," a similarly abstract love too easily unmoored from the restraints of law and principle and too fervent to permit self-examination and critique.[11] Despite her fondness for the fraternity shared among pariah peoples, which she experienced during her Paris years, she also expressed concerns about the way such love can enclose a group within their own narrow perspective and prevent them from drawing upon the enlarged mentality of the common world.[12] At one point, Arendt goes as far as to say that love is not only "unworldly" and "apolitical," but also "antipolitical, perhaps the most powerful of all antipolitical human forces" (HC 242). While she does not specify which kind of love she means, all of these dangers are surely not far from her mind.

Such strident statements have earned Arendt a reputation for "misamorism," that is, the belief that love is antithetical to political life, which is perhaps justly deserved given her criticisms of charity and other forms of love.[13] Nonetheless, she continued to speak of her own vision of worldliness in terms of *amor mundi*, or love for the world, suggesting that there might be more to her views on love than such passages let on. We will have more to say about this below, but before we do, we need to assess her reading of Augustine and broader claims about Christianity. They have certainly not gone unnoticed—or uncontested.

III. Contending with Arendt on Worldliness and Love

No area of Arendt's work has generated more criticism—indeed, more exasperation—among theologians than her reading of Augustine and the broader Christian tradition on worldliness.[14] In responding to her criticisms, they shift the burden back to Arendt and suggest that it is ultimately her account that fails to be sufficiently public, as she remains captive to the ancient world's divisions and inadequately specifies the motivational dispositions necessary to sustain her own commitment to the common world. In this section, I examine the specific criticisms raised by Rowan Williams and Eric Gregory, both of whom use Arendt's reading of Augustine as a lens for illuminating the shortcomings of her own account.

Rowan Williams takes as his point of departure Arendt's paradoxical claim that Augustine was the last to know what it meant to be a citizen even though he allegedly did more than anyone else to bring about the demise of the public realm.[15] Williams suggests that she was ultimately right, but for the wrong reasons. He argues that Augustine did not intend to shift the locus of citizenship from the *polis* to the church, but rather was "engaged in a *redefinition* of the public itself," showing that it is the classical conception of the public realm "which fails to be truly public, authentically political."[16] "The opposition," he says, "is not between public and private, church and world, but between political virtue and political vice."[17]

Augustine's redefinition of the public, Williams argues, begins by interrogating the ancient world's assumption that political community is best sustained through the striving for immortality. If Augustine's *City of God* teaches us anything, Williams suggests, it is the utter folly of such a motivation. Striving for immortality may restrain certain vices and prevent tyranny; it may even unite a society negatively against a foreign enemy, but it can hardly be said to generate a genuine interest in a common world. On the contrary, Augustine famously unmasks the quest for immortality as an expression of the *libido dominandi*, the lust to dominate others. It is completely fixated upon the self's own interests and leads to an agonistic and elitist vision of politics. Inevitably, its outward-facing enmity turns inward and plunges political society into discord. Rather than produce an enduring world, it produces a perpetual state of political and moral ruin, as Rome's various civil wars and other disasters attest.

Williams goes on to argue that in appealing to such striving, it is Arendt, not Augustine, who attempts to escape from the limits of our mortal condition.[18] He writes:

> Augustine would have replied that the decision to "inscribe" ourselves within the human conversation in the terms described by Hannah Arendt is bound to that quest for reputation and secular immortality that actually itself represents a deep denial of the temporal. The guarantee of a place in the human story, gained by active participation in the public realm, seeks to assuage the fundamental restlessness that is *constitutive* of our human creaturehood by offering us the glamour of an assured historical future.[19]

As Williams sees it, Arendt is trying to confer upon the world a "final security and 'finishedness.'"[20] Augustine's thought suggests that, on the contrary, no such security is possible: "there is no guaranteeable future such as Arendt's neo-classical vision might suggest: real temporality is more vulnerable."[21] "It is the awkwardness and provisionality," Williams writes, "the endlessly *revisable* character (morally speaking) of our social and political relationships, that, in the Augustinian world, keep us faithful to the insight of humility—that we are timebound in everything here below, that our love is an unceasing search."[22]

By reconceiving all human relationships on the basis of charity, Augustine does not, Williams argues, seek to replace the world with love or go into hiding, but to re-imagine the terms by which the ancient world understood the relation between body and soul, household and *polis*. In this way, he gives us resources for questioning the instrumental way in which it conceived these spheres, and by extension, for going beyond these dichotomies in Arendt's own thought. The household, "far from being the sphere of bondage and necessity," becomes "a 'laboratory of the spirit,' a place for the maturation of souls" while the city is re-envisioned as "a creative and pastoral community," one that shares power and accepts limits.[23] Instead of opposing these spheres to one another, Augustine unites them under a broader purpose: "both the small and large-scale community are essentially purposive, existing so as to nurture a particular kind of human life."[24] For Augustine, the choice at the end of the day is not between love or the world, but what kind of world our loves will foster: a competitive, atomized world of scarcity born from the love of self, in which freedom is the right of the few exercised at the expense of the many, or a genuinely common world of abundance born from the love of God and neighbor, in which freedom is exercised as the common possession of all.

Extending Williams' critique, Eric Gregory questions Arendt's specific claims about the world-alienating effects of Augustine's views on the love of God. "Augustine's God," Gregory explains, "does not compete with the neighbor for the self's attention, as if God were simply the biggest of those rival objects considered worthy of love."[25] Rather, "the Augustinian self loves the neighbor *in* God."[26] Defending Augustine's use/enjoyment distinction, Gregory argues that in light of God's identification with humanity through the Incarnation, the love of neighbor and love of God are not conflated but rather become correlative:

> Augustine's God is a worldly God ... recognized in the intersubjectivity accomplished through the revelation of Christ as the divine neighbor. To love God is to love the whole of creation existing in God. The love of God is expressed in an ordered love that loves God *in loving* God's world, a world that bears "His footprints" (CD 11.28).[27]

This does not rule out love for the world or neighbor, but clarifies the kind of love that is appropriate to each, not confusing the creature with the Creator. Rather than instrumentalize the neighbor as a means to God, such love has the opposite effect: it "aims to morally protect the neighbor from the self's prideful distortion that the neighbor exists only in terms of one's own ends, or that the neighbor is a threat to the self's relation to this infinite God."[28] In this way, the love of God plays a mediating role between self, other, and world, serving to restrain precisely those paternalistic forms of love that Arendt rightly warns against. Like the world itself, it relates us without causing us to stumble over one other.

The problem with Arendt's rejection of these and other forms of love in politics, Gregory argues, is that it is based solely upon a consideration of love's pathological expressions and ignores its more constructive possibilities: "In Augustinian terms, by focusing on the hubris of disordered love, she allows sin to overwhelm the possibilities of love. She fails to discern the legitimacy and, at times, the necessity of love for healthy politics."[29] Echoing feminist criticisms of Arendt, Gregory contends that she "consistently characterizes love as a passionate sentiment appropriate only to a private, domesticated sphere" while limiting public behavior to the allegedly more rational, disinterested, and universal virtues of respect and solidarity.[30] Such a division of labor comes at a high cost, as it excludes the very motivational dispositions that are required to fund her commitment to the public world.[31] "Emotions," Gregory writes, "are not simply sentiments"; they are "complex evaluative cognitions and energies that focus ethical attention and develop understanding and judgment."[32] "In moving us to action, they become instruments of justice in accord with right reason."[33] Neighbor-love has a particularly important role to play, with the potential to transform minimalistic conceptions of justice and cultivate the kind of care that is necessary to sustain civic life at the institutional and grassroots level. "If it truly involves giving each his or her due in all respects, justice must also involve loving what merits love and securing, as best possible, the conditions for persons to flourish."[34] Augustine's thought can be said to reduce politics to an activity focused merely upon remedies for sin only if his emphasis upon sin is divorced from this corresponding commitment to love. Love for Gregory is what allows us to strive for more in our politics, not to be content with negative liberalism or even Arendt's civic republicanism. In separating liberty and equality from considerations of need and desert, Arendt ultimately aims too low.[35] Gregory thinks we can aim higher. Augustine's love-informed vision challenges us to aim as high as an "ethics of citizenship [that is] *perfectionist* without trading in sentimentalism, Pelagian notions of achieved *perfectibility*, or elitist conceptions of undemocratic politics."[36]

This review suggests that Arendt's concerns about the unworldly character of the love of God and neighbor were largely unfounded. While there are certainly varieties of Christianity and Augustinianism that have tended in this direction, this is hardly the only way to understand Augustine's own vision or the kind of citizenship his theology can inspire. Williams and Gregory help to show that rather than come at the expense of a commitment to the world, the love of God and neighbor can help deepen it. Such loves motivate the kind of non-paternalistic, non-instrumental relationship to the world that Arendt desires, but more than this, they can improve upon her own conception of the world by more fully attending to questions of need and desert without thereby drowning politics in necessity.[37]

Arendt may have misjudged the relevance of the love of God and neighbor, but this should not cause us to overlook the important affinities that remain between her and Augustine's respective visions of worldliness. As Gregory himself observes, her "concerns about self-absorption and the demise of the public realm amidst a plurality of fleeting, fragile, and inauthentic human loves mirror Augustine's own concerns."[38] As mentioned in the last chapter, Charles Mathewes suggests there remains a profound symmetry between their constructive outlooks: both ascribe to the world a kind of ontological priority over evil, and both respond to evil by reaffirming the goodness of the world. Mathewes insists that we cannot understand her vision of worldly belonging "if we do not appreciate her long-running engagement with Augustine," an engagement that "is not simply an opposition to Augustinian thought" but one that "builds on insights shared with Augustine."[39] In the next chapter, we will have an opportunity to explore how her account of natality builds upon insights gained from his creation theology, but two other areas of influence are worth mentioning in the present context, as they speak to concerns raised by Williams and Gregory.

The first has to do with Arendt's views on the relationship between the world and temporal existence. Above Williams identified the concern that in her various appeals to secular immortality and worldly permanence, Arendt ultimately seeks to secure a place outside temporal existence, one safe from its various contingencies and vulnerabilities. But Arendt's writings on worldliness suggest that she never abandons Augustine's insights on this score. As Ronald Beiner observes, "Arendt actually shared Augustine's vision of the precariousness of human temporality, and it constituted one of the major sources of impetus for her philosophical reflection."[40] From her earliest studies of the concentration camps to her account of the worldlessness of modern citizens, Arendt consistently brings her discussion back to the fragility of the conditions that allow individuals to exercise their basic human capacities. She was under no illusion that the preservation of such conditions was ever assured. The very events that taught her the importance of the world's endurance also taught her that it always remains the product of mortal makers and that without continual repair and renewal, it will decay like all other things. It is tempting to read Arendt's various appeals to immortality as an attempt to escape this situation, but as Peg Birmingham rightly points out, we should be careful about identifying her own views with those she attributes to the ancient Greeks. Birmingham observes, "While Arendt's discussion of immortality in *The Human Condition* is often read as an argument for heroic deeds and speech that distinguish the actor in the public realm and thereby ensure individual endurance in time," her real concern is not individual glory but the endurance of "the common world itself."[41] Echoing this, Patrick Boyle notes that Arendt's particular conception of the world bears a closer resemblance to Augustine's than that of the Greeks; unlike the Periclean ideal of the *polis*, hers is a world that remains ever subject to the ruin of time, one that is always "passing away" and, for this very reason, one that demands our care and attention.[42] In her 1955 remarks, "The History of Political Theory," Arendt puts it this way:

> In the last analysis, the human world is always the product of man's *amor mundi*, a human artifice whose potential immortality is always subject to the mortality of those who build it and the natality of those who come to live in it. What Hamlet said is always true: "The time is out of joint; O cursed spite/ That ever I was born to set it right!" (PP 203)

For Arendt, the world, no less than its inhabitants, exists "between past and future," and the task of sustaining it is never finished. It falls to each new generation to renew.

That Arendt uses the specific language of *amor mundi* to capture this task suggests that despite all of her criticisms of the role of love in politics, she never fully abandons another core Augustinian insight—that the world is a product of our loves. In a letter written to Karl Jaspers, Arendt writes: "I've begun so late, really only in recent years, to truly love the world that I shall be able to do that now. Out of gratitude, I want to call my book on political theories '*Amor mundi*'" (HAKJ 264). Arendt eventually settled upon her editor's choice of title, *The Human Condition*, but her use of the phrase to summarize a book largely hostile to the role of love in politics is suggestive, if not perplexing. Gregory is skeptical whether such *amor* amounts to love in any meaningful sense, writing: "The 'love' for the world relevant to Arendt's vision of political citizenship is a particular notion of love. It is a love drained of religious affectivity or moral passion so as to be suitable for the responsibilities of the political world of action."[43] Yet when we look at some of the specific practices and attitudes that Arendt has in mind, we see that it entails more than this, something closer to the kind of care that Gregory thinks is vital for democratic citizenship. It is a vision of how to abide in the world in a manner consistent with its fragility, and worth a closer look.

IV. Revisiting Arendt's Vision of *Amor Mundi*

The place to begin to understand Arendt's vision of *amor mundi* is her neglected essay, "The Crisis in Education." There she discusses how the wider crises of tradition and authority have manifested themselves in the realm of education, with the effect that we are no longer sure we have anything to teach our children or that teachers are even the ones best equipped to do the teaching. Hence our experimentation with a variety of pedagogical techniques that effectively hand over the teaching to children themselves. Arendt sees this situation as symptomatic of our basic estrangement from the world, a sign that we are no longer acquainted with the world enough to share it with our children, and no longer invested in the world enough to see ourselves as responsible for passing it on to them. Yet this, she takes it, is exactly the purpose of education:

> Education is the point at which we decide whether we love the world enough to assume responsibility for it and by the same token save it from that ruin which, except for renewal, except for the coming of the new and young, would be inevitable. And education, too, is where we decide whether we love our children enough not to expel them from our world and leave them to their own devices, nor to strike from their hands their chance of undertaking something new, something unforeseen by us, but to prepare them in advance for the task of renewing a common world. (BPF 196)

Several things are striking about the way Arendt frames love for the world here. First, the lines that typically separate public and private in her thought are noticeably blurred. Love for children manifests itself in the form of love for the world; love for the world takes the form of love for children. The roles of parent, teacher, and citizen overlap in the same activity, and the meeting of a need, namely, the initiation of children into the world, is a framed as an explicitly political task, part of the renewal of the world. Here we also note Arendt's characteristic emphasis upon responsibility, but it is not framed in terms of respect or friendship. Throughout the essay,

Arendt repeatedly uses the language of care, not only in relation to the child, but the world as well:

> the child requires special protection and care so that nothing destructive may happen to him from the world. But the world, too, needs protection to keep it from being overrun and destroyed by the onslaught of the new that bursts upon it with each new generation. (186)

Such care, Arendt suggests, is necessary in order to see each student through to their full development: "Insofar as the child is not yet acquainted with the world, he must be gradually introduced to it; insofar as he is new, care must be taken that this new thing comes to fruition in relation to the world as it is" (189). Arendt's argument also appeals to other features of love, particularly love's capacity to conserve and cherish: "conservation," she says, "is of the essence of the educational activity, whose task is always to cherish and protect something—the child against the world, the world against the child, the new against the old, the old against the new" (192). Perhaps most strikingly, Arendt plainly appeals to our love as a motivation for assuming our role in this process. The task of education, the task of conserving and passing on the world, is not simply a question of having the right knowledge, of having the latest statistics or pedagogical methods; it is a question of our love. Do we *love* the world enough to take responsibility for it? Here love is hardly peripheral to action; it is what focuses our attention and moves us to act. Later, in her reflections on the will in *The Life of the Mind*, Arendt comes back to Augustine's notion of love as the "weight of the soul." She observes that for Augustine, love "exerts its influence through the 'weight'—'the will resembles a weight'—it adds to the soul, thus arresting its fluctuations. Men do not become just by knowing what is just but by loving justice" (LMW 104). In her reflections on education, we see Arendt framing love for the world in similar terms. We only come to be committed to education when the world, and the children in it, have become a genuine object of our love. As Shin Chiba puts it, it is this love that for Arendt "restrains the fluctuation, contingencies, and arbitrariness of the will by giving 'weight' and 'permanence' to the soul, so that a sustained commitment to the world may become possible."[44]

While we are accustomed to thinking of children and other individuals as objects of love, we may be less inclined to think of the tangible world in such terms. That our ability to love persons might be caught up in a correlative love of things is the subject of Arendt's companion essay, "The Crisis in Culture." Here she appropriates Cicero's notion of the *cultura animi*, or the cultured mind, and re-defines it as "an attitude that knows how to take care and preserve and admire the things of the world" (BPF 225). Arendt plays upon the etymological roots of the word culture, derived from *colere*, meaning "to cultivate, to dwell, to take care, to tend and preserve" (211). Cultivation, she explains, "indicates an attitude of loving care and stands in sharp contrast to all efforts to subject nature to the domination of man" (212); it regards worldly objects "independently of all utilitarian and functional references" (210) and protects them from "processes of consumption and usage" (209). Here love for the world serves as an antidote to the consumptive attitude described above, one that see the world as merely another object to be consumed. Arendt likens it to a kind of *philokalia*, or love of beauty, which loves things for their own sake, for the sheer goodness of their appearance independent of what we do with them. Above we saw that Arendt left her dissertation asking why we should make a desert out of the world. Many readers take her later overtures to love for the world as an attempt to invert Augustine's outlook and replace *amor dei* with *amor mundi*, transforming *cupiditas* from a vice into a virtue. But as Chiba again perceptively observes, *amor mundi* is not the love of self that defines Augustine's earthly city; here, in Arendt's reflections on culture, we see it is precisely the desire to possess the world for our own selfish ends that she is trying to combat.[45] *Amor mundi* is instead a non-possessive love for the world, one that wills its ongoing existence independent of our personal stake in it.[46] Here Arendt points to a kind of love that Augustine appears to have overlooked, one which, if falling short of the love of God and neighbor, reaches higher than the love of self to the good of what is common to all. As Jennifer Herdt points out, Augustine tended not to distinguish between love for the common good and love for the self, believing the former to be merely another form of the latter:

> Augustine had granted that the best Romans acted for the sake of the common good, but he had insisted at the same time

that they did so for the sake of glory, and thus out of vicious self-love; "Virtue which is employed in the service of human glory is not true virtue" (CD V 19).⁴⁷

Later medieval thinkers, Herdt goes on to say, sought to account for "the possibility of pursuing some good other than self even in the absence of ordering all things to God," which led Aquinas to his notion of true, but imperfect virtue.⁴⁸ Arendt is pointing to a similar possibility, a civic virtue that seeks the good of the common world and restrains the self-love that sees the world as another object to be consumed.

Among contemporary democratic theorists, we find a striking parallel to Arendt's vision of *amor mundi* in Sheldon Wolin's notion of "tending." Playing upon the same etymological roots of culture as Arendt, Wolin suggests that to tend "is to be concerned about something that exists, something that requires being taken care of, if it is to perdure."⁴⁹ "The idea of tending," he observes, "is one that centers politics around practices, that is, around the habits of competence or skill that are routinely required if things are to be taken care of."⁵⁰ This is a politics attuned to the historicity of things, one that emerges organically from the "biography of a place," as opposed to the politics of "intending," which attempts to escape the vulnerabilities of temporal existence through top-down organization and planning.⁵¹ The power of a politics of tending "lies in the multiplicity of modest sites dispersed among local governments and institutions under local control (schools, community health services, police and fire protection, recreation, cultural institutions, property taxes)."⁵² This echoes Arendt's own focus on ordinary practices at the level of education, work, and culture, which unceremoniously carry out the task of repairing and conserving the world so that it serves as a space for citizens from one generation to the next, grounding a people's memory in the process.

All of this may be true, but what of Gregory's lingering concern about *amor mundi* being stripped of moral passion? Does such a love actually speak to questions of need and desert? Does it appeal to our emotions and affections? Clearly Arendt has concerns about limiting the role of politics to meeting our basic needs, but the circumstances that prompted her turn to worldliness indicate that she was hardly indifferent to them. It was the plight of the stateless—the abuse suffered by minority populations, the inability of refugees to find a home, the horrors of the concentration camps—that led her to emphasize the importance of worldly belonging. As we have seen, statelessness revealed for Arendt a major gap in the prevailing liberal conception of justice based upon human rights.[53] In shifting her attention to worldliness, Arendt was trying to articulate those deeper conditions that provide the social texture in which such rights are intelligible. She was pointing to what she regarded as our deepest need, the need for a home, a place in the world. In the process, she was trying to challenge some of the unspoken assumptions about where we draw the boundaries of citizenship, who we include, who we exclude, whose needs we are prepared to recognize, whose needs we choose to ignore. In championing the political good of plurality in particular, she was not only resisting the nationalist trend of reducing citizenship to one ethnic identity, but also offering a vision of political community that is inherently open to the arrival of strangers and newcomers. Arendt saw the issue of immigration in much the same terms as education: it was ultimately a question of whether we love the world enough to welcome newcomers into it.[54] Moreover, in continually bringing our attention back to the varieties of worldlessness that can exist within modern society—unemployed workers, pariah peoples, and the growing alienation of most citizens from public life in general—Arendt was reminding us that the basic need for place is not simply an issue for strangers outside our community, but for those within it as well. In these ways, her turn to worldliness can be read as an important attempt to open a deeper conversation about our most fundamental needs and the conditions necessary to meet those needs.

As for whether *amor mundi* appeals to our emotions and affections, one could point to areas of her work where she has more to say about our affective relationship to the world, such as her essay, "On Humanity in Dark Times," where she notes how anger "reveals and exposes the world" and laughter "seeks to bring about reconciliation with the world ... help[ing] one to find a place in the world ... without selling one's soul to it" (MDT 6). But it may be most instructive to consider the example of Arendt herself. When the first reviews of *The Origins of Totalitarianism* came out, critics made a point of attacking her "emotional" and "prophetic" style. "She is neither cool, aloof, nor impartial," Philip Rieff wrote. "Plainly, detachment is, for her, morally despicable."[55] Eric Voegelin observed:

> [T]here can be no doubt that the fate of the Jews, the mass slaughter and the homelessness of displaced persons, is for the author a center of emotional shock, the center from which radiates her desire to inquire into the causes of the horror, to understand political phenomena in Western civilization that belong to the same class, and to consider means that will stem the evil.[56]

How Arendt responded to these criticisms, as Seyla Benhabib points out, provides a revealing glimpse into some of the core assumptions that inform her overall outlook.[57] She flatly rejects the tradition of *sine ira et studio* that her critics presumed and questions the desirability of any sensibility that would respond to the camps or some other gross injustice without emotion. In her reply to Voegelin, she writes:

> Let us suppose—to take one among many possible examples—that the historian is confronted with excessive poverty in a society of great wealth, such as the poverty of the British working classes during the early stages of the Industrial Revolution. The natural human reaction to such conditions is one of anger and indignation because these conditions are against the dignity of man. If I describe these conditions without permitting my indignation to interfere, I have lifted this particular phenomenon out of its context in human society and have thereby robbed it of part of its nature, deprived it of one of its important inherent qualities. For to arouse indignation is one of the qualities of excessive poverty insofar as poverty occurs among human beings. (EU 403)

It is hard to imagine a stronger statement of the interconnection between the emotions and truthful description, of the inextricability of our moral passions and our ability to perceive the world accurately. She drives home the point:

> I therefore cannot agree ... that the "morally abhorrent and the emotionally existing will overshadow the essential," because I believe them to form an integral part of it ... To describe the concentration camps *sine ira* is not to be "objective," but to condone them; and such condoning cannot be changed by a

condemnation which the author may feel duty bound to add but which remains unrelated to the description itself. (403–4)

Arendt makes no apologies for offering an analysis of totalitarianism that begins from horror, for to describe totalitarianism accurately is to recognize that it is something that is inherently horrible. To connect this back to Arendt's vision of *amor mundi*, our love for the world is measured by the anger we express in response to the injustices that happen within it, the outrage we feel at the occurrence of systematic murder or the subjection of individuals to inhumane conditions, the indignation we feel at the moral detachment of perpetrators who participate in such crimes or the complicity of wider society. Likewise, it is measured in the wonder that we feel at a resistance movement or the joy we find in a joint enterprise with our peers. These emotional energies come through on nearly every page that Arendt wrote. At the end of the day, she not only described a vision of *amor mundi*, but also modeled it with the passion with which she wrote, using her own voice to stir another generation to love this world as their own.

V. "This-Worldliness"

As we have seen in this chapter, Arendt's turn to worldliness represented an attempt to reflect more deeply upon the underlying conditions that enable us to exercise our basic human capacities. It was a way of re-envisioning citizenship in terms of the everyday task of forging a common world, a task sustained by the *amor mundi* of each citizen. Along the way, Arendt made her share of misjudgments about Christian views on the world, but she also remained indebted to key Augustinian insights about the world's fragility and the importance of love in ensuring its ongoing existence. It remains for us to consider what Arendt's vision of worldliness might offer those working in Christian theology today. I mentioned at the outset of the chapter that this area of Arendt's work offers particularly valuable resources for advancing recent investigations at the intersection of ecclesiology, radical democracy, and civic virtue. It does so by highlighting the importance of place, materiality, and culture for democratic life, providing especially helpful conceptual tools for naming the ways that the church can contribute to the civic task of world-building.

Arendt's conception of the world as an in-between that gathers and separates persons suggests that the church contributes to the task of world-building first by serving as a worldly space itself. This, of course, is not a move Arendt herself made. As we know, she saw the church primarily as a social "body" bound together through charity, not the worldly in-between of things. Yet not even Arendt could deny the church's worldly dimension, noting how it became an institution of tremendous durability in the medieval age through its organizational authority and traditions. In a discussion of religious architecture in "The Crisis in Culture," Arendt goes a step further, acknowledging that the very love of God that she usually takes to enjoin an instrumental outlook on the world has had, at least in this area, the opposite effect. Reflecting upon the medieval cathedrals and the spirit with which they were built, she observes:

> The cathedrals were built *ad maiorem gloriam Dei*; while they as buildings certainly served the needs of the community, their elaborate beauty can never be explained by these needs, which could have been served quite as well by any nondescript building. Their beauty transcended all needs and made them last through the centuries; but while beauty, the beauty of a cathedral like the beauty of any secular building, transcends needs and functions, it never transcends the world, even if the content of the work happens to be religious. On the contrary, it is the very beauty of religious art which transforms religious and other-worldly contents and concerns into tangible worldly realities. (BPF 208)

In a departure from her usual anxieties about the otherworldly effects of the love of God, Arendt observes here that it is precisely because the cathedrals were built to the glory of God that they became structures of such enduring permanence. This suggests that there is an inherent worldliness to worship, just to the extent that what is offered in worship is removed from the usual economy of use and consumption. Precisely because they are not built for us, the cathedrals exist more freely for us. The same point applies to the many other dimensions of the church's material culture: its sacraments, texts, and icons; its offices and canons; its relics and pilgrimage sites. Worship makes the church worldly, suggesting that one of the most important contributions that the church can make to the task of world-building is simply to remain faithful to its life of worship, which in building up a lasting ecclesial community also builds up an important edifice of the broader common world.

In a particularly suggestive appropriation of Arendt's work, Mary McClintock Fulkerson takes the point beyond material culture to consider how the church can be seen as a "space for appearing" for those denied visibility in broader society.[58] Drawing upon fieldwork in a church in North Carolina, Fulkerson emphasizes how racial, gender, and other bodily disciplines often shape the way worship space is configured, reinforcing wider societal patterns of blindness and obliviousness; at the same time, she notes how these disciplines can also be challenged. In reorganizing its worship space to accommodate the presence and voices of the mentally disabled and other marginalized groups, redistributing power roles historically monopolized by privileged members, and offering a place where citizens of a largely segregated city can interact, Fulkerson emphasizes how the church can be a place of worldly transformation. She writes:

> What is needed to counter the diminishment and harm associated with obliviousness is a *place to appear*, a place to be seen, to be recognized and to recognize the other. Being seen and heard by others, being acknowledged by others—these are said to be essential to the political life; my point is that they are also essential to a community of faith as an honoring of the shared image of God.[59]

In appropriating Arendt's concept of worldliness in this way, Fulkerson shows how it applies more broadly than Arendt herself acknowledged. Indeed, she challenges Arendt's tendency to privilege the singular space of the "public realm," the place of politics properly speaking, at the expense of taking more seriously the worldly character of a variety of other spaces and groupings. As Seyla Benhabib argues in relation to the salons of early nineteenth-century Germany, which feature prominently in Arendt's biography of Rahel Varnhagen, these kind of spaces are not merely "social" and certainly not unworldly; on the contrary, they serve as powerful alternative or experimental "publics" that offer glimpses of new possibilities for the broader common world.[60]

Luke Bretherton articulates a similar vision of the church as a space for appearing, extending it to a group of particular relevance for Arendt: refugees.[61] Recalling Arendt's conclusion that the most urgent need of refugees is not humanitarian assistance but a home, Bretherton observes, "the church's duty of care to refugees must involve creating places for the recognition and expression of their ability to act on their own behalf."[62] Bretherton agrees with Arendt that citizenship is what ultimately meets this need, but in contexts where the claim of refugees to asylum has been denied, he envisions a role for the church in standing in the gap and providing an intermediary space, where their claims to citizenship can be more effectively heard. As an example, he cites the Sanctuary movement, which emerged in the United States in the 1980s as a response to the influx of refugees from Central America. While the general practice of the US government at the time was to deny these individuals refugee status, classifying them as illegal aliens or migrants instead, the Sanctuary movement set up a network of safe houses to protect them from deportation.[63] In the process, the movement challenged the boundaries that separated American citizens and those seeking asylum, creating an imaginative space in which a new community could be glimpsed. Bretherton cites the following summary from Hilary Cunningham:

> In redefining what a "church" was, the participants of the Sanctuary movement profoundly reconstituted their social reality and their place within it. This process of "articulation" altered the ways in which the individuals identified themselves vis-à-vis their families/kin groups, their denominational churches, their nation/government, and, ultimately, the international community.[64]

As in the case of Fulkerson's study above, the Sanctuary churches not only modeled a different way of being church, but also displayed a possible future for the broader common world. In Bretherton's words, their witness "call[ed] forth just judgment on a contested political issue," demonstrating how a local politics of place can have implications for policy at the national and international level as well.[65]

Bretherton goes on to emphasize the role that churches can play in cultivating what he calls "complex space," which is fostered when a range of partners collaborate in the pursuit of shared goods, or to use the Augustinian language, "common objects of love."[66] He cites the work of the Industrial Areas Foundation, in which churches are one of many partners who join in issue-campaigns on such matters as wages, schools, and policing. For Bretherton, the complex civic space that is produced as a result recalls Augustine's notion of the "*saeculum*," the time (and space) that the two cities share during their sojourn on earth. For Bretherton, such a local, place-based politics "allow[s] the church to be the church, cooperate with religious others in pursuit of earthly goods in common, and contradict the totalizing tendencies of the market and the state."[67] In addition to the work of the Industrial Areas Foundation that Bretherton mentions, one could point to a variety of other models of partnership. One that resonates particularly strongly with Arendt's emphasis upon building lasting worldly institutions is the Christian Community Development Association, a consortium of inner city churches which promote community revitalization at the neighborhood level.[68] Inspired by the work of the civil rights leader John Perkins, these churches apply a comprehensive approach to community development through home ownership, neighborhood-based schools, community health clinics, small business loans, and public gardens, among many other initiatives. In this way, a worldly church contributes to the building of a broader world by reclaiming the neighborhood as one particularly vital nexus for democratic life.

The abiding challenge of Arendt's vision of *amor mundi* is to ask who is denied a place in the world today, and how we can deepen our own place within it. For those whose sense of place is shaped by a religious tradition, this is not simply a question about a deeper experience of citizenship or even the fuller realization of our basic human capacities. It is ultimately a question about entering more fully into the life of God. Quoting John Inge, Bretherton notes that places are "the seat of relations" between human beings and God.[69] This renders theologically articulate Arendt's basic intuition above about the building of cathedrals *ad maiorem gloriam Dei*: to love God is to enter more deeply into the world, and because God identifies with the world—with the world God has made, with the body God has assumed, with the bread God has broken, and the wine God has poured—to enter more fully into the world is to enter more fully into God.

Strikingly, this was the insight that Arendt's fellow German, Dietrich Bonhoeffer, came to while living through the same totalitarian experience as Arendt.[70] "The church, like Christ, has become world ... It is entirely world," he writes. "For the sake of real people, the church must be thoroughly worldly. It is a worldly reality for our sakes."[71] In one of the last letters he wrote, Bonhoeffer put it this way:

> I discovered later, and I'm still discovering right up to this moment, that it is only by living completely in this world that one learns to have faith ... By this-worldliness I mean living unreservedly in life's duties, problems, successes and failures, experiences and perplexities. In so doing we throw ourselves completely into the arms of God, taking seriously, not our own sufferings, but those of God in the world—watching with Christ in Gethsemane. That, I think, is faith.[72]

One cannot help but find the language of "watching," of abiding in a deserted and ruined place, an apt way to summarize the spirit of Arendt's own understanding of worldliness.[73] It was out of the deprivation of the concentration camps and the plight of refugees that her own vision of worldliness arose. It was from there that she longed for a world that once again might offer a place fit for human habitation, a world that will always stand in need of repair, and thus a world worthy of nothing less than our love.

Notes

1. For more background on Arendt's conception of the world, see Margaret Canovan, "Politics as Culture: Hannah Arendt and the Public Realm," in *Hannah Arendt: Critical Essays*, eds. Lewis P. Hinchman and Sandra K. Hinchman (Albany: State University of New York Press, 1994), 179–205. See also her discussion in *Hannah Arendt: A Reinterpretation of Her Political Thought* (Cambridge: Cambridge University Press, 1992), 99–154.
2. Hannah Arendt, "Public Rights and Private Interests," in M. Mooney

and F. Stuber, eds. *Small Comforts for Hard Times: Humanists on Public Policy* (New York: Columbia University Press, 1977), 104.

3 While much attention focuses upon Arendt's understanding of the episodic character of political action, less focuses upon her emphasis upon the stabilizing role of law. Her clearest statement on the centrality of law in maintaining "worldly fences" between citizens comes in "Ideology and Terror," the final chapter added to the 1958 version of OT 460–8.

4 In HC, she notes that our capacity to introduce man-made processes into nature brings with it the same dangers that accompany political action, namely, irreversibility and unpredictability: "The very fact that natural sciences have become exclusively sciences of process and, in their last stage, sciences of potentially irreversible, irremediable 'processes of no return' is a clear indication that, whatever the brain power necessary to start them, the actual underlying human capacity which alone could bring about this development is no 'theoretical' capacity, neither contemplation nor reason, but the human ability to act—to start new unprecedented processes, whose outcome remains uncertain and unpredictable whether they are let loose in the human or natural realm" (231–2). Later she observes that the capacity for action "has become the exclusive prerogative of the scientists, who have enlarged the realm of human affairs to the point of extinguishing the time-honored protective dividing line between nature and the human world" (323–4).

5 Arendt is drawing from Kant's *Critique of Judgment* on this point. In "Truth and Politics," she writes: "Political thought is representative. I form an opinion by considering an issue from different viewpoints, by making present to my mind the standpoints of those who are absent ... The more people's standpoints I have present in my mind while I am pondering a given issue, and the better I can imagine how I would feel and think if I were in their place, the stronger will be my capacity for representative thinking and the more valid my final conclusions, my opinion. (It is this capacity for an 'enlarged mentality' that enables men to judge; as such, it was discovered by Kant in the first part of his *Critique of Judgment*, though he did not recognize the political and moral implications of his discovery)" (BPF 241).

6 Roxanne Euben, "Killing (for) Politics: Jihad, Martyrdom, and Political Action," *Political Theory* 30:1 (February 2002), 23.

7 The full quote suggests that Tertullian is actually targeting the parochialism of conceiving citizenship within the limited horizon of one *res publica*: "Nothing is more foreign to us than the *res publica*.

One *res publica* we know, of which all are citizens—the universe." *Apologeticus* 38, quoted in Oliver O'Donovan, *Ways of Judgment* (Grand Rapids: Eerdmans, 2005), 212.

8 Ronald Beiner, "Love and Worldliness: Hannah Arendt's Reading of Saint Augustine," in Larry May and Jerome Kohn, eds. *Hannah Arendt: Twenty Years Later* (Cambridge: MIT Press, 1996), 281.

9 Arendt echoes many of these themes in *On Revolution*, where she addresses the related love of compassion. She contends that compassion is unworldly because it does not lend itself to discourse: "Such talkative and argumentative interest in the world is entirely alien to compassion, which is directed solely, and with passionate intensity, towards suffering man himself; compassion speaks only to the extent that it has to reply directly to the sheer expressionist sound and gestures through which suffering becomes audible and visible in the world" (86). For Arendt, this is a function of the fact that compassion is literally "suffering with another," by definition a direct form of engagement, and thus incapable of considering change that may be needed at a structural level: "As a rule, it is not compassion which sets out to change worldly conditions in order to ease human suffering, but if it does, it will shun the drawn-out wearisome processes of persuasion, negotiation, and compromise, which are the processes of law and politics, and lend its voice to the suffering itself, which must claim for swift and direct action, that is, for action with the means of violence" (86–7).

10 This is a point that Arendt emphasizes in several places throughout her work, which weakens her own claims about the inherent otherworldliness of Christianity. Samuel Moyn notes that the this-worldly effects of Christianity are front and center in *On Revolution*, commenting: "The baseline for appreciating the challenge of finding a secular basis for modern politics, as Arendt sees it, is a sense of the political or quasi-political functions that Christianity has played in European civilization. Arendt is renowned for arguing in *The Human Condition* that 'the victory of the Christian faith in the ancient world ... could not but be disastrous for the esteem and the dignity of politics.' But she qualifies or upends this thesis in *On Revolution* with a depiction of religion as playing a collective function that modern politics will have to inherit ... For a thinker usually thought uninterested in or opposed to religion in general and Christianity in particular, Arendt thus attributes an extraordinary efficacy to them in providing an absolute in a way that irreligious politics cannot easily rival" (74–5). See Moyn, "Hannah Arendt on the Secular," *New German Critique* 35:3 (Fall 2008): 71–96.

11 See her section entitled "Tribal nationalism" in OT 227–43. See also her July 24, 1963 letter to Scholem, in which she writes: "I have never in my life 'loved' any people or collective—neither the German people, nor the French, nor the American, nor the working class or anything of the sort" (JW 466–7).

12 In "On Humanity in Dark Times," she observes that fraternity "is the advantage that the pariahs of this world always and in all circumstances can have over others" but that it is "dearly bought." This is because "it is often accompanied by so radical a loss of the world, so fearful an atrophy of all the organs with which we respond to it—starting with the common sense with which we orient ourselves in a world common to ourselves and others and going on to the sense of beauty, or taste, with which we love the world—that in extreme cases, in which pariahdom has persisted for centuries, we can speak of real worldlessness" (MDT 13).

13 See Gregory, *Politics and the Order of Love*, 204, 207. See also Kateb, *Hannah Arendt*, 25–6.

14 See Rowan Williams, "Politics and the Soul: A Reading of the *City of God*," *Milltown Studies* 19/20 (1987): 55–72; Thomas Breidenthal, "Jesus Is My Neighbor: Arendt, Augustine, and the Politics of the Incarnation," *Modern Theology* 14:4 (1998): 489–503; Bernd Wannenwetsch, *Political Worship* (Oxford: Oxford University Press, 2004), 117–206; and Eric Gregory, *Politics and the Order of Love* (Chicago: University of Chicago Press, 2008), 197–240.

15 Williams, "Politics and the Soul," 57.

16 Williams, "Politics and the Soul," 58.

17 Williams, "Politics and the Soul," 58.

18 For a similar criticism of Arendt, see John E. Seery, *Political Theory for Mortals: Shades of Justice, Images of Death* (Ithaca: Cornell University Press, 1996), 12–17.

19 Williams, "Politics and the Soul," 68–9.

20 Williams, "Politics and the Soul," 69.

21 Williams, "Politics and the Soul," 69.

22 Williams, "Politics and the Soul," 69.

23 Williams, "Politics and the Soul," 64. In *The End of Work* (Oxford: Blackwell, 2006), John Hughes emphasizes that Arendt's debts to Greek thought lead her to undervalue the human activities of labor and work. While "sympathetic with her critical account of the degeneration of notions of human activity in modernity through rational utilitarian instrumentalization to bestial self-interest,"

Hughes does not agree "that manual subsistence labour is necessarily sub-human, nor that fabrication need be violent, nor that either are somehow 'private' and sub-political, as distinct from the active life of the *polis*" (226–7). The dignity of labor is suggested in the Eucharist, "where our most animal-like activities of consumption are also the highest art, and the very creation of community. Even subsistence is cultural for humanity, and as such, like art, is also always social and political, and crucially need not be agonistic" (227).

24 Williams, "Politics and the Soul," 64. For a similar critique along these lines, see Bretherton, *Christianity and Contemporary Politics*, 198.
25 Gregory, *Politics and the Order of Love*, 41.
26 Gregory, *Politics and the Order of Love*, 42, my italics.
27 Gregory, *Politics and the Order of Love*, 323. Earlier, he puts it this way: "To love an eternal and incomprehensible God, for Augustine, stretches the soul to allow for a qualitatively different kind of love which can now include all that is not God ... In his God, 'our love will know no check'" (40).
28 Gregory, *Politics and the Order of Love*, 42.
29 Gregory, *Politics and the Order of Love*, 208.
30 Gregory, *Politics and the Order of Love*, 210. For feminist responses to Arendt, see Bonnie Honig, ed. *Feminist Interpretations of Hannah Arendt* (University Park, PA: Pennsylvania State University Press, 1995).
31 Gregory, *Politics and the Order of Love*, 68. He argues that her thought, like liberalism more generally, could be enriched "by attending to the emotionally involved motivational qualities of those dispositions and traits of character that are necessary to be a good citizen" (68).
32 Gregory, *Politics and the Order of Love*, 38, 249.
33 Gregory, *Politics and the Order of Love*, 38.
34 Gregory, *Politics and the Order of Love*, 157.
35 For more on the importance of supplementing the liberal values of liberty and equality with considerations of need and desert, see Gregory, *Politics and the Order of Love*, 116–17.
36 Gregory, *Politics and the Order of Love*, 9.
37 I develop this point further in my discussion of Arendt's theory of action in Chapter 4.
38 Gregory, *Politics and the Order of Love*, 198.
39 Mathewes, *Evil and the Augustinian Tradition*, 152.

40 Ronald Beiner, "Love and Worldiness," 277.

41 Peg Birmingham, "Arendt and Hobbes: Glory, Sacrificial Violence, and the Political Imagination," *Research in Phenomenology* 41 (2011), 17. Roxanne Euben argues that regardless of whether Arendt herself endorsed the Greek striving for immortality, she performs a great service by naming the kind of expectations that citizens once brought to the public realm. In this way, Euben thinks Arendt breaks silences in political theory surrounding "the connections and tensions among political action, identity, immortality, death, and violence" ("Killing (for) Politics," 9). Our tendency only to talk about public reason and epistemic justification elides the deeper anxieties about death that inform the actual practice of politics, and in Euben's view, it is the particular analytic strength of Arendt's work to bring these anxieties to the surface. Arendt's mistake, she argues, is to assume that citizens no longer carry such expectations to the public realm; indeed, as Euben sees it, Arendt's account remains all too relevant in analyzing the kind of motivations that drive a host of political misadventures today.

42 Patrick Boyle observes that "the concept of a 'common world' she describes in *The Human Condition* as related to 'the human artifact, the fabrication of human hands as well as to the affairs which go on among those who inhabit the man-made world together,' bears a striking resemblance to the 'human world' she finds in Augustine—constituted 'by the lovers of the world and by that which they love" ("Elusive Neighborliness," 97). It should be said that against Arendt's assertions to the contrary, the fact that Augustine thinks the world is passing away does not mean he believes caring for the world is futile. Rather, it means that the world stands all the more in need of it. This comes across especially clearly in his sermons on the sack of Rome, where in the course of reminding the Romans that their city is finite and subject to ruin, he still expresses hope that the end is "not yet" and appeals to his listeners to take up the task of repair. See Sermon 105 in *Nicene and Post-Nicene Fathers*, vol. 6, trans. R. G. MacMullen (Peabody, MA: Hendrickson Publishers, 1994).

43 Gregory, *Politics and the Order of Love*, 206.

44 Shin Chiba, "Hannah Arendt on Love and the Political: Love, Friendship, and Citizenship," *The Review of Politics* 57:3 (1995), 534.

45 Chiba, "Hannah Arendt on Love and the Political," 534.

46 As Boyle puts it, "The loves of Augustine and Arendt have a common locus: the world and the people who constitute it. Their seemingly contrary visions, *amor mundi* or *amor dei*, are linked insofar as they affirm possibilities for a truly human world without adding to

those the illusions either of 'perfectibility' or 'progress'" ("Elusive Neighborliness," 101). Compare to Charles Mathewes: "Like Augustine, she begins with the affirmation that we are love-oriented beings, whose loves are a primary clue to the real character of our existence and to the existence of the world we inhabit, and which seeks most fully to exegete and articulate the significance of these loves in a full and systematic manner" (*Evil and the Augustinian Tradition*, 151).

47 Jennifer Herdt, *Putting on Virtue: The Legacy of the Splendid Vices* (Chicago: University of Chicago Press, 2008), 75.

48 Herdt, *Putting on Virtue*, 74.

49 Sheldon Wolin, *The Presence of the Past: Essays on the State and the Constitution* (Baltimore: Johns Hopkins University Press, 1989), 90.

50 Wolin, *The Presence of the Past*, 89.

51 Wolin, *The Presence of the Past*, 93.

52 Wolin, *Politics and Vision* (Princeton: Princeton University Press, 2006), 603.

53 In *Hannah Arendt and Human Rights* (Bloomington: Indiana University Press, 2006), Peg Birmingham suggests that this point should be kept in mind when weighing criticisms that suggest she is inattentive to questions of social justice: "Indeed, Arendt's location of freedom and justice in the more foundational issue of the right to have rights goes far in answering her critics, such as Dana Villa, who charge Arendt with ignoring the liberal tradition, especially its notion of justice. In her discussion of modern human rights, Arendt does not dismiss the liberal tradition; rather, she shows how this tradition, with its paramount concern for freedom and justice, does not grasp that politically there is something more fundamental ... For Arendt, more fundamental than the rights of justice and freedom is the right to action and opinion and the right to belong to a political community in which one's speech and action are rendered significant" (36).

54 In "The Crisis in Education," she observes, "For America the determining factor has always been the motto printed on every dollar bill: *Novus Ordo Seclorum*, a New Order of the World. The immigrants, the newcomers, are a guarantee to the country that it represents the new order ... its magnificence consists in the fact that from the beginning this new order did not shut itself from the outside world ... [but rather] welcomed all the poor and enslaved of the earth" (BPF 175–6).

55 Philip Rieff, "The Theology of Politics: Reflections on Totalitarianism

as the Burden of Our Time," *The Journal of Religion* 32:2 (April 1952), 121.

56 Eric Voegelin, "The Origins of Totalitarianism," *Review of Politics* 15:1 (January 1953), 70.

57 Seyla Benhabib summarizes Arendt's position this way: "The moral resonance of one's language does not, or even primarily, reside in the explicit value judgments that an author may pass on the subject matter; rather, such resonance must be an aspect of the descriptive narrative itself. The language of narration must match the moral quality of the narrated object" (*Reluctant Modernism of Hannah Arendt*, 90–1).

58 Mary McClintock Fulkerson, *Places of Redemption: Theology for a Worldly Church* (Oxford: Oxford University Press, 2007).

59 Fulkerson, *Places of Redemption*, 21.

60 See Benhabib, *Reluctant Modernism*, 14–22. See also Lisa Stenmark, *Religion, Science, and Democracy: A Disputational Friendship*, 142–57.

61 Luke Bretherton, *Christianity and Contemporary Politics: The Conditions and Possibilities of Faithful Witness* (Oxford: Blackwell, 2010), 126–74.

62 Bretherton, *Christianity and Contemporary Politics*, 146.

63 Bretherton, *Christianity and Contemporary Politics*, 152.

64 Bretherton, *Christianity and Contemporary Politics*, 151. The passage is from Hilary Cunningham, *God and Caesar at the Rio Grande: Sanctuary and the Politics of Religion* (Minneapolis: University of Minneapolis Press, 1995), 102.

65 Bretherton, *Christianity and Contemporary Politics*, 155.

66 Bretherton, *Christianity and Contemporary Politics*, 83. He borrows the term "complex space" from John Milbank, taking it in a direction that both challenges Milbank's aversion to ecclesial alliances with other political actors and clarifies that it can actually alleviate Milbank's legitimate concerns about complicity and co-option. He writes: "Discovering and tending common objects of love is a precondition of forging the kind of multifaceted or 'complex space' and 'hazy' boundary between different forms of life and institutional arrangements, including church and state, that Milbank seeks" (84).

67 Bretherton, *Christianity and Contemporary Politics*, 106.

68 See Mark Gornik, *To Live in Peace: Biblical Faith and the Changing Inner City* (Grand Rapids: Eerdmans, 2002) and Charles Marsh, *The Beloved Community* (New York: Basic Books, 2005), 153–216.

69 Bretherton, *Christianity and Contemporary Politics*, 147.
70 For more on the similarities between Bonhoeffer and Arendt, see James Bernauer, "Bonhoeffer and Arendt at One Hundred," *Studies in Christian-Jewish Relations* 2:1 (2007): 77–85, and Charles Mathewes, "A Tale of Two Judgments: Bonhoeffer and Arendt on Evil, Understanding, and Limits, and the Limits of Understanding Evil," *The Journal of Religion* 80:3 (July 2000): 375–404.
71 Dietrich Bonhoeffer, "The Nature of the Church," in *A Testament to Freedom*, eds. Geoffrey B. Kelly and F. Burton Nelson (New York: Harper Collins, 1995), 87; cited in Bernauer, "Bonhoeffer and Arendt," 79.
72 Dietrich Bonhoeffer, *Letters and Papers from Prison* (New York: Simon and Schuster, 1971), 369–70; cited in Bernauer, "Bonhoeffer and Arendt," 79.
73 Peg Birmingham does not mention Bonhoeffer, but she evokes Gethsemane in her own description of Arendt's vision of worldliness: "A post-sacrificial imagination is one in which immortality and glory mean nothing other than finding our bearings in an enduring world without ultimate meaning [i.e., a world that is penultimate] and therefore without ultimate sacrifice ... Peter Eisenman's 'Stones: Memorial to the Murdered Jews of Europe,' in the center of Berlin, is perhaps one site of a post-sacrificial imagination. The site is a gash, a wound in the middle of Potsdamer Platz. There is nothing beautiful here. Nothing grows ... The memorial acknowledges that it was murder, not sacrifice. This is not Calvary, but Gethsemane. If the stones speak, they say only, 'Stay here and keep watch with me'" ("Arendt and Hobbes," 22).

4

"That a Beginning Be Made": Natality, Action, and the Politics of Gratitude

Arendt's vision of *amor mundi* was born from a recognition of the world's fragility and its need for ongoing care if it is to remain a place fit for human habitation. For Arendt, the world only endures provided that each new generation takes up the task of *amor mundi* as its own. As we saw in the last chapter, this involves an important element of conservation: tending our homes and gardens, replacing worn-out use-objects with new ones, preserving cultural treasures, repairing civic institutions and infrastructure, and passing the world on to the young through education. But Arendt makes clear that the role of newcomers is not limited to conservation. The world's endurance is also contingent upon their resolve "to intervene, to alter, to create what is new" (BPF 192). For Arendt, the opportunity to undertake something new is what we conserve the world for, and it is this capacity for new beginnings, the action that takes place within the world, that in turn contributes to the world's renewal. As she puts it:

> The miracle that saves the world, the realm of human affairs, from its normal, "natural" ruin is ultimately the fact of natality, in which the faculty of action is ontologically rooted. It is, in other words, the birth of new men and the new beginning, the action they are capable of by virtue of being born. (HC 247)

With these words Arendt captures one of her most important, if least understood, contributions to political theory: her concept of natality. Referring broadly to the human condition of birth, the concept has, as this passage indicates, a close association with the faculty of action. Arendt worked with a specific understanding of action that, like her conception of worldliness, differs considerably from our ordinary usage of the term. She had in mind the words and deeds that transpire directly between citizens in the public realm, activities that do not result in a tangible object, like many of the world-building activities discussed in the last chapter, but whose end is realized in the course of acting itself. This understanding of action owes much to Aristotle's distinction between *praxis* and *poiēsis*, as well as her fondness for the debate and deliberation that animated the Greek *polis*. But it was just as decisively shaped by the events through which she lived. Think of the workers' councils that fuelled the 1956 Hungarian Revolution, the gatherings in churches and meeting halls that propelled the civil rights movement, the student uprisings on college campuses in the 1960s, or the acts of civil disobedience in American streets during the Vietnam War. Or in more recent times, think of the intense democratic activity that prompted the fall of the Berlin Wall or the Arab Spring. Action in Arendt's sense is performative and dramatic: it involves individual citizens acting in concert to bring new possibilities into existence, possibilities that become lasting features of our common world when legislators, poets, and historians transform these "enacted stories" into more tangible form. It is this "birthing" quality inherent in action that led Arendt to see it as the activity that has the closest connection with the human condition of natality, and in turn, what led her to see natality, not mortality, as the central category of political thought (9). She observes:

> The life span of man running toward death would inevitably carry everything human to ruin and destruction, if it were not for the faculty of interrupting it and beginning something new, a faculty which is inherent in action like an ever-present reminder that men, though they must die, are not born in order to die but in order to begin. (246)

Arendt may have considered natality the central category of political thought, but she was struck by its relative neglect in the broader political tradition. Certainly there was no shortage of speculation on the question of the origins of political society and plenty of due consideration to acts of founding and constitution-making, but on the whole, Arendt found surprisingly little emphasis upon the relevance of beginnings for the ongoing life of citizens. Instead she found a division of labor between rulers, to whom fell the responsibility for initiating new ventures, and subjects, who executed what the rulers began. The capacity to make a beginning appeared to demand sovereignty over others, yet what Arendt observed among the various democratic movements of her time was that new beginnings arose only when claims to such sovereignty were relinquished, and citizens acted in concert with one another. With a view to developing a more adequate political theory of this kind of action, Arendt took to pearl diving among resources excluded or overlooked by the tradition. In addition to Athenian democracy, the town councils and communes of revolutionary America and France, and the early Russian soviets, Arendt drew upon a striking number of religious sources. As she saw it, one of the reasons that her discipline of political philosophy lacked an adequate theory of action is that it arbitrarily excluded a number of authentically political experiences and insights on account of their "allegedly exclusively religious nature" (239). But this did not stop Arendt from trying to learn from them. She found in the first Genesis account of creation a rich picture of human plurality as the condition for action, took inspiration from the Abrahamic notion of covenant in her account of promising, and appealed to the teachings of Jesus in demonstrating the relationship between doing and forgiving, likening the "originality and unprecedentedness" of his insights into action "to Socrates' insights into the possibilities of thought" (247). But by far the figure she drew upon the most was Augustine, whom she claims "discovered" the importance of beginnings in "its full significance" (EU 321). Evidently, Arendt did not think Augustine's alleged otherworldliness carried over into his views on freedom. Throughout her writings on action, she repeatedly cites her favorite passage from the *City of God*, "that a beginning be made, man was created, before whom nobody was" (12.21), finding in these words a powerful account of the human being as a beginner.[1]

Neither Arendt scholars nor Augustinians have known quite what to do with her use of such sources. In a fascinating study,

Mara Willard suggests that Arendt is appropriating theological idioms for her own strictly immanent, post-metaphysical purposes, but admits that her appeals to Genesis and Augustine's creation theology are instances where she "enters ambiguously theological territory."[2] Susannah Gottlieb and Mavis Biss point to the influence of Walter Benjamin and suggest that her account of natality may be best illumined through the lens of Jewish messianic thought, observing that her appeals to the notion of time collapsing and redemptive new beginnings are classic messianic motifs.[3] Among Augustinians, Arendt's reading of the *City of God* passage has been the subject of considerable dispute. George McKenna voices a common concern when he writes:

> Augustine was not talking about any "capacity of man" but the capacity of *God* to start something new in the universe ... To find in his remark a celebration of man's capacities or even a glimmer of hope for some sort of secular renewal is to find something that is not there.[4]

Others take less issue with her exegetical claims and focus more on the perils of selectively appropriating from his thought. As Charles Mathewes sees it, Arendt identifies authentically Augustinian insights on creation and freedom, but extracts these from his deeper anthropology, thereby neglecting the innumerable internal and external constraints that limit our freedom.[5] He takes Arendt to be suggesting that we have an unlimited capacity to make spontaneous new beginnings, a capacity that remains undetermined by the legacy of the past (sin, habit, virtue, historical context, etc.) and any consideration of political or moral ends that guide our actions into the future. This, he concludes, sounds less like Augustine than the Pelagianism that he rejected.

Below I will take some time to further unpack Mathewes' criticisms, for they help to highlight the range of concerns that Arendt's thinking on natality has generated. Indeed, as many see it, her link between natality and action flatly contradicts one of her most enduring insights: that we are *conditioned* beings who depend upon a variety of factors in order to speak or act at all. Was this not the central takeaway from our earlier discussions of her writings on evil and worldliness? Yet what upon first glance appears as a departure from these insights in fact represents the area of Arendt's thought in which she explores them in the deepest way. For as Arendt makes clear, natality is itself a human condition, one that not only enables us to act, but limits our capacity to act as well. As early as her dissertation on Augustine and her biography of Rahel Varnhagen, we find her turning to the past and exploring how the circumstances of our birth continue to shape our existence in decisive ways. As a persecuted Jew under totalitarianism, this became an intensely personal wrestling with how one retains the capacity to act when these very features become the basis of one's exclusion. By shifting the conversation to natality, she sought to take the discussion of action to a level that addresses the very heart of politics in our age, which all too often makes the differences of birth, to say nothing of the link between citizenship and birth, all-decisive for politics. Thus what initially appears to be the chief liability of Arendt's thought turns out to be one of its greatest strengths. Arendt sought a politics that learns to see our natality as a source of gratitude rather than resentment. To think about action and natality together was to reflect upon how we reconcile ourselves to all that we cannot change and find in such reconciliation one important source of our freedom. Action for her is the process through which we disclose and discover our unique identities in the company of others. New beginnings emerge out of this process of discovery, and politics becomes the art of being born.

To envision a politics that embraces and nourishes our natality in all of these senses is to stake a claim on the broader question of the ends of politics. This is crucial to keep in mind in weighing where Arendt ultimately stands on the matter of teleology. As I clarify in the chapter's penultimate section, Arendt certainly rejected those teleological outlooks that approach politics instrumentally, as a means to achieving external goods such as wealth, security, or the contemplative rest of leisure. But she did not reject all forms of teleology. She carried forward a version of the Aristotelian teleological framework that governs the first nine books of the *Nicomachean Ethics*, emphasizing those ends that are "inclusive" to action, realized in the very course of acting. In an age dominated by instrumental rationality, she sought to recover a sense for the internal goods of politics, including self-discovery, recognition, and, most importantly, what she calls "public happiness," the joy that accompanies the fellowship that we find in the common world.

Appreciating this allows us to bring into sharper focus the real shortcoming of Arendt's account, which is not that it claims too much for human beings, but that it is ultimately content to settle for too little. Arendt at times seems strangely enamored with beginnings as such, and she can be surprisingly undiscriminating when it comes to the various beginnings she extols. As I argue in the concluding section, Augustine himself was perfectly willing to grant the Romans the capacity to found political communities, to form new alliances abroad, and to realize a certain happiness in the *res publica*, yet he pined for a more radical beginning and a deeper transformation of our loves. I follow this longing further than Arendt was willing to go, and close the chapter by considering how it might extend her own important challenge to keep politics ever open to the inbreaking of the new, which is to say, a politics open to grace.

I. The Human Condition of Natality

To understand the connection Arendt makes between action and natality, we first need to say more about her account of natality itself.[6] Arendt considers natality, along with mortality, the two most general conditions of human existence. Mortality, of course, was the central preoccupation of her teacher Heidegger, who, in *Being and Time*, famously characterizes our temporal situation as one of "being-towards-death." As Anne O'Byrne observes, Heidegger was not entirely neglectful of the importance of birth.[7] His notion of "thrownness" was an attempt to capture the way that birth entangles us in an already existing world and a variety of relationships and circumstances from which we cannot easily extract ourselves. Yet, as O'Byrne observes, "By approaching our finitude as initially and for the most part *mortal* finitude, Heidegger sets himself squarely in philosophy's necrophilic tradition and orients our being in time toward the future."[8] Arendt sought to redress this imbalance and consider how we are no less conditioned by birth and our relationship to the past.

We see Arendt first making this shift in her doctoral dissertation on Augustine. In the first part, she focuses on Augustine's views on desire, and the picture that she paints is one that is broadly consistent with Heidegger's: through our desire, we stretch out towards the future and all that we do not yet possess, but no sooner do we possess the object of our desire than we are overwhelmed by the anxiety and fear of losing it. Death looms over everything that we love, as it guarantees that we will eventually lose all temporal goods, including our own life, only further intensifying our anxiety. Yet in Augustine's thought, we are not just creatures of desire; we are also creatures of memory. In fact, there is an element of remembrance in every desire just to the extent that in order to desire something, we have to know that it is desirable, which presupposes some experience of the object in the past. Thus desire sends us back to the past, in search of the source of what we desire. In the second part of the dissertation, Arendt notes how, for Augustine, the search for the source of our desire brings us to the very limit of our existence and the discovery that we are the source of neither our desire nor our very life. Our source lies outside our self, in the Creator. We can choose to return to God and accept the limits of our creatureliness, or reject this relationship and attempt to elevate ourselves to the position of Creator. Either way, our existence is determined by how we remember and make our peace with our origins, and this often proves more determinative than the objects that we choose to desire. Indeed, it shapes which objects we will desire.

In the course of revising her dissertation in the 1960s, Arendt takes the liberty of inserting her mature concept of natality into the manuscript, spelling out her understanding of the implications of Augustine's discussion for how we think about birth more specifically:

> To put it differently, the decisive fact determining man as a conscious, remembering being is birth or "natality," that is, the fact that we have entered the world through birth. The decisive fact determining man as a desiring being was death or mortality, the fact that we shall leave the world in death. Fear of death and inadequacy of life are the springs of desire. In contrast, gratitude for life having been given at all is the spring of remembrance, for a life cherished even in misery ... What ultimately stills the fear of death is not hope or desire, but remembrance and gratitude: "Give thanks for wanting to be as you are that you may be delivered from an existence that you do not want. For you are willing to be and unwilling to be miserable." (LSA 51–2)

This latter quote, taken from Augustine's *De libero arbitrio*, provides, as O'Byrne perceptively observes, a striking counter to the desolate wisdom of Silenus, the drunken sage of Sophocles' *Oedipus at Colonus*, whose famous words Arendt cites at the end of *On Revolution*: "Not to be born prevails over all meaning uttered in words; by far the second best for life, once it has appeared, is to go as swiftly as possible whence it came" (OR 281).[9] For Arendt, Silenus represents the attitude that sees in the gift of birth a source of resentment rather than gratitude. Given that death will eventually swallow up everything, why be born at all? For Augustine, on the other hand, the fact that we have been given life is a source of gratitude, which in turn stimulates our memory, which, as we see most clearly in the *Confessions*, expands our gratitude to all the things that we have experienced, which ultimately acts as a counterweight to our fears and anxieties. In her revisions, Arendt makes a point of relating this back to Heidegger, who if not as despairing as Silenus, sees the looming prospect of death as more determinative than the gift of birth: "Since our expectations and desires are prompted by what we remember and guided by a previous knowledge, it is memory and not expectation (for instance, the expectation of death as in Heidegger's approach) that gives unity and wholeness to human existence" (LSA 56).

We see Arendt carrying forward the theme of gratitude for birth in her next work, her biography of Rahel Varnhagen, the late eighteenth/early nineteenth-century writer whose Berlin salon served as a gathering place for various luminaries of German society. Arendt later calls Varnhagen "my closest friend, though she has been dead for some hundred years" (RV 5), identifying with her struggle to navigate the various inhospitable demands of assimilation. The opening lines of the book, a quote that Varnhagen uttered from her deathbed, sets the tone for the study: "The thing which all my life seemed to me the greatest shame, which was the misery and misfortune of my life—having been born a Jewess—this I should on no account now wish to have missed" (85). For much of her life, Varnhagen chose the path of the "parvenu," Arendt's term for those who, by denying the circumstances of their birth, strive to obtain what everyone else enjoys by birthright.[10] Arendt observes:

> Rahel's struggle against the facts, above all against the fact of having been born a Jew, very rapidly became a struggle against

herself. She herself refused to consent to herself; she, born to so many disadvantages, had to deny, change, re-shape by lies this self of hers, since she could not very well deny her existence out of hand. (92)

Arendt takes us through each agonizing step of Varnhagen's struggle, from broken engagements to name changes, Gentile marriage, and eventually Christian baptism. To assimilate, she had "to sacrifice every natural impulse, to conceal all truth, to misuse all love, not only to suppress all passion, but worse still, to convert it into a means for social climbing" (244). In short, "One had to pay for becoming a parvenu by abandoning truth," and this, ultimately, Rahel could not do (242). Assimilation was not only a form of self-betrayal, but also a futile means of social reform; it meant obtaining privileges by fraud, and merely for oneself (258). "In a society on the whole hostile to the Jews," she learned, "it is possible to assimilate only by assimilating to anti-Semitism" (256). At the end of her life, she moved towards the position of what Arendt calls the "conscious pariah," one who makes the question of Jewish emancipation what "it really should have been—an admission of Jews *as Jews* to the ranks of humanity, rather than a permit to ape the gentiles or an opportunity to play the parvenu" (JW 275). For the conscious pariah, being Jewish ceases to be a source of shame and becomes a source of gratitude, a ground for political action and a basis of freedom.

We see Arendt assuming the position of the conscious pariah herself when her own Jewishness came under attack under totalitarianism.[11] "If one is attacked as a Jew, one must defend oneself as a Jew," she recalls thinking at the time. "Not as a German, not as a world-citizen, not as an upholder of the Rights of Man, or whatever. But: What can I specifically do as a Jew?" (EU 12). For Arendt, totalitarianism represented a fundamental rejection of "everything merely given" (OT 627).[12] Birth stood as the ultimate obstacle to its ideological vision because it revealed the limit of what it could not change and exposed the lie of its claim that "everything is possible." In totalitarianism, we find Silenus' resentment of birth in its fiercest and most annihilating form. Yet lest we think such resentment is limited to totalitarianism, Arendt warns:

The reason why highly developed political communities, such as the ancient city-states or modern nation-states, so often insist on ethnic homogeneity is that they hope to eliminate as far as possible those natural and always present differences and differentiations which by themselves arouse dumb hatred, mistrust, and discrimination because they indicate all too clearly those spheres where men cannot act and change at will, i.e., the limitations of the human artifice. The "alien" is a frightening symbol of the fact of difference as such, of individuality as such, and indicates those realms in which man cannot change and cannot act and in which, therefore, he has a distinct tendency to destroy ... No doubt, wherever public life and its law of equality are completely victorious, wherever a civilization succeeds in eliminating or reducing to a minimum the dark background of difference, it will end in complete petrifaction and be punished, so to speak, for having forgotten that man is only the master, not the creator of the world. (301–2)

One can hear the echoes of her dissertation in these last lines. No state, Arendt argues, is immune to the danger that even as it seeks the laudable goals of equality and growth, it will come to see difference as an obstacle to be overcome, as something to be expelled rather than accepted, a temptation that is strongest when it comes to its treatment of minorities and asylum seekers. We can respond with resentment, by expelling such difference, or, Arendt says, we can strive for a different politics, one rooted in "a fundamental gratitude for the few elementary things that indeed are invariably given us, such as life itself, the existence of man and the world" (630).[13] She invokes Augustine again in referring to "all that which is mysteriously given us by birth and which includes the shape of our bodies and the talents of our minds" which "can be adequately dealt with ... by the great and incalculable grace of love, which says with Augustine, '*Volo ut sis*' (I want you to be)" (301).[14] Here, in the specific context of the needs of the stateless, we see love assuming a directly political relevance, affirming the differences that the political tends to exclude. In a 1963 letter to Scholem, Arendt expresses her doubts about the possibility of loving a whole people, but she does extend the point about gratitude to her own Jewish identity: "To be a Jew belongs for me to the indisputable facts of my life, and I have never had the wish to change or disclaim facts of this kind. There is such a thing as a basic gratitude for everything that is as it is; for what has been *given* and not *made*" (JW 466).

Thus for Arendt, to respond as a Jew to totalitarianism was to affirm, in the very midst of domination, the possibility of a different kind of politics, a politics that sees difference not as a threat to action, but one of its grounds. As she will later formulate it, these very differences—collectively understood as the human condition of plurality—enable and enhance our capacity to act, giving us a reason to disclose ourselves to each other, as well as diverse perspectives from which to view the common world, a basis for multiplying our energies, and ultimately deeper understanding and judgment of ourselves and one another.

Arendt's experience of totalitarianism brought to light one additional feature of natality, which, from the perspective of her later action theory, may be most important of all. Recall from Chapter 2 how totalitarian ideologies view history as a realm of necessity, subject to laws of race or class. From this vantage point, human freedom cannot stop the ultimate triumph of such laws, but it can slow their progress down. The point of total terror is to eliminate individuality and freedom as such, to make individuals act as one whole, thereby creating a universe in which nothing new can ever happen. In such a universe, the fact that individual persons are born comes to be seen as an "annoying interference with higher laws." What this suggested to Arendt was a tacit acknowledgment that there is something about our freedom that is intimately caught up with birth itself, that with our very uniqueness comes the guarantee that none of us will inhabit the world in quite the same way, that birth brings with it an inevitable element of newness and unpredictability. This is why total terror must "eliminate from the process not only freedom in any specific sense, but the very source of freedom which is given with the fact of the birth of man and resides in his capacity to make a new beginning" (OT 466). Henceforth Arendt will emphasize a core, programmatic connection between natality and the capacity to make new beginnings. It is, appropriately, the note upon which she concludes *Origins*:

> Beginning, before it becomes a historical event, is the supreme capacity of man; politically, it is identical with man's freedom.

> *Initium ut esset homo creatus est*—"that a beginning be made, man was created" said Augustine. This beginning is guaranteed by each new birth; it is indeed every man. (479)

Here we see Arendt returning once more to Augustine, citing a passage from the *City of God* that will appear in nearly all her subsequent discussions of natality and which becomes foundational to her theory of action.[15] Strikingly, the passage does not appear in her dissertation, where, as we saw, she is focused primarily upon the link between birth, gratitude, and remembrance.[16] This suggests the experience of totalitarianism caused Arendt to see something new in Augustine. That a contemporary event served as the impetus for a return to an ancient thinker and yielded fresh insights is what we would expect from a pearl diver such as Arendt. Yet as mentioned above, some Augustinians remain wary. Can he really have been suggesting that we have a capacity to make new beginnings simply in virtue of our birth? Given its centrality for Arendt's theory of action, it warrants a closer look.

II. Pearl Diving in the *City of God*

The key passage in question is found in *City of God* 12.21, where Augustine concludes a broad discussion of the creation of man and is engaged in a response to critics who argue that God cannot create anything new (12.18–21).[17] Upon first glance, this indeed appears to be a strange place to look for insights into the nature of human action, given that, as George McKenna points out, Augustine's primary focus is God's creative capacity, not our own. But let's see where the discussion leads. Augustine's main target in this chapter are certain Neoplatonist philosophers who defend the teaching of eternal recurrence, the idea that human souls do not have a beginning in time, but arise and perish in eternal cycles.[18] Augustine acknowledges that these philosophers have God's best interests in mind, as they subscribe to this teaching only because they think it is necessary in order to protect God's immutability and omniscience. As they see it, a God who creates is a God who changes, a God who, as it were, awakens from "a duration of slothful leisure" and bursts into "an improvident and impulsive creation" (12.18). To avoid this, they argue that what appears to be new must be part of a pattern of change that remains eternally the same. Augustine counters by arguing that eternal recurrence arises as a philosophical necessity only when we assume that the temporal categories that apply to human activity also apply to divine activity. He clarifies that the time by which we measure beginnings and endings is part of the created order that God transcends; while we experience God's creative activity as new, God Himself does not. Thus Augustine writes: "it is not impossible for God both to create new things never before created, and, by his ineffable foreknowledge, to preserve His will unaltered in doing so" (12.21).

The passage Arendt cites comes towards the end of 12.21, where Augustine addresses the implications of eternal recurrence for how we think about human happiness. If such a view is true, Augustine argues, then we are led to believe that human beings journey through life, experience its various trials and tribulations, enter blessedness, and finally enjoy the vision of God, only to be plunged back into mortal existence, renewing the cycle all over again. Augustine protests that this is no happiness at all: "For what happiness can be more false and fallacious than that in whose greatest light of truth we nonetheless remain ignorant of the fact that we shall presently be miserable, or in whose highest citadel of happiness we nonetheless fear that we shall be so?" (12.21). It would be closer to the truth "to say that we shall always be miserable than that we may sometimes be happy" (12.21). True happiness, Augustine argues, *lasts*, and to last, it must have a beginning, an authentic beginning that is not merely the return to a previous happiness. And for this happiness to begin, human life itself must have a beginning, one that is not merely a return to a previous life. Augustine concludes by considering whether the number of those who will enjoy eternal felicity is fixed or constantly increases, and argues that either way, these souls must have a beginning. "In order that there might be this beginning" he writes, "a man was created, before whom no man existed" (12.21).[19]

Arendt takes this discussion to carry two broad implications for how Augustine thinks about human beings. The first is that each human being is a "beginning," in the ontological sense of having never existed before. In "Understanding and Politics," she puts the point this way:

According to Augustine, who might rightly be called the father of all Western philosophy of history, man not only has the capacity of beginning, but is this beginning himself. If the creation of man coincides with the creation of a beginning in the universe ... then the birth of individual men, being new beginnings, re-affirms the *original* character of man in such a way that origin can never become entirely a thing of the past; the very fact of the memorable continuity of these beginnings in the sequence of generations guarantees a history which can never end because it is the history of beings whose essence is beginning. (EU 321)

Here Arendt makes explicit what Augustine's defense of God's creative capacity presupposes: namely, that the human being is a new creation. The whole debate with the Neoplatonists turns on this point; indeed, if the human being is not new, then God creates nothing new, and there is no basis of disagreement between them. Elsewhere Arendt conflates important differences between Augustine's theology and Neoplatonism, but here she puts her finger upon a significant difference and exploits it to show that Augustine's creation theology entails a radical affirmation of the uniqueness of each human life. It suggests that each one of us is unprecedented, a "somebody" who has never existed before. We are not reducible to what has come before, not a mixture of something new and old, but wholly new. Arendt's extension of the point from the creation of the first man to all human beings is also in keeping with the text, as Augustine makes clear that the happiness that God promises each human being would be artificial if each human soul did not have such a beginning.

If Arendt is on relatively firm ground with her first claim, it is her second claim that warrants closer scrutiny. Here is how she puts it in *The Human Condition*:

This beginning [the creation of human beings] is not the same as the beginning of the world; it is not the beginning of something but of somebody, who is a beginner himself. With the creation of man, the principle of beginning came into the world itself, which, of course, is only another way of saying that the principle of freedom was created when man was created but not before. (HC 177)

Arendt actually makes two claims here. The first is that human beings have the capacity to make beginnings in virtue of their birth, which, as Arendt suggests, means they are capable of acting freely. This in itself is no small claim. But she makes an even stronger claim: that the creation of man coincides with the creation of the very principle of beginning in the world, suggesting that human beings are beginners in an exclusive sense (i.e., the only creatures capable of making beginnings). Arendt defends this assertion by arguing that Augustine uses a different word for the beginning of man (*initium*) than the beginning of the world (*principium*). On her reading, the difference is indicated by Augustine's insertion of the phrase "before whom nobody was" (*ante quem nullus fuit*), suggesting that the beginning that is *initium* is tied up with the introduction of personhood and agency. The human being, as *initium*, is the first somebody, the first being capable of making beginnings into the world.

Does Augustine actually make such a distinction? A quick survey of his use of the word *initium* in Books 11 and 12 reveals a fairly broad application across a variety of contexts, from the beginning of the world (11.4) to the beginning of angels (11.13) and human beings (12.21).[20] Augustine betrays very little sense that *initium* carries an exclusively anthropocentric meaning. Moreover, in his discussion of the fall of angels, he makes clear that they exercise free will no less than human beings, weakening Arendt's case that the principle of beginning/freedom came into creation with human beings.[21] If the *initium/principium* distinction does not hold in the way that Arendt contends, what about her more basic claim, that regardless of whether it is unique to them, human beings have the capacity to make beginnings? Here the broader context of Book 12 does offer some evidence to support her claim. At several points, Augustine frames his objection to philosophers who deny human beings a beginning in terms of what their position would mean for human initiative. In 12.10, for example, Augustine rejects the notion of an everlasting human race this way:

> But if the human race has always existed, how can those histories be true which tell us who were the first inventors, and what they invented, and who first instituted the liberal studies and other arts, and who first inhabited this or that region or part of the earth, and this island and that? (12.10)

Here Augustine draws attention to the fact that if the human race did not have a beginning in time, the very notion of discovery and invention would lose all meaning. In such a world, there would have always been human beings in existence who had the opportunity to do things before others, *ad infinitum*, rendering any human "firsts" impossible. Philosophers who defend such a view find themselves forced to devise elaborate explanations about "floods and conflagrations" that reduced the human race to a remnant, such that "the things which seem to be newly discovered and originated at such times are in fact only being renewed" (12.10). "But," Augustine replies, "they say what they think, not what they know" (12.10). Here he does seem to be quite invested in the link between creation and the capacity to make beginnings. At the very least, he wants to press the point that in a world that is created, human beings will quite naturally find themselves doing things that have never been done before, a possibility which proponents of eternal recurrence are forced to deny.

Augustine expands upon the point in 12.14. He notes that some Christian authors have taken to defending the doctrine of eternal recurrence on the basis of the famous saying in Ecclesiastes 1:9, "there is nothing new under the sun." But Augustine quickly interjects that the passage refers to "the passing and arising of the generations, the turning of the sun, the descent of the rivers," not to individual human beings or, crucially, their actions. Here is how he frames his objection:

> God forbid, however, that we of the true faith should believe these words of Solomon to signify those cycles in which, according to the philosophers, the same things are repeated time and time again. On their view, for example, just as, during a certain period of time, the philosopher Plato taught in the town of Athens at a school called the Academy, so, during innumerable past ages, at long but fixed intervals, the same Plato, the same city, the same school and the same pupils existed repeatedly, and will exist repeatedly during innumerable ages to come. God forbid, I say, that we should believe this. (12.14)

Why is eternal recurrence objectionable? Augustine says look where it leads. It leads to the absurdity of suggesting that everything we do over the course of our lifetime is merely a repetition of what we have done before. And so Plato has taught the same pupils, at the same school, in the same city from time immemorial. But Augustine deliberately mentions these accidental features to underscore the contingency of it all: Plato could have easily been born in another city, come under the tutelage of a different teacher, founded (or not founded) a different school, taught other students, etc. It could have all been otherwise. It stretches the mind to consider how many forces would have had to align to recreate the same circumstances in another life, if another life were even possible. It is the contingency of Plato's life, not its necessity, that strikes us, and we know that what actually happened can never be repeated. There may be other teachers, there may be other schools, but there will never be another Plato who taught at the Academy in fourth-century Athens. The point is not limited to Plato. It extends to each one of us. The unique and unrepeatable quality of our lives comes back to the unique and unrepeatable nature of each one of us, the fact that we are created, that we are each a new beginning. Everything we do, regardless of whether it is historically unprecedented in the sense described above, is new just to the extent that it is *we* who do it, we who have never existed on this earth before, never lived in this city before, never held this job before, never come into contact with these neighbors before, and so on. In rejecting eternal recurrence from this angle, one does get the sense that Augustine sees an important link between being a beginning and the capacity to make new beginnings in the world. The latter follows from the former.[22]

Of course, for Augustine, there are deeper, Christological reasons for rejecting eternal recurrence. He concludes his discussion in 12.14 by writing: "God forbid, I say, that we should believe this [eternal recurrence]. For Christ died for our sins once, and 'being raised from the dead dieth no more; death hath no more dominion over Him'" (12.14). As Augustine sees it, eternal recurrence is theologically unacceptable because it suggests that Christ would have to go on redeeming the world again and again, which is to say, his redemption would never be effective enough. But Christ entered history once, died once, and his redemptive acts are effective for all time. They explode the endless cycles of the philosophers. For Augustine, Christ's acts define the very shape of history, revealing it not to be the eternal repetition of the same, but a genuine drama, one in which a free God acts and human beings freely respond. Arendt actually cites this same passage in *The Life of the Mind*, and makes a point of emphasizing just how dramatically this view of history differs from that of the Greeks:

> Whatever its indebtedness to Greek philosophy and especially to Aristotle, [Christian philosophy] was bound to break with the cyclical time concept of antiquity and its notion of everlasting recurrence. The story that begins with Adam's expulsion from Paradise and ends with Christ's death and resurrection is a story of unique, unrepeatable events: "Once Christ died for our sins; and rising from the dead, He dieth no more." The story's sequence presupposes a rectilinear time concept; it has a definite beginning, a turning-point—the year One of our calendar—and a definite end. (LMW 18)

Here Arendt comes to the heart of the matter, recognizing that for Augustine, eternal recurrence is objectionable not only because it denies God's capacity to create the world, but because it denies God's capacity to do new things within it.[23] It jeopardizes the integrity of salvation history, its distinctive character as a historical narrative defined by unique and unrepeatable events. In the process, it jeopardizes the new things that human beings do as well, actions both tragic (Adam's fall) and awe-inspiring (their inventions and discoveries). Eternal recurrence trivializes both God's capacity to do new things and our own, and this is why Augustine so adamantly rejects it.

Thus while the specific passage in the *City of God* to which Arendt points does not support her exegetical claims in quite the way she thinks, one could say that both claims—that human beings are an ontological beginning and have the capacity to make beginnings—are recognizably Augustinian commitments. Of course, just how much of a capacity to do new things survives the effects of sin and can be exercised independent of grace is a much thornier issue in Augustine's thought, one that I will come back to below. For now, the point is to appreciate the place this passage occupies in the broader context of her concept of natality. For her, to be conditioned by birth means that we are each ontologically new, born with unique features and differences, which both enables and limits the capacity to make new beginnings in the world. What does action rooted in such natality actually look like? This is what

Arendt explores in her theory of action, to which I now want to turn.

III. Arendt's Theory of Action

To say Arendt has a "theory" of action is a bit misleading because she nowhere offers a systematic account of such a faculty.[24] Her most extensive discussion comes in a chapter from *The Human Condition* entitled "Action," but many of her most important insights are found, as they often are, in her occasional writings on various political events such as revolutions and resistance movements. A distinctive vision of action nonetheless emerges out of these writings that consistently frames our capacity to act as an expression of our natality.

Action expresses our natality in two broad ways. First, it discloses the unique identities that each of us has in virtue of our birth; and second, it represents the beginning of something new. Arendt announces the first theme in one of the epigraphs to the "Action" chapter, a quote from Dante's *De Monarchia*: "For in every action what is primarily intended by the doer, whether he acts from natural necessity or out of free will, is the disclosure of his own image ... nothing acts unless [by acting] it makes patent its latent self" (HC 175). Putting this point in her own words, Arendt suggests, "In acting and speaking, men show who they are, reveal actively their unique personal identities and thus make their appearance in the human world" (179). Here she is drawing attention to action's revelatory quality, its capacity to display not simply "what" we are (our profession, our class or social status, our skills, etc.), but "who" we are: our irreducible particularity, who we alone are and no one else can be. It is this unique "who" that is first disclosed when we are born and reappears every time we act. Thus Arendt likens action to a kind of second birth, in which we take on the uniqueness of our existence and realize it more fully.

This is one of many places where Arendt, following Aristotle, finds it helpful to distinguish action (*praxis*) from work (*poiēsis*).[25] We explored the activity of work in some detail in the last chapter, noting its close association with worldliness. Work produces tangible objects that have the potential to become a lasting part of the human artifice. A defining characteristic of work is that the objects that it produces have the potential to exist independently of the production process. This "reified" quality gives them their tremendous durability and enables them to outlast their makers. But what such objects gain in durability they lose in their power to reveal. Such objects can certainly tell us about their maker's "what" (that she is a carpenter or potter, skilled or unskilled, and so on), but not about her "who." According to Arendt, a person's who is tied to his or her actual presence. And this is where action is perhaps most fundamentally different from work. Action does not produce a tangible object; rather, the end of action lies in the activity itself. It "produces" a word spoken, a deed done, and as in the performing arts, the person must be present in order to say the word or do the deed. This is what gives action its revelatory power. In every action, we *see* a person's who disclosed, and the disclosure of a person's who represents one of the primary ends of action (179–80). This is what we hear Dante emphasizing above: "what is primarily intended by the doer ... is the disclosure of his own image." Crucially for Arendt, this means that action may realize its internal end even if its various external aims (say, bringing about a political reform) are not successful.

Of course, this presupposes the presence of others to whom we can disclose ourselves. Here Arendt identifies another difference between work and action. If work is not only compatible with but requires a certain degree of isolation, action is only possible in the company of others. In the last chapter we saw that the common world provides one important means of gathering citizens together, offering a tangible space in which to appear and shared interests around which to organize. But this space must be inhabited and "humanized" by the actual presence of citizens. Thus Arendt speaks of what she calls the "web of human relationships" (183), a less tangible in-between that exists directly between human beings, held together not by things but the concerted action of citizens, or what Arendt calls power. Power is different from strength, which is an attribute of individuals, and violence, which uses implements to compel when all power has been lost.[26] "Power is what keeps the public realm, the potential space of appearance between acting and speaking men, in existence ... [it] springs up ... when they act together and vanishes the moment they disperse" (200). Here it may be helpful to picture protesters in Tahrir Square in Egypt in

2011: the square is the common world, but the people themselves form the web of human relationships. Their power is a function of the in-between that has arisen directly between them and it lasts as long as they are together. It is in this web that we disclose ourselves to one another in word and deed. Just as we do not know quite who we disclose when we are first born in the world, we are never quite sure who it is we reveal when we act, which is why we disclose ourselves in the first place, to enlist the help of others in coming to a better understanding of ourselves, as we help them come to a better understanding of themselves. In the process, a common story arises in the space between us (179).

In the background here are not only the many democratic movements that Arendt witnessed during her lifetime, but the lives of individuals such as Rahel Varnhagen and her own experience under totalitarianism. As a form of self-disclosure, action is one concrete way we work out our relationship to our birth, as well as many other features of our existence, and such a coming to terms is only possible in the company of others, who help us discern the ongoing, ever-changing shape of our identity. So long as Varnhagen remained bound to the conventions of German high society, she could not disclose who she really was; only when she ventured in the direction of becoming a "conscious pariah" could she begin to come to a truthful relationship to her self. Likewise, when Arendt joins with Kurt Blumenfeld and other German Zionists in resistance to totalitarian domination, she comes to a more profound awareness of her identity as a Jew, a woman, a German, an intellectual, and a political actor. For a thinker famous for her public/private distinction, Arendt's action theory actually blurs the line considerably, as we come to know our innermost self only in our willingness to appear in public.

These are all ways of talking about how action reflects the uniqueness of our birth. Arendt notes a second way in which action reflects natality, namely, that each action initiates something new. Playing on the etymological root of action, *archein*, meaning to begin or set in motion, Arendt writes: "It is in the nature of beginning that something new is started which cannot be expected from whatever may have happened before" (177–8). In developing this point, Arendt distinguishes action from labor. Labor, as mentioned in the last chapter, is the activity that corresponds to the human condition of life. We must labor in order to stay alive, and by producing goods that sustain the life process, we confirm that we are creatures bound by biological necessity. When we labor, we participate in nature's circular movement of growth and decay, where, strictly speaking, nothing new can ever happen. Action is an interruption of this cycle. When we act, we move beyond the realm of necessity and nature's law of cause and effect and actualize our freedom. "The touchstone of a free act," she writes, "is always that we know that we could also have left undone what we actually did" (LMW 26). Much as for Augustine the creation of each human being marks an interruption of the eternal cycles of the philosophers, action for Arendt breaks the eternal recurrence of the cyclical life process: "It is the faculty of action that interferes with this law because it interrupts the inexorable automatic course of daily life, which in its turn, as we saw, interrupted and interfered with the cycle of the biological life process" (HC 246).[27] For Arendt, each of our actions reflects something of the unprecedented quality of our births, a newness that is ontologically rooted in the newness of our very being:

> The fact that man is capable of action means that the unexpected can be expected from him, that he is able to perform what is infinitely improbable. And this again is possible only because each man is unique, so that with each birth something uniquely new comes into the world. (178)

In her later work, Arendt grew fond of referring to action as man's "miracle-working faculty," her provocative way of drawing attention to the way it disrupts automated patterns and processes, defies statistical and behavioral norms, and unsettles our penchant for narratives of progress and decline. Some may dismiss miracles in the realm of nature as superstition, she says, but in the realm of human history, "the miracle of accident and infinite improbability occurs so frequently that it seems strange to speak of miracles at all" (BPF 170). It is a "counsel of realism," she observes, "to look for the unforeseeable and unpredictable, to be prepared for and to expect 'miracles' [in the realm of human affairs]" (170).

Arendt's work is full of memorable accounts of individuals whose ability to defy the norm and surprise us with their actions clearly inspired this dimension of her action theory. Among them include Anton Schmidt, the German lieutenant who, in the midst of a general atmosphere of moral collapse and complicity, acted on behalf of the Jews; Rosa Luxemburg, a passionate advocate for workers' rights who defied traditional gender roles to play a leading part in the Spartacist Movement; and Pope John XXIII, whom Arendt notes was elected as a "provisional and transitional Pope" and was widely regarded "as a figure without consequence" but, to the surprise of everyone, set the Catholic Church on a dramatic new course by convening the Second Vatican Council (MDT 58).[28] While Arendt takes each individual action to involve an element of spontaneity, she especially has in mind the unpredictability of collective actions, which involve a number of actors and whose course is not reducible to any one will. Here she is thinking of events such as the Hungarian Revolution, the French Resistance, and the student protest movements of the 1960s.[29] Such events only take on the air of inevitability in hindsight, when historians can act as "prophets turned backward"; when we actually live through them, it is not clear what prompted them or where they will lead. Hence Arendt will often talk about the "abyss" of freedom, the causal gap that opens up in the middle of time when citizens act in concert with their peers.[30]

Given that our actions take place in the web of human relationships, there is an important sense in which each action, even the most isolated act of courage on the fringes of society, has a collective dimension. Arendt notes two consequences that follow from this. The first is what she calls the "boundlessness" of action (HC 190), which refers to the way that our actions ripple out into the world in ways that we cannot foresee in advance. Once these effects are set in motion, they prove impossible to reverse. Arendt calls this the "irreversibility" of action (236). Taken together, the boundlessness and irreversibility of action means that to act in freedom, we must relinquish the illusion that we can exercise control over everything we do. This connects to a final difference between action and work. In work, the craftsman remains a master over his activity, steering it to its predictable conclusion; in action, however, such mastery is exactly what we must give up. Arendt observes: "Because the actor always moves among and in relation to other acting beings, he is never merely a 'doer' but always and at the same time a sufferer. To do and to suffer are like opposite sides of the same coin, and the story that an act starts is composed of its consequent deeds and sufferings" (190). "If men wish to be free," she says, "it is precisely sovereignty they must renounce" (BPF 165).

Given the inherent risks and dangers of action, Arendt finds it unsurprising that many political philosophers have preferred to think about politics through the lens of work rather than action. Arendt cites Plato and his followers as the earliest and most influential example of this tendency. In place of action, Plato substitutes the concept of rule, "the notion that men can lawfully and politically live together only when some are entitled to command and the others forced to obey" (HC 222). In isolation, the ruler perceives the forms and applies these "as the craftsman applies his rules and standards; he 'makes' his City as the sculptor makes a statue" (227). Political activity comes to be associated with legislation and voting because they, like the fabrication process, result in tangible products and come to a definite end (195). Arendt observes: "It as though [these philosophers] had said that if men only renounce their capacity for action, with its futility, boundlessness, and uncertainty of outcome, there could be a remedy for the frailty of human affairs" (195). In our own age of bureaucratic administration and centralized planning, Arendt fears we have come to accept a similar bargain.

She was not convinced, however, that such a bargain was necessary. Arendt sought remedies for action's various hazards within the "potentialities" of action itself. She identified two in particular: for the unpredictability of action, she cited the human capacity to make and keep promises; for the irreversibility of action, she pointed to the human capacity to forgive. Arendt makes a point of emphasizing that both experiences originated in "a religious context" (238) and that such experiences thereby tend to be dismissed as politically irrelevant.[31] But it is precisely such arbitrary exclusions, as we have heard her say in other contexts, that have led to our distorted understanding of action. So she seeks to bring them back in. Promising, as she famously puts it, establishes "islands of security" in "the ocean of uncertainty" (237). It offers a kind of stability that remains receptive to the unpredictability that inevitably accompanies human action. When we promise, we voluntarily bind ourselves to one another and give up some of the freedom we enjoy in isolation. What we gain is a new condition of equality and the freedom to act in the company of others. Rather than relinquish power, promising multiplies it, allowing each individual to do more than they could alone. Promising in this respect is different from contracting, the idea popular among political theorists in the seventeenth and eighteenth centuries in which individuals give up their power and consent to be governed in exchange for the protection of their negative liberties. One "gains as much power by the system of mutual promises," Arendt observes, "as he loses by his consent to a monopoly of power in the ruler" (OR 170). Here Arendt continues to counter the modern emphasis upon sovereignty by emphasizing that it is only when we bind ourselves to a common purpose that we are free. Promising provides an alternative "to a mastery which relies on domination of one's self and rule over others; it corresponds exactly to the existence of a freedom which was given under the condition of non-sovereignty" (HC 244).

If promising gives us the security necessary to set our actions in motion, it cannot reverse the consequences of these actions once they have occurred. In fact, nothing can do this. This means we stand under the burden of all the consequences that we did not originally intend, but that nonetheless arise as a result of our action. These unintended consequences would overwhelm us and completely determine our subsequent actions if it were not for forgiveness, which releases us from these consequences and allows us to begin again. In explaining forgiveness, Arendt contrasts it to vengeance, "which acts in the form of re-acting against an original trespassing, whereby far from putting an end to the consequences of the first misdeed, everybody remains bound to the process, permitting the chain reaction contained in every action to take its unhindered course" (240–1). Forgiveness, on the other hand, "is the only reaction which does not merely re-act but acts anew and unexpectedly, unconditioned by the act which provoked it and therefore freeing from its consequences both the one who forgives and the one who is forgiven" (241). In this way, forgiveness epitomizes Arendt's identification of action with natality: it is undetermined by what came before, and through it, it expresses the uniqueness of the person who performs it—and in this case, the person who receives it: "Forgiving and the relationship it established is always an eminently personal (though not necessarily individual or private) affair in which *what* was done is forgiven for the sake of *who* did it" (241).

In the course of her discussion of forgiveness, Arendt makes a number of claims that are sure to give theological readers pause. One is that Jesus only intends forgiveness for the unintended consequences of our action ("trespasses") but not for willed evil (*skandala*).³² She also argues that forgiveness can be motivated sufficiently through respect, not neighbor-love.³³ But most contestable is her claim that Jesus believed that the power to forgive "does not derive from God ... but on the contrary must be mobilized by men toward each other" (239).³⁴ Such claims leave even her most sympathetic theological readers wondering if her partial appropriation of theological sources does not end up haunting her in the end. The issue is not simply that she attributes to human beings powers that properly belong to God. It is the more basic link she makes between action and natality, suggesting a kind of naïve humanism that trusts we can make new beginnings at will, unbound by any determining forces, whether the weight of sin or any wider consideration of the ends of our actions. In the introduction, I mentioned that this is the line of criticism adopted by Charles Mathewes, whose concerns raise fundamental issues about whether Arendt's attempt to root action in natality is advisable at all. Having placed her action theory on the table, I now want to return to his critique.

IV. Pelagianism Redux?

As we have seen in previous chapters, Charles Mathewes is one of Arendt's most sympathetic readers. For him, Arendt's banality thesis, along with her constructive vision of *amor mundi*, strongly parallel Augustine's own views on the privative effects of evil and the ontological priority of goodness. In his view, these dimensions of her work effectively model how the insights of the Augustinian tradition can continue to illumine our contemporary world. Her action theory, however, represents a significant departure. Despite the fact that it is the area of her thought in which she draws mostly explicitly upon Augustine, Mathewes concludes that her account ends up resembling something closer to the Pelagianism that Augustine rejected.

Pelagianism, in the words of Peter Brown, "appealed to a universal theme: the need of the individual to define himself, and to feel free to create his own values in the midst of the conventional, second-rate life of society."³⁵ It was a movement of "heroic individuality" in which Christians took upon themselves the task of self-perfection, convinced that the restraints of sin, social context, and history were minimal, and could be overcome through sheer will and determination. For Mathewes, Arendt's theory of action is "essentially Pelagian" because it "depicts us as acting from a position of no prior commitments" and expresses an "absolute faith in the *ex nihilo* spontaneity of human agency."[36] It "refuses to place any metaphysical limits on the will, and thus invests agents with a radical originality in their actions," assuming that "freedom is not real unless the action is uninfluenced by any determining forces."[37]

Mathewes points to a particularly notorious passage from "What is Freedom?" in which Arendt appears to suggest that action must remain uninfluenced by our very motives and aims:

> Action, to be free, must be free from motive on one side, from its intended goal as a predictable effect on the other. This is not to say that motives and aims are not important factors in every single act, but they are its determining factors, and action is free to the extent that it is able to transcend them. (BPF 151)

Here Mathewes takes Arendt to be suggesting that the motives and intentions that most of us would regard as expressions of freedom are among the forces that threaten it. As he paraphrases her point, "If we know what we are always going to do, we will never transcend our narrow and captivating self-understanding, we can never really become something new."[38] Action, it would appear, can only be free if it is free of *us*, free of our narrow horizons and our desire to determine the outcomes of actions in advance. Following Dana Villa, Mathewes takes this to represent a fundamental rejection of all teleological approaches to action, an "explicit voluntarist" account that refuses to subordinate our willing to any specification of ends.[39] Such independence, Mathewes argues, comes at a heavy price: "if this is so—if the nature of action is absolutely unpredictable—human agents must be surprised not only at the effects of what they will, but at the very character of their willing, the form and direction it takes."[40] For Mathewes, it is unclear how we remain responsible for our actions at all, given that they seem to arise from "a fountain of novelty, a source which is foreign to our conscious selves."[41] The agent becomes, in Mathewes' words, "simply a rider on a runaway train—or, rather, on a train that was never under its control in the first place."[42] This not only leads to an "irrational" and "anarchist" conception of action, but also reproduces the very determinism it was meant to avoid, as it renders the agent completely passive before the arbitrary whims of the will.[43] Arendt herself seems resigned to such a conclusion, Mathewes points out, when she writes: "we are *doomed* to be free by virtue of being born, no matter whether we like freedom or abhor its arbitrariness."[44]

Mathewes goes on to argue that Arendt's account not only threatens our freedom, but also the very self capable of exercising such freedom. As he puts it:

> [I]f an action is, properly speaking, spontaneous, it can have no connection with what came before, and this undermines the basic framework of the self's continuity, a continuity necessary for the self's actions—and indeed the self itself—to be intelligible.[45]

Even though action is supposed to reveal a person's "who," the fact that each action is a new beginning means a different "who" appears every time we act. This implies, for Mathewes, that we have as many selves as we have actions. Constantly re-inventing ourselves, we become "episodic beings," splintered reflections of our arbitrary whims.[46] For all of her attentiveness to the temporal situation of the self, Mathewes argues that Arendt's account of action denies our basic historicity, the fact that we are subjects whose existence extends in time, whose dispositions and attributes persist and shape our capacity to act in decisive ways. This explains why she senses the need to supply a source of stability through such practices as promising and forgiving, and why this attempt must fail because she cannot call upon the deeper stability of self that such practices require. Arendt's picture of the self mirrors her conception of politics: one of "permanent revolution," one that is so busy beginning it never breaks out of this circle to allow the story of the self to unfold.

In the end, Mathewes detects in Arendt's work that recognizable spirit of Pelagian pride that believes that human beings are ultimately capable of redeeming themselves. Citing Arendt's depiction of natality as the "miracle" that saves the world from ruin, Mathewes observes that for her, "What saves us from action's caprices can only be action itself; as such, the fragility of life must be met not by theoretical or philosophical solutions, but by ongoing *political* engagements ... Action is thus the only guard against itself we can have."[47] If Arendt relied upon Augustine for his basic insistence upon freedom, her own account of action "effectively Pelagianizes" his thought by unmooring it from any account of grace:

> Arendt recognized that for Augustine the "outside" force of natality was not ultimately human will, but always human will under the direction of divine providence. She thought that interpretation of natality was not essential to the structure of willing; so she sought in her own work to "demystify" it, to strip it of its theological pretenses and show it to be solely a human capacity—properly miraculous, to be sure, but not in need of any supernatural powers to back it up.[48]

Summarizing his critique, Mathewes observes that her account offers "too narrow a picture of human agency, and leaves uninvestigated both agency's interesting interrelations with the world outside it, and its internal complexities as well."[49] He goes on: "Arendt fails to see that there are significant determinants of our actions, determinants that we must recognize and explicitly acknowledge, if we are responsibly to address them."[50] Her account is at best "a partial Augustinianism," failing to incorporate his insights into all that constrains our willing. "We need instead an account of action which affirms that, from the beginning, humans are 'always already' responding to the more primary action of the larger reality within which they find themselves," one that places our actions "within a rich picture of human life as an integrated whole."[51]

Of course, Arendt's defenders would insist that this is exactly what she offers in *The Human Condition*. "It is an ironic comment on the presuppositions of her readers," Margaret Canovan observes, "that a work concerned as much with the limits as with the possibilities of the human condition has often been read as an invitation to unlimited action."[52] Canovan notes that it was precisely the resentment of limits—the imperialist claim that "everything is permitted," the totalitarian assertion that "everything is possible," the scientist's hope for liberation from the earth, the industrialist's dream of being freed from labor, the engineer's desire to replace "human existence as it has been given" for "something he has made himself" (HC 3)—that led Arendt to write the book in the first place. As we have seen, a sensitivity to the ways in which our capacity to act is contingent upon a variety of conditions pervades her work. Her writings on evil taught her the importance of a common world in which to appear, and her writings on action continually come back to the importance of plurality and the web of human relationships. Mathewes acknowledges all of this, but still insists that Arendt's specific emphasis upon the link between natality and action represents a departure from these insights. Can her attention to conditionedness be reconciled with her claim that action represents a new beginning?

V. Political Freedom and the Limits of Action

In answering this question, we need to return to one of Arendt's core insights discussed above: that natality is itself a human condition, one that not only enables but also limits the capacity to act. As we saw, it was the way that birth acts as a determinant upon our existence that initially alerted Arendt to the connection between action and natality. Varnhagen was stifled as an actor just to the extent that she attempted to deny her origins and reinvent herself in the image of anti-Semitic German society. It was only in coming to terms with her Jewish identity that she was able to act freely. Likewise, for Arendt, it was only by embracing the identity that totalitarianism attacked that she found a free way to respond. In "On Humanity in Dark Times," she states that those who believe they can act completely undetermined by the reality of persecution "may feel wonderfully superior to the world, but their superiority is then truly no longer of this world; it is the superiority of a more or less well-equipped cloud-cuckoo-land" (MDT 18). Arendt does not abandon these insights in her more formal action theory. Rather, in insisting that action is a disclosure of our who, she suggests that our ability to act is caught up in our willingness to maintain an ongoing relationship with "who" we are. The life of action just is this constant, ongoing task of remembering and discerning who it is that first appeared when we were born, which is caught up in the task of discerning who we have become ever since. Arendt's very first insight into natality as a human condition, drawn from Augustine, was the way it "determines" us as remembering beings, giving us a past that continues to shape us in the present. Interestingly, when Arendt inserts her beloved *initium* passage into her revised dissertation, she does so to underscore the link between our capacity to make beginnings and remembrance: "Since man can know, be conscious of, and remember his 'beginning' or his origin, he is able to act as a beginner" (LSA 55). We also recall her point against Heidegger: what we remember proves more determinative than what we desire because what we desire is in large measure a function of what we remember, and whether remembrance is born from gratitude or resentment will shape the kind of actions we undertake. "For Arendt," Young-Bruehl observes, "temporality, far from having to be overcome for man to be, is the source of his possibility for action in which his being is intensified," which accounts for her fondness for Pindar's line "become what you are," or as Young-Bruehl paraphrases, "gratefully acknowledge what the fact of having been born grants you."[53]

Of course, we are conditioned by more than what we choose to remember. Eichmann's capacity to act creatively diminishes under the weight of years of bureaucratic repetition and rote ideological deduction. He remains a free actor, responsible for what he does, but he has become entirely predictable, "the last man," she says, "to be expected to challenge these notions and to strike out on his own" (EJ 135). He is the epitome of thoughtless habituation.[54] In her portrait of Robespierre in *On Revolution*, habituation takes the form of an excessive and sentimental pity thinly veiling a deeper will to power. His resort to terror, Arendt observes, is symptomatic of his inability to create or build anything. Terror is always the weapon of choice for those who have not only lost power over themselves, but are no longer capable of eliciting the cooperation of others. In this regard, Arendt considers the will to power *the* political vice of politics, "that quality which tends to destroy all political life, its vices no less than its virtues" (OR 119–20).

Arendt may have been prepared to acknowledge various determinants that weigh upon our actions from the direction of the past, but what about those future determinants that give our actions their distinctive shape and intelligibility? Mathewes identifies two specific concerns: her appeals to spontaneity and her apparent rejection of motives and ends. To start with her appeals to spontaneity, some clarity can be gained by turning to her discussion of Augustine in *The Life of the Mind*, where Arendt distinguishes between two kinds of beginning: an absolute beginning, which she identifies with creation *ex nihilo* and the beginning of the heavens and the earth; and a relative beginning, which she identifies with human beginnings that take place within time.[55] Borrowing words from Kant, she states: "a series occurring in the world can have only a relatively first beginning, being always preceded by some other state of things" (LMW 29). Here she makes clear that within human affairs, the notion of absolute spontaneity, a spontaneity that breaks in from nowhere and is unconditioned by any external factors, is impossible. As she observes in her essay, "Lying in Politics": "A characteristic of human action is that it always begins something new, and this does *not* mean that it is ever permitted to start *ab ovo*, to create *ex nihilo*" (CR 5, my italics). So what does she mean by a new beginning? Arendt goes on to say that there is another way to think about beginnings, not with respect to time but with respect to causality. Here it becomes possible to speak of "a *relatively* absolute spontaneity" (LMW 110), a kind of beginning which, while conditioned by what comes before it, is not reducible to it. Her authority on this is none other than Augustine who, in *De libero arbitrio*, observes: "For either the will is its own cause or it is not a will" (3.17.49; LMW 89). For Arendt, the point is not that our actions cannot be subject to any external determinants; it is that our freedom is ultimately not reducible to any one of them. Her discussion of forgiveness is perhaps most instructive in this regard. A paradigm case of new beginnings, forgiveness is nothing if not a response to a prior act. Her point, however, is that it is not determined by what came before: "Forgiving, in other words, is the only reaction which does not merely re-act but acts anew and unexpectedly, unconditioned by the act which provoked it" (HC 241). One could point to other examples: her response to totalitarianism, acts of civil disobedience, Char's participation in the French Resistance, all of which represent the possibility of newness in the course of a response to various determinants and provocations. In each case, Arendt is trying to highlight what Mathewes himself calls the "causal hiccup" of every "willed, intentional act."[56]

This brings us to the vexed question of motives and aims. As Mathewes reads Arendt, action can only be free to the extent that it is free of all motives and aims. Above we reviewed the passage from "What is Freedom?" that he cites in support of this view. Here is the passage again, in its full context:

> Action, to be free, must be free from motive on one side, from its intended goal as a predictable effect on the other. This is not to say that motives and aims are not important factors in every single act, but they are its determining factors, and action is free to the extent that it is able to transcend them. *Action insofar as it is determined* is guided by a future aim whose desirability the intellect has grasped before the will wills it, whereby the intellect calls upon the will, since only the will can dictate action. (BPF 151, my italics)

As the latter part of this passage makes clear, Arendt is not claiming action can only be free if it is undetermined. She explicitly states that action *is* determined, and determined in a way that appears to affirm the conventional wisdom of Thomistic practical reasoning: the intellect specifies, the will moves.[57] As with the circumstantial determinants discussed above, she sees no tension in the suggestion that an act may be determined by certain motives and aims and still be free. That is not the issue for her. The issue is when freedom is reduced to these determinants. Arendt has two specific dangers in mind. The first, prevalent in philosophical discussions of free will, is when freedom is conceptualized in a way that limits its experience to the mind alone. This is to see freedom as inner freedom, an inward state of consciousness that occurs "in the intercourse between me and myself" (158). Freedom here is freedom of choice, freedom as a mental exercise antecedent to and independent from action, a state of mind that would not be diminished even if the action never came to pass. The opposite danger is when freedom is identified exclusively with the outcome of action. Here freedom is associated with the successful realization of our aims, the state of affairs that action brings about. Such freedom comes into being when action is complete, experienced as the cessation of activity, as rest or leisure. If the first approach psychologizes freedom by making it a matter of the mind alone, the second approach instrumentalizes action, rendering it a mere means on the road to freedom. For Arendt, both views overlook the freedom that inheres in action itself: "Men *are* free—as distinguished from their possessing the gift for freedom—as long as they act, neither before nor after; for to *be* free and to act are the same" (153). This is what she means when she says the freedom of action transcends its determinants: while action is motivated by certain reasons and is directed toward certain aims, the freedom of action is reducible to neither; it is experienced in the action itself. She has in mind a freedom which is "a worldly reality, tangible in words which can be heard, in deeds which can be seen, and in events which are talked about, remembered, and turned into stories" (154–5).[58] She calls this "political freedom," the freedom that accompanies the introduction of a new beginning into politics. It is the creativity on display when a political actor has devised a novel approach to a problem, or the new reality that comes into existence when a group acts in concert with one another. Think of the freedom tangibly embodied in those who marched from Selma to Montgomery, or the hunger strikers in Northern Ireland, or Gandhi's nonviolent protests. In each of these instances, the participants have, to borrow the words Arendt uses to describe those who joined the French Resistance, "set a table for freedom to come and sit down." They are determined in innumerable ways, indeed radically constrained, but they have tasted a tangible freedom.

Arendt notes that freedom is often seen as a presupposition for action, but for her, political freedom is better seen as an end of action, the sign of a certain fullness or actualization of creative capacity. Appreciating this helps shed important light on where she ultimately stands on the question of teleology. She clearly rejects teleological approaches that frame action in instrumental terms, where action is a means to some external end.[59] But this does not mean she rejects all teleological thinking. What she is after are the ends that are realized in the course of acting, among which include political freedom itself. To get at this, Arendt appropriates Aristotle's notion of *energeia*, those activities, like flute-playing and stage-acting, "that do not pursue an end ... and leave no work behind ... but exhaust their full meaning in the performance itself" (HC 206). Here action has an end, but the end is a kind of sheer activity or performance; the excellence is realized in the very course of acting. The "work" is the performance. In a key passage, she writes:

> Aristotle, in his political philosophy, is still well aware of what is at stake in politics, namely, no less than the *ergon tou*

anthrōpou (the "work of man" *qua* man), and if he defined this "work" as "to live well" (*eu zēn*), he clearly meant that "work" here is no product but exists only in sheer actuality. This specifically human achievement lies altogether outside the category of means and ends; the "work of man" is no end because the means to achieve it—the virtues, or *aretai*—are not qualities which may or may not be actualized, but are themselves "actualities." In other words, the means to achieve the end would already be the end; and this "end," conversely, cannot be considered a means in some other respect, because there is nothing higher to attain than this actuality itself. (206–7)

For Joseph Dunne, this passage "goes a long way toward showing an appreciation on Arendt's part of the Aristotelian provenance of much of what she wants to say about action."[60] Elsewhere Arendt expresses the worry that Aristotle falls into a more instrumental approach to action when, in Book 10 of the *Nicomachean Ethics*, he identifies *eudaimonia* with the contemplative life, appearing to relativize the internal goods of a life devoted to action. In the above passage, however, Arendt recognizes that there is another way to read Aristotle, one in which teleology does not operate instrumentally, but, in the words of J. I. Akrill, "inclusively."[61] Here living well is not a state achieved when action is complete, but a state of activity. Action is not a means to *eudaimonia*, but constitutive of *eudaimonia*; likewise, the virtues are not simply tools that help us eventually arrive at happiness, but are themselves a tangible taste of happiness.

Arendt is so well known as a critic of *eudaimonistic* accounts of politics that her own deep investment in the question of happiness often goes overlooked. Throughout her writings, she repeatedly brings her discussions back to the specific kind of happiness that awaits us in the public realm, one that accompanies the realization of the political freedom described above. Arendt points to the testimony of the René Char, whose famous saying "our inheritance was left to us by no testament" we discussed in Chapter 2. At the height of his involvement in the French Resistance, Char wrote: "If I survive, I know that I shall have to break with the aroma of these essential years, silently reject (not repress) my treasure" (BPF 4). This treasure, Arendt explains, refers to Char's discovery "that he who joined the Resistance, *found* himself," that "he no longer suspected himself of 'insincerity', that he needed no mask and no make-believe to appear, that wherever he went he appeared as he was to others and to himself" (OR 280). It relates to the fact that he and his peers "had become 'challengers,' had taken the initiative upon themselves and therefore, without knowing or even noticing it, had begun to create that public space between themselves where freedom could appear" (BPF 4). Arendt suggests that the American revolutionaries possessed a name for this treasure: "public happiness," which for them "consisted in the citizen's right of access to the public realm, in his share in public power—to be a 'participator in the government of affairs'" (OR 127). They distinguished this from "the generally recognized rights of subjects to be protected by the government in the pursuit of private happiness" (127). Both meanings, Arendt suggests, can be heard in the Declaration's famous preamble, but our association of happiness with the pursuit of private welfare has caused us to lose sight of the fact that it was the happiness that the colonists experienced in their town meetings and convention halls that fuelled their revolutionary struggle:

> The very fact that the word "happiness" was chosen in laying claim to a share in public power indicates strongly that there existed in the country, prior to the revolution, such a thing as "public happiness," and that men knew they could not be altogether "happy" if their happiness was located and enjoyed only in private life. (127)

It is in the "pursuit" of such happiness, Arendt argues, that we act politically.[62] This is the goal, the *telos* toward which we strive and which we experience in the very course of acting, the treasure that endows life "with splendor" (281).

If Arendt's discussion of public happiness helps to fill in some of her thinking on the ends of action, it also helps to illumine her thinking on the deeper dispositions that enable us to make beginnings and realize such happiness. To stay with Arendt's discussion of the American Revolution, she cites John Adams' observation that "the revolution was effected before the war commenced" (118), noting that he refers not to "any specific revolutionary or rebellious spirit" but the fact that "the inhabitants of the colonies were 'formed by law into corporations, or bodies politic' and possessed 'the right to assemble'" (118). It was "in these assemblies of towns or districts that the sentiments of the people were formed in the first place" (118). What this suggests is that the capacity to launch the revolution did not arise from nowhere, but was cultivated over many years of assembling, debating, and organizing. The capacity to do the unexpected was not a break from this culture, but one important manifestation of it. Arendt captures the relationship this way: "Public or political freedom and public or political happiness were the inspiring principles which prepared the minds of those who then did what they never had expected to do, and more often than not were compelled to acts for which they had no previous inclination" (123).

We see Arendt emphasizing this same point throughout her writings: it was in the Berlin salons that Rahel Varnhagen formed new habits of sociability that enabled her to begin to question the dominant strategy of assimilation;[63] it was in Rosa Luxemburg's Polish-Jewish peer group, "a highly significant and totally neglected source ... of the revolutionary spirit in the twentieth century" (MDT 40), that she developed the moral passion to defend the rights of workers in the 1919 Spartacist strike;[64] and it was through the revival of voluntary associations that the tradition of civil disobedience was renewed among anti-war and student demonstrators during the 1960s.[65] This emphasis upon formation should not sound altogether surprising, as this is the same Arendt who stresses in "The Crisis in Education" that our children must be initiated into the world lest we strike from them their chance at undertaking something new. As we saw in the last chapter, this commitment was itself contingent upon the cultivation of *amor mundi*, the civic virtue par excellence, the "weight of the soul" that grounds, inspires, and sustains our commitment to the world as a space for such action. Scattered across her writings we find appeals to several other virtues, including courage, "which we still believe to be indispensible for political action, and which Churchill once called 'the first of human qualities, because it is the quality which guarantees all others'" (BPF 156). "It requires courage," Arendt suggests, "even to leave the protective security of our four walls and enter the public realm, not because of particular dangers which may lie in wait for us, but ... because in politics not life but the world is at stake" (156). Courage, like *amor mundi*, helps us to move beyond narrow self-interest to act in the interest of what is common to all. To this Arendt adds self-control, "one of the specifically political virtues" which helps to lift the internal and external constraints that stand in between the I-will and the I-can (159); respect, which is the equal regard that is required in order to receive and support the disclosure of one's who (HC 243); and solidarity, through which citizens establish "a community of interest with the oppressed and exploited" (OR 88).[66] In the next chapter we will explore how Arendt reclaims thinking, understood in the Socratic sense of self-examination, as a kind of intellectual virtue, an antidote to the tyranny of thoughtless know-how. Growth in these and other virtues presupposes civic friendships that provide the enduring relationships and support through which we humanize the common world.[67] In the contexts of such relationships, through imitation and repetition, virtues such as courage "become second nature or a habit" (LMT 36). "Out of such acts," Arendt writes, "arises finally what we call character or personality, the conglomeration of a number of identifiable qualities gathered together into a comprehensible and reliably identifiable whole, and imprinted, as it were, on an unchangeable substratum of gifts and defects peculiar to our soul and body structure" (37). It is out of this enduring character that our capacity to make new beginnings arises.

In *The Human Condition*, Arendt notes the ancient conviction that "where *aretē* is, oblivion cannot occur" (208). She echoes the point in the preface to *Men in Dark Times*, where she suggests that the light that shines from the men and women described therein is enough to keep the public realm lit even in the darkest of times. This owes not simply to the fact that they are beings whose essence is beginning, but because they were each schooled in that *amor mundi* that enabled them to make such beginnings, and in doing so, still taste that public freedom and happiness that is our birthright.

VI. The Grace of Natality

Where does all of this leave Arendt on the question of Pelagianism? Let's recall what Pelagianism actually was. It was not simply the view that freedom is only free if it is completely unlimited, although that was certainly part of it. I hope our discussion above has made sufficiently clear that Arendt does not hold this view. Pelagianism, as Eleonore Stump reminds us, refers more precisely to the belief that human beings are capable of achieving perfect righteousness without the need for grace.[68] Pelagius and his followers were moral perfectionists of the most extreme sort. They were ascetics who believed that once the divine commandments and teachings of Jesus had been given, Christians really had no excuse but to fulfill them. In his letter to Demetrias, a woman on the verge of entering the religious life, Pelagius quotes his favorite passage from Paul: "Be blameless and innocent, as children of God without blemish" (Phil. 2.15), adding: "Now, therefore, direct your mind's attention to complete moral perfection and prepare yourself to lead a heavenly life for a heavenly reward."[69] Arendt can hardly be taken to enjoin this. On the contrary, as we saw in the last chapter, she believed goodness and neighbor-love were fundamentally unworldly and had little place in politics. While she certainly speaks of the power to forgive, it is a stripped down version of forgiveness, motivated not by *agape* but respect, extending only to the unintended consequences of our actions. Arendt's writings on natality and action are many things, but they are not perfectionist. On the contrary, one is tempted to say they are not perfectionist *enough*. We often find Arendt content with beginnings as such, with merely setting an action in motion, and while she does discriminate between different beginnings (we will say more about her important call to "think what we are doing" in the next chapter), the beginnings that captivate her often leave us wanting more. Thus the shortcomings that we identified in the last chapter on the question of neighbor-love come back to influence, and ultimately limit, all that Arendt's account of natality could be.

A case in point is the founding of Rome. Arendt routinely cites this as a quintessential expression of our capacity to make new beginnings, as it brought a new people into existence and defied, as all genuine new beginnings do, straightforward chains of cause and effect. For the Romans, all subsequent political activity came to be seen as a way of "binding oneself back" to the founding, a way of augmenting this singular, people-defining event (OR 201). Contrast Arendt's sense of the importance of this event to Augustine's. He does not deny that it gave birth to a new republic, nor does he deny its obvious importance in world history, but he is not convinced it represented a genuinely new beginning. After all, Rome was founded in fratricide, when Romulus slew Remus, which only repeated the primordial crime that founded the first city, Cain's slaying of Abel. Strikingly, he observes that the founding of Rome was a "kind of reflection ... an event of the same kind" (15.5). A less original event, he suggests, can scarcely be found. Rome was merely extending the cycle of violence characteristic of the earthly city as a whole. It did not make the fundamental break. It was not new.

Arendt herself does not appear to be entirely satisfied with the founding of Rome, certainly not this dimension of it, as it runs counter to everything she has to say about action being rooted in power rather than violence. This explains her attempt to move the founding back to the alliance Aeneas establishes with the native Italians (OR 209). But wherever she locates it, one suspects Augustine would not have been satisfied. He longed for a more transformative founding, one that ushered in a new beginning of an entirely different sort, one that could offer deliverance from this long history of violence. He found it, of course, in the City of God, whose founder was the Prince of Peace, the *principium* who created the world and all that is in it, the Mediator who took on flesh, and whose death and resurrection offered "the remission of sins," "the grace of justification," "the abolition of the worship of idols," "the purification of those who persevere and their liberation from all evil" (10.32). Membership in this city entailed the transformation of our deepest loves, birthing in its citizens "a love inspired by its founder" (11.1). The markings of this city were patience, humility, mercy, and peace: "For they do not give orders because of a lust for domination but from a dutiful concern for the interests of others, not with pride in taking precedence over others, but with compassion in taking care of others" (19.14). Commingling with the earthly city, the presence of these citizens was felt in the impact their love of God and neighbor has upon the peace they seek with others, the signs of which are manifested when leaders submit to correction, as in the case of Theodosius, when clemency is granted to prisoners, as in the case of Macedonius, when unjust wars are abandoned, when consolation is extended to the injured, and when relief is given to the poor.

Arendt, as we know, was wary of the love of God for its potential to instrumentalize our relationship with others and the love of neighbor for the ways it threatens to drown politics in necessity or set up paternalistic relationships between citizens. In the last chapter, Williams and Gregory gave us good reason to believe that while such dangers remain ever present, our politics would be diminished without citizens motivated by such loves. These loves have often motivated actors at the forefront of the very movements Arendt celebrates as extending political freedom and new beginnings. And when we survey the periods in history in which she claims Christian charity was chipping away at the dignity of politics, we see that it often manifested itself in a creativity and inventiveness befitting her own emphasis upon new beginnings. Strikingly, when Gregory of Nazianzus eulogized Basil of Caesarea, he enumerated the many institutions that came into existence under his watch, from hospitals to poor houses, and likened his actions to the founding of a "new city," a "common treasury ... unexposed to the moths and no source of joy to the thief, escaping the assaults of envy and the corruption of time."[70]

At the same time, let us not miss what Arendt might have to teach Augustine. For all the anxieties about unlimited freedom that her writings on natality have generated, it is unlikely that Augustine himself would have denied that we have the capacity to make the kind of beginnings that she mentions. We have already noted the example of the founding of Rome. The *City of God* is full of other such actions, from political compacts and resistance movements to individuals performing daring feats of courage. One thinks of Regulus voluntarily returning to his captors, the Sanguntines dying rather than break faith with Rome, and the nameless Horatian woman who protests the death of her betrothed, to say nothing of the historic first voyages, discoveries, and inventions mentioned above. Yet Augustine remained convinced that absent the love of God, all such actions remained tainted by *superbia*, the disordered love of self, and thus could only be considered a mere semblance of virtue. As mentioned in the last chapter, he lacked the kind of distinctions that we find in later thinkers such as Aquinas, who can better account for the dignity of such actions because he appreciates that while they may not be rooted in the love of God, they may not be rooted in the vicious love of self or glory either.[71] Arendt's appeal to new beginnings motivated by *amor mundi* testifies to a similar kind of possibility. Specifically, she directs our attention to actions which, while not salvific, are nonetheless generative and life-giving, which ennoble our politics and humanize our common world.

In the history of theology, such actions have gone by many names. Barth called them parables of the kingdom. In *Gaudium et spes*, they are called "signs of the times." Whatever we call them, they highlight the basic truth that to the extent that we act as creatures, we are already acting under a state of grace, and that we should not be entirely surprised to see the Spirit moving in places we might not expect. From this angle, that Arendt appeals to Augustine's creation theology to ground our capacity to make beginnings seems entirely appropriate, suggesting it may have contained more riches than Augustine himself knew. That we are each a new beginning means that it is indeed a counsel of realism to expect the unexpected in human affairs. Whether it is the inbreaking of a movement that no one had foreseen, or the unanticipated arrival of an individual whose presence has no precedent, what is Arendt pointing us to if not a politics open to grace? And what would be left of politics without it?

Notes

1 The quote appears in the following works: "Understanding and Politics," (1954, EU 321), OT (1958 2nd edn, 479), HC (1958, 177), BPF (1961, 167), OR (1963, 211), LSA (inserted early 1960s, 55), LMW (finished 1975, published 1978, 18, 108, 217).

2 Mara Willard, "'Recasting the Old Questions': Theological Reliance and Renunciation in the Political Thought of Hannah Arendt' (Ph.D. diss., Harvard University, 2011), 21. See also 200–53.

3 Susannah Young-ah Gottlieb, *Regions of Sorrow: Anxiety and Messianism in Hannah Arendt and W.H. Auden* (Stanford: Stanford University Press, 2003); Mavis Louise Biss, "Arendt and the Theological Significance of Natality," *Philosophy Compass* 7/11 (2012): 762–71.

4 George McKenna, "Augustine Revisited," *First Things* (April 1997), 44.

5 Charles T. Mathewes, *Evil and the Augustinian Tradition*, 149–97.

6 For more background on Arendt's concept of natality, see Patricia Bowen-Moore, *Hannah Arendt's Philosophy of Natality* (New York: St. Martin's Press, 1989); Peg Birmingham, *Hannah Arendt and Human Rights* (Bloomington: Indiana University Press, 2006); Anne O'Byrne, *Natality and Finitude* (Bloomington: Indiana University Press, 2010); Jeffrey Champlin, "Born Again: Arendt's 'Natality' as Figure and Concept," *The Germanic Review* 88 (2013): 150–64;

Miguel Vatter, "Natality and Biopolitics in Hannah Arendt," *Revista de Ciencia Politica* 26:2 (2006): 137–59; Stephan Kampowski, *Arendt, Augustine, and the New Beginning* (Grand Rapids: Eerdmans, 2008).

7 O'Byrne, *Natality and Finitude*, 3–4.
8 O'Byrne, *Natality and Finitude*, 4.
9 O'Byrne, *Natality and Finitude*, 88.
10 Arendt borrowed the terms "parvenu" and "pariah" from the French-Jewish journalist and activist Bernard Lazare, whom she regarded as the epitome of the "conscious pariah." See her essays, "The Jew as Pariah: A Hidden Tradition" and "Herzl and Lazare" in JW 275–97, 338–42. For more on the influence of Lazare, see Dagmar Barnouw, *Visible Spaces: Hannah Arendt and the German-Jewish Experience* (Baltimore: Johns Hopkins Press, 1990) 38–9.
11 For more on how this period shaped Arendt's thinking on Jewish identity, see Richard J. Bernstein, *Hannah Arendt and the Jewish Question* (Cambridge: MIT Press, 1996). See also the essays in the section "Judaism and Cosmopolitanism," in Roger Berkowitz and Thomas Keenan, eds. *Thinking in Dark Times: Hannah Arendt on Ethics and Politics* (New York: Fordham University Press, 2010), 161–220.
12 This page reference comes from the 2004 hardcover version of *Origins*, which includes an appendix and the original conclusion to the 1951 version.
13 For more on Arendt's appeals to gratitude as an alternative to resentment, see Birmingham, *Hannah Arendt and Human Rights*, 70–103; Willard, "'Recasting the Old Questions,'" 221–35; and Kampowski, *Arendt, Augustine, and the New Beginning*, 219–21.
14 Birmingham argues that an appreciation of this affirmation of difference in *Origins* provides a helpful lens for reading *The Human Condition* and its apparent relegation of the bodily and the given to the private. She observes: "Arendt's analysis of *zoe* and the *bios politikos* in *The Human Condition*, and especially her critique of the social as replacing both the political and private, can be differently understood if grasped on the basis of Arendt's early insistence on the unqualified affirmation of givenness and her recognition that the Western political space is characterized not by affirmation of but by violence toward this dimension of natality ... she is insisting that this fundamental exclusion be overcome such that givenness, unqualified mere existence, occupies a rightful place in the political domain" (*Hannah Arendt and Human Rights*, 76).

15 As Kampowski points out, Arendt first cites the passage in a 1952 Heidelberg lecture entitled "Ideologie und Terror" (*Arendt, Augustine, and the New Beginning*, 6). This was published in 1953 as part of a *Festschrift* for Karl Jaspers. A slightly different version of this lecture then appeared as the final chapter to the second edition of *The Origins of Totalitarianism* in 1958.

16 In the course of summarizing Arendt's revisions to the dissertation, Scott and Stark observe, "The theme of life experience as a 'story' linked to natality as *initium* was also inserted in the 1960s revisions" (LSA 133).

17 Not all English translations of *City of God* number the chapters in Book 12 the same way. Arendt always cites the source as 12.20, which corresponds to the *Patrologia*, but readers of most English translations (including the Dyson translation I use here) will find this passage in 12.21.

18 In what follows, I draw upon Kampowski's discussion of this passage in *Arendt, Augustine, and the New Beginning*, 47–54. See his especially helpful analysis of Arendt's failed attempt to justify Augustine's alleged *initium/principium* distinction, 51–4.

19 *Si autem oportet ut certus sit liberatarum aliquis numerus animarum, quae ad miseriam numquam redeant, neque iste numerus ulterius augeatur: etiam ipse sine dubio, quicumque erit, ante utique numquam fuit; qui profecto crescere et ad suae quantitatis terminum pervenire sine aliquo non posset initio; quod initium eo modo antea numquam fuit. Hoc ergo ut esset, creatus est homo, ante quem nullus fuit.* But suppose, on the other hand, it is more suitable to say that the number of souls which have been redeemed and are never to return to misery is fixed, and that this number will never be further increased. In this case, there is still no doubt that this number, whatever it is, never existed before; also, it cannot increase and reach its final quantity without having some beginning, and this beginning itself never before existed. In order that there might be this beginning, therefore, a man was created before whom no man existed (Dyson).

20 In 11.4, Augustine uses *initium* to refer to the beginning of the world as a whole: "There are, indeed, those who confess that the world was made by God, but who wish to say that, although it was created, it did not have a beginning [*initium*] in time, so that, in some scarcely intelligible sense, it was always created." In 11.13, Augustine uses *initio* to refer to both the beginning of the Devil and the human race: "Perhaps, however, someone will say that what the Lord said of the devil in the Gospel—'He was a murderer from the beginning [*ab initio*], and abode not in the truth'—is to

be understood to mean not only that he was a murderer from the beginning of the human race [*initio humani generis*], when man, whom he could not kill by his deceit was made, but also that he did not abide in the truth from the time of his own beginning [*ab initio suae conditionis*]."

21 In 11.13, Augustine says the wicked angels "were deprived of that light by their own depravity." In 11.17, he observes that the devil was not evil by nature, but "became wicked by his own will." Once more in 12.1: "It is not permissible for us to doubt that the contrasting appetites of the good and bad angels have arisen not from a difference in their nature and origin—for God, the good Author and Creator of all substances, created them both—but from a difference in their wills and desires … The cause, therefore, of the blessedness of the good angels is their cleaving to God; so too, the cause of the misery of the wicked angels is to be found in the opposite, that is, in their not cleaving to God." This is also a prominent theme in one of Arendt's favorite Augustinian texts, *De libero arbitrio*. In Book 3, Augustine treats the objection that God "should have made us such that we always want to enjoy His unchangeable truth and never want to sin," to which he responds: "They should not rant and rage! God did not force them to sin merely because he gave to those whom He made the power whether they would so will. Indeed, there are some angels who never have sinned and never will sin … Believe that there is such a creature in the loftier realms of the heights of the heavens!" (3.5.14.52–4).

22 In LMW, Arendt suggests a more straightforward theological basis for the human capacity to make beginnings: the fact that human beings are created in the image of God (18). She writes: "With man, created in God's own image, a being came into the world that, because it was a beginning running toward an end, could be endowed with the capacity for willing and nilling" (109). She immediately adds: "In this respect, he was the image of a Creator-God; but since he was temporal and not eternal, the capacity was entirely directed toward the future" (109). Later she makes clear that this does not mean that we have the capacity to create *ex nihilo* (110).

23 While he does not mention this specific passage, Kampowski notes that salvation history could offer another way to justify Arendt's exegetical claim. See *Arendt, Augustine and the New Beginning*, 53.

24 For more on Arendt's theory of action, see George Kateb, *Hannah Arendt: Politics, Conscience, Evil* (Totowa, NJ: Rowman & Allanheld, 1984), 1–51; Canovan, *Hannah Arendt: A Reinterpretation of Her Political Thought*, 99–154; Dana Villa,

Arendt and Heidegger, 3–109; Maurizio Passerin D'Entrèves, *The Political Philosophy of Hannah Arendt* (London: Routledge, 1994), 64–100; and Birmingham, *Hannah Arendt and Human Rights*, 35–69.

25 See her discussion of Aristotle in HC 12–13, 195.
26 For a more extensive discussion of her distinction between power and violence, see OV 43–56.
27 On the parallels between Arendt and Augustine on this score, see Kampowski, *Arendt, Augustine, and the New Beginning*, 50–1.
28 Arendt discusses Anton Schmidt in EJ 230–3. Her essays on Rosa Luxemburg and Pope John XXIII can be found in MDT 33–69.
29 For her discussion of the Hungarian Revolution, see OR 271; the French Resistance, BPF 3–14; and student protest movements, OV 3–31. For her account of civil disobedience, see CR 51–102.
30 See OR 179–214; LMW 195–217.
31 On promising, she observes that "we may see its discoverer in Abraham, the man from Ur, whose whole story, as the Bible tells it, shows such a passionate drive toward making covenants that it is as though he departed from his country for no other reason than to try out the power of mutual promise in the wilderness of the world, until eventually God himself agreed to make a Covenant with him" (HC 243–4). As for forgiveness, "The discoverer of the role of forgiveness in the realm of human affairs was Jesus of Nazareth" (238). She notes that the fact that Jesus discovered forgiveness "in a religious context and articulated it in religious language is no reason to take it any less seriously in a strictly secular sense. It has been in the nature of our tradition of political thought (and for reasons we cannot explore here) to be highly selective and to exclude from articulate conceptualization a great variety of authentic political experiences, among which we need not be surprised to find some of an even elementary nature" (238–9). See her similar discussion in PP 55–9.
32 Arendt lays out the difference between trespasses and *skandala* this way: "The reason for the insistence on a duty to forgive is clearly 'for they know not what they do' and it does not apply to the extremity of crime and willed evil, for then it would not have been necessary to teach: 'And if he trespass against thee seven times a day, and seven times in a day turn again to thee, saying, I repent; thou shalt forgive him' [Lk. 17.3–4]. Crime and willed evil are rare, even rarer perhaps than good deeds; according to Jesus, they will be taken care of by God in the Last Judgment … But trespassing is an everyday occurrence which is in the very nature of action's constant

establishment of new relationships within a web of relations, and it needs forgiving, dismissing, in order to make it possible for life to go on by constantly releasing men from what they have done unknowingly" (HC 239–40). In support of the identification of *skandala* and willed evil, she cites Luke 17.1–5, where Jesus refers to offenses (*skandala*) and says "woe unto him, through whom they come! It were better for him that a millstone were hanged about his neck, and he cast into the sea" (240 n.80).

33 As Arendt sees it, love is concerned with a person's "who" to the point of complete disregard for "what" the person may be. "If it were true, therefore, as Christianity assumed, that only love can forgive because only love is fully receptive to *who* somebody is, to the point of being always willing to forgive him whatever he may have done, forgiving would have to remain altogether outside our considerations" (HC 242–3). Respect, she says, is also a regard for the person, but from more of a distance: "Respect, at any rate, because it concerns only the person, is quite sufficient to prompt forgiving of what a person did, for the sake of the person" (243).

34 In a footnote, she cites Mt. 6.14–15: "If ye forgive men their trespasses, your heavenly Father will also forgive you: But if ye forgive not men their trespasses, neither will your Father forgive your trespasses." She observes: "In all these instances, the power to forgive is primarily a human power" (HC 239 n.77).

35 Peter Brown, *Augustine of Hippo: A Biography* (Berkeley: University of Berkeley Press, 1967), 346–7.

36 Mathewes, *Evil and the Augustinian Tradition*, 177.

37 Mathewes, *Evil and the Augustinian Tradition*, 152, 175.

38 Mathewes, *Evil and the Augustinian Tradition*, 159.

39 Mathewes, *Evil and the Augustinian Tradition*, 153. In *Arendt and Heidegger*, Dana Villa writes, "*Arendt's theory of political action should be read as the sustained attempt to think of praxis outside the teleological framework*. Her argument is that teleological accounts of action are irreconcilable with the freedom born of human plurality and the public sphere. They deny the open-endedness of action, demanding a prior positing of goals in order for the activity—now viewed as *process*—to have either meaning or value" (47, original italics). I provide a different reading of Arendt's relationship to teleology, highlighting her appropriation of a non-instrumental strand of Aristotle's teleological framework.

40 Mathewes, *Evil and the Augustinian Tradition*, 175.

41 Mathewes, *Evil and the Augustinian Tradition*, 176.

42 Mathewes, *Evil and the Augustinian Tradition*, 176.
43 Mathewes, *Evil and the Augustinian Tradition*, 176, 171.
44 Mathewes, *Evil and the Augustinian Tradition*, 176.
45 Mathewes, *Evil and the Augustinian Tradition*, 176.
46 Mathewes, *Evil and the Augustinian Tradition*, 8.
47 Mathewes, *Evil and the Augustinian Tradition*, 159.
48 Mathewes, *Evil and the Augustinian Tradition*, 196.
49 Mathewes, *Evil and the Augustinian Tradition*, 177.
50 Mathewes, *Evil and the Augustinian Tradition*, 175.
51 Mathewes, *Evil and the Augustinian Tradition*, 153, 175.
52 Margaret Canovan, "Hannah Arendt as a Conservative Thinker," in *Hannah Arendt: Twenty Years Later*, eds. Larry May and Jerome Kohn (Cambridge: MIT Press, 1996), 19.
53 Young-Bruehl, *Hannah Arendt*, 495.
54 As early as her dissertation, Arendt explores the role that habit plays in diminishing our freedom. She discusses Augustine's notion of *consuetudo*, or habituated sin, and the way it locks the sinner inside a world of his or her own making. She quotes the *Confessions*: "For the law of sin is the force of habit, by which the mind is dragged along and held fast, even against its will, but still deservedly so, since it was by its will that it slipped into the habit" (*Conf.* 8.5.12), and adds: "Hence, habit is the realization of that 'second nature' from which man can estrange himself only if he recollects his real source" (LSA 82).
55 Arendt again cites Augustine's distinction between *principium* and *inititum* in support of this: "The distinction between an 'absolute' and a 'relative' beginning points to the same phenomenon we find in Augustine's distinction between the *principium* of the Heaven and the Earth and the *initium* of Man" (LMW 110). While I remain doubtful that the distinction between *principium* and *initium* is operative in Augustine's thought, I take her to be making an Augustinian point here: that the human capacity to begin is not the same as God's, that we cannot create or act *ex nihilo*.
56 Mathewes, *Evil and the Augustinian Tradition*, 78.
57 Arendt reiterates this priority later in LMT: "It would be wrong, I believe, to try to establish a hierarchical order among the mind's activities, but I also believe that it is hardly deniable that an order of priorities exists. It is inconceivable how we would ever be able to will or to judge, that is, to handle things which are not yet and things

which are no more, if the power of representation and the effort necessary to direct mental attention to what in every way escapes the attention of sense perception had not gone ahead and prepared the mind for further reflection as well as for willing and judging. In other words, what we generally call 'thinking,' though unable to move the will or provide judgment with general rules, must prepare the particulars given to the senses in such a way that the mind is able to handle them in their absence" (76–7).

58 In OR, Arendt reaffirms the limits under which such tangible freedom is exercised: "Freedom, wherever it existed as a tangible reality, has always been spatially limited … What is true for freedom of movement is, to a large extent, valid for freedom in general. Freedom in a positive sense is possible only among equals, and equality itself is by no means a universally valid principle but, again, applicable only with limitations and even within spatial limits" (275).

59 Arendt is not rejecting instrumentality as such. As she writes: "The issue at stake is, of course, not instrumentality, the use of means to achieve an end, as such, but rather the generalization of the fabrication experience in which usefulness and utility are established as the ultimate standards of life and the world of men" (HC 157).

60 Joseph Dunne, *Back to the Rough Ground: Practical Judgment and the Lure of Technique* (South Bend: University of Notre Dame, 1993), 102.

61 See J. I. Akrill, "Aristotle on *Eudaimonia*," in Amélie Oksenberg Rorty, ed. *Essays on Aristotle's Ethics* (Berkeley: University of California Press, 1980), 15–33. For an example of how "inclusive" teleology works in another thinker influenced by Aristotle, consider the following passage from Alasdair MacIntyre's *After Virtue* (South Bend: University of Notre Dame Press, 1981): "We need to remember however that although Aristotle treats the acquisition and exercise of the virtues as means to an end, the relationship of means to end is internal and not external. I call a means internal to a given end when the end cannot be adequately characterized independently of a characterization of the means. So it is with the virtues and the *telos* which is the good life for man on Aristotle's account. The exercise of the virtues is itself a crucial component of the good life for man" (184).

62 See her unpublished lecture, "Action and the 'Pursuit of Happiness,'" delivered at the American Political Science Association, September 8–10, 1960 (Hannah Arendt Papers at the Library of Congress).

63 Suzanne Duvall Jacobitti notes Arendt's emphasis upon character formation in "Thinking about the Self," *Hannah Arendt: Twenty*

Years Later, 203–5. On the role of the Berlin salons in shaping new forms of sociability, see Seyla Benhabib, *Reluctant Modernism*, 19–30.

64 See "Rosa Luxemburg" in MDT 40–3.

65 See "Civil Disobedience" in CR 94–102.

66 On the importance of moral exemplars in the role of character formation, see KPP 76–7.

67 Arendt writes: "We are wont to see friendship solely as a phenomenon of intimacy, in which friends open their hearts to each other unmolested by the world and its demands … Thus it is hard for us to understand the political relevance of friendship. When, for example, we read in Aristotle that *philia*, friendship among citizens, is one of the fundamental requirements for the well-being of the City, we tend to think that he was speaking of no more than the absence of factions and civil war within it. But for the Greeks the essence of friendship consisted in discourse. They held that only the constant interchange of talk united citizens in a *polis*. In discourse the political importance of friendship, and the humanness peculiar to it, were made manifest … We humanize what is going on in the world and in ourselves only by speaking of it, and in the course of speaking of it we learn to be human" (MDT 24–5).

68 In *Aquinas* (London: Routledge, 2003), Stump writes: "Pelagianism was condemned at the Council of Carthage in 418 because it denied the doctrine of original sin, maintained the view that a person can achieve perfect righteousness without the grace of God, and understood grace to be, for example, the sort of mental illumination which comes from reading the Bible" (381).

69 B. R. Rees, ed. *Pelagius: Life and Letters* (Rochester, NY: Boydell Press, 1998), 54.

70 Gregory of Nazianzus, "Funeral Oration on S. Basil," in *The Fathers of the Church*, vol. 22 (Washington, DC: Catholic University Press, 1953), para. 63.

71 See Jennifer A. Herdt, *Putting on Virtue: The Legacy of the Splendid Vices* (Chicago: University of Chicago Press, 2008), 73–6. See also David Decosimo, *Ethics as a Work of Charity: Thomas Aquinas and Pagan Virtue* (Stanford: Stanford University Press, 2014), esp. 253–72.

5

In the Region of the Spirit: Thinking Between Past and Future

"We are still looking ..."
– AUGUSTINE, *DE TRINITATE* 9.1

Arendt concludes *The Human Condition* with a curious quote from Cato: "Never is he more active than when he does nothing, never is he less alone than when he is by himself" (325). For a book devoted primarily to recovering the meaning of political action, this is a strange note on which to close. Arendt has spent many of the previous pages trying to demonstrate how philosophy's traditional exultation of the theoretical life has distorted our understanding of the active life, blurring important distinctions between labor, work, and action, and abasing the dignity of politics. Yet here she is at the end of the book appearing to reinstate the very priority of the theoretical life that she rejected. Have the seductions of the *vita contemplativa* proved too irresistible even for its greatest critic?

The Human Condition was never just a book about action. In the book's opening pages, Arendt explicitly states that her aim is to "*think* what we are doing" (HC 5), convinced that "what we are doing" in the modern age increasingly transcends our ability to comprehend. The triumph of thoughtless know-how and the inability to subject new technologies to scrutiny and deliberation, she says, has alienated our minds from reality, and no call to action can provide a remedy for this. Thus Arendt could not follow the lead of the modern rebels against tradition and seek to realize philosophy through action. For her, our very ability to remain political actors depended upon our willingness to continue to think. In addition to recovering the meaning of action, the book was also an attempt to make our thinking more responsive to the challenges of the modern age and begin the long, ongoing process of reconciling our minds to reality.

This helps to clarify where Arendt's real objection to the *vita contemplativa* lies. It is not with contemplation itself. Rather, it is with the attempt to transform contemplation into a way of life, separate and detached from the active life. In her view, such a separation severs the life of the mind from the very wellsprings that keep it responsive to the world around us, valorizing the quiet of contemplation to such an extent that it makes all other activities appear the same. She believed this not only led to the blurring of distinctions within the *vita activa*, but those within the life of the mind as well. Specifically, it led to a neglect of the importance of thinking in its more active dimension, precisely that critical, dialogical thinking that can help us challenge unexamined assumptions and interrupt the thoughtlessness that submits to "every gadget that is technically possible, no matter how murderous it is" (3). It was this thinking to which Cato was referring, and this thinking that Arendt wanted to recover.

In a symposium on her work over a decade later, Arendt shared that she was working on a sequel to *The Human Condition* and that her point of departure was "this business of Cato."[1] True enough, the epigraph to what became *The Life of the Mind* was the Cato passage, and in the introduction to the first volume, *Thinking*, Arendt notes its role in stimulating the inquiry's two main questions: first, "What are we 'doing' when we do nothing but think?" and second, "Where are we when we, normally always surrounded by our fellow-men, are together with no one but ourselves?" (LMT 8). Her coverage of the Eichmann trial in 1961 raised an additional moral question: "Could the activity of thinking as such, the habit of examining whatever happens to come to pass or to attract attention, regardless of results and specific content, could this activity be among the conditions that make men abstain from evil-doing or even actually 'condition' them against it?" (5). Finally, each of these questions presupposed a more basic question, namely, what makes us think in the first place?

These are the questions that Arendt takes to *Thinking*, and they are the questions that I want to take up in this chapter. The vision of thinking that they yield, as we will see, defies easy classification. Arendt conceives thinking as the inner dialogue of the self, made possible by the fact that the self is not one, but a "two-in-one." While such thinking is active, she insists that it not be confused with other forms of cognitive reasoning, such as deducing or inducing. Emphasizing its aporetic character, Arendt sees thinking as the activity that asks the unanswerable questions upon which our capacity for asking answerable questions is based. For the inner dialogue with the self to ensue, a degree of withdrawal is necessary, not so much to a physical location but to the region of the thinking ego, the realm of representation, where we deal with images and "thought-things." Given the mind's capacity to generalize, transcend distance, and make present what is absent, she concludes that the *topos* of thinking is really a "nowhere." In light of this, she prefers to frame the location of thinking in terms of time, as the gap between past and future, one that is unique to each person who thinks and which each of us must inhabit if we are to understand and respond to the challenges of our time. Such thinking does not make us moral, but it has the potential to condition us against evil in two ways: first, at an individual level, the desire to sustain the self's dialogue provides an incentive not to contradict oneself with wrongdoing; and second, the critical mode of thinking has the power to question accepted values and release the faculty of judgment. The question of what makes us think, with which I begin the chapter, is of central importance because it clarifies that while Arendt's primary aim was to recover an active dimension of the life of the mind, her intention was not to compel a choice between thinking and contemplation. On her account, the two are related: thinking begins in a posture of contemplative wonder (or the related affects of love, gratitude, grief, or horror) and ends in wonder, but should be understood as a distinct activity. It is the active, searching dialogue that our wonder (or grief, horror, etc.) inspires.

Arendt's account of thinking has received relatively little attention in Christian theology.[2] It offers a welcome opportunity to reflect upon the diversity of modes of theological reflection, and a particularly valuable invitation to consider what thinking in its more active and dialogical dimension might mean for the task of theology. I explore those possibilities in the final section of the chapter, following up on leads that she suggests (the medieval practice of meditation, Augustine's *Confessions*) as well as more recent movements (*ressourcement* theology) that endeavor to inhabit the gap between past and future and strive for an ever higher synthesis between the life of action and the life of the mind, without losing sight of the difference between them or the need of one upon the other.

I. "The Spark of Fire Between Two Flint Stones"

Like her concepts of worldliness and action, Arendt's understanding of thinking is distinctive and requires some careful unpacking.[3] A logical place to begin is the question of what makes us think in the first place. Arendt provides a survey of responses from the history of philosophy, the most famous of which is the one Plato offers through the voice of Socrates in the *Theaetetus*: "For this is chiefly the passion (*pathos*) of the philosopher, to wonder (*thaumazein*). There is no other beginning of philosophy than this one" (LMT 142). Readers will recall from Chapter 1 the importance of this passage for Arendt's own work. As she explains, Platonic wonder is different from mere puzzlement at an unsolved problem or surprise in the face of something new, although puzzlement and surprise are essential to the experience. It is closer to the "wonderstruck beholding" that Homer reserved for the appearance of gods among men, but which Plato extends to the invisible harmony made manifest in the world of appearances, "the totality of all things that were not man-made" (143). Such wonder is prompted not by what is contingent, but what is necessary and unchanging, "that which is as it is" (PP 32), what "swings in itself in changeless eternity without any interference or assistance from outside" (HC 15). "Since Parmenides," Arendt observes, "the key word for this invisible imperceptible whole implicitly manifest in all that appears has been *Being*" (LMT 144). Too general for words, the encounter with Being is a *pathos*, "something to be suffered, not acted" (143);

it stops one in one's tracks, demanding stillness as long as it lasts. When one emerges from the experience, the natural response is to express admiration, and thinking as a distinctive activity arises for Plato out of the need to praise what we have beheld. On this account, we think in order "to say 'yes' and confirm the factuality of sheer existence" (148). Yet because the wonder is unspeakable, such thinking "will not begin with statements but will formulate in unending variations of what we call the ultimate questions—What is being? Who is man? What meaning has life? What is death? etc." (PP 33). The inexhaustibility of the source of wonder will make the answers to such questions inexhaustibly elusive, thus firing our love for what we have beheld all the more.

As Arendt sees it, there is a notable tension between the intensely active, dialectical character of the Platonic dialogues and the contemplative ideal that emerges from them, most notably in the *Republic*, where the *polis* is re-envisioned as a means for realizing the philosopher's way of life. As Arendt reads the cave allegory, the ideal life for Plato is one in which the philosopher, having turned from the shadows on the wall to the open sky of the ideas outside it, would not have to return to the cave at all, but could enjoy contemplative wonder as one, uninterrupted state of being. In such a state, there would no longer be a need for thinking or speaking; one could simply stand rapt in the presence of truth, in complete quiet and rest. Arendt suspects that such an ideal arose out of the bitter experience of the trial and death of Socrates, which exposed the futility of the philosopher trying to engage in dialogue with his fellow citizens. For Plato, Arendt suggests, to engage in dialogue about truth is ultimately to make truth one more *doxa*, or opinion, and in a realm where persuasion and sophistry reign, truth in the form of *doxa* will always suffer defeat. Better, then, not to submit to the tyranny of opinion and rule the *polis* with truth, with the ultimate aim of achieving liberation from the *polis* altogether. In this vision, the speechlessness and singularity that mark the experience of wonder become defining features of the *bios theoretikos*, as opposed to the dialogue and plurality that characterize the *bios politikos*. Plato's philosopher "puts himself outside the political realm in which the highest faculty of man is, precisely, speech ... He is to an extent alienated from the city of men, which can only look with suspicion on everything that concerns man in the singular" (PP 35).

Socrates, on the other hand, remains "a citizen among citizens," equally at home in thinking and acting, able to move from one to the other "with the greatest apparent ease" (LMT 167), too in love with both to substitute one for the other.[4] He belonged more to the world of his Pythagorean forebears than that of his pupil, regarding anything that appeared, whether natural or man-made, divine or human, an object worthy of wonder. Rather than an experience that we seek to extend indefinitely, he took wonder to be the "flying spark of fire between two flint stones" (PP 37), a spur to thinking, and he saw the life of the mind as a circular movement from wonder to thinking back to wonder again. Thinking was quite simply a demand of citizenship. It was the courageous act that prompted the question, "What is courage?" and the just deed that made one ask, "What is justice?" Sustaining the conversation was as important as finding answers because the good of the *polis* hinged on the friendships that such questions made possible, including friendship with the self.

The contrast that Arendt makes between Socrates and Plato is overdrawn, and her own criticisms of Plato are weakened by her acknowledgment of the role that dialogical thinking plays in his own work. As her comments elsewhere indicate, not even she seems to have believed he proposed anything so simple as replacing thinking with contemplation, at least not in this life, even if uninterrupted *theōria* was for him, as for Aristotle, our ultimate *telos*.[5] The same kind of oversimplification reappears in her account of Christian conceptions of the *vita contemplativa*, with similar costs.[6] Laying this aside for the moment, it is important to appreciate that despite her criticisms of contemplation conceived as a way of life, Arendt herself remained committed to a certain practice of contemplation. Indeed, that thinking begins from contemplative wonder, she says, is a view that "in my opinion, has lost nothing of its plausibility," although she adds: "I am quite sure that it runs counter to present-day opinion on the subject" (151). Arendt provides an account of "present-day opinion" in the sweeping last chapter of *The Human Condition*, where she tracks the growth of the conviction that truth and knowledge can only be won through the work of our hands rather than anything given to our senses:

> It was an instrument, the telescope, a work of man's hands, which finally forced nature, or rather the universe, to yield

its secrets ... Nothing indeed could be less trustworthy for acquiring knowledge and approaching truth than passive observation or mere contemplation. In order to be certain one had to *make sure*, and in order to know one had to do. (HC 290)

The costs of this shift in attitude, Arendt stresses, have been steep. The "ubiquitous functionalization of modern society" and the restriction of knowledge to what we have made ourselves has deprived the life of the mind of "one of its most elementary characteristics—the instilling of wonder at that which is as it is" (BPF 40). It is as if in the modern age, Plato's view has been reversed, and we can only know the *nomō* rather than the *physei*. Against this backdrop, Arendt's remarks to Scholem, cited in the last chapter, are all the more striking: "There is such a thing as a basic gratitude for everything that is as it is; for what has been *given* and not *made*; for what is *physei* and not *nomō*" (JW 466). Here Arendt signals the basic importance of opening ourselves to a world beyond what we have made, to life itself and to nature. In this sense, she is trying to recapture a spirit of wonder that has been eclipsed by the outlook of *homo faber*. Yet in the manner of Socrates, she also seeks to extend our wonder to givens that lie outside the traditional purview of philosophy, such as human plurality. Hence her programmatic claim that if the philosophers "were ever to arrive at a true political philosophy, they would have to make the plurality of man, out of which arises the whole realm of human affairs—in its grandeur and misery—the object of their *thaumazein*" (PP 38).

Thus while Arendt is deeply critical of contemplative wonder transformed into a way of life, she by no means rejects wonder. She does, however, identify an important danger in thinking that begins from admiring wonder alone. "Admiring wonder conceived as the starting-point of philosophy leaves no place for the factual existence of disharmony, of ugliness, and finally of evil" (LMT 150). Relating this to the outlook of Socrates, she writes:

> Because thought's quest is a kind of desirous love, the objects of thought can only be lovable things—beauty, wisdom, justice, and so on. Ugliness and evil are almost by definition excluded from the thinking concern. They may turn up as deficiencies, ugliness consisting in lack of beauty, evil, *kakia*, in lack of the

good. As such, they have no roots of their own, no essence that thought could get hold of. (179)

Of course, Arendt had some sympathy for the view that evil has no ontological depth, but she did not think this meant that instances of evil merited any less of our thinking attention or posed questions of any less gravity than instances of goodness. As noted in previous chapters, she believed the experience of horror was as much a source of questions as wonder, and she took the aversion of contemporary philosophers to reckon with the experience of evil in the twentieth century to be an extension of the ancient aversion to wonder at human affairs (EU 445). Given the experiences of the twentieth century, Arendt believed that our very ability to think may very well hinge upon our capacity to awaken and expand our capacity to feel horror.[7]

Here we see Arendt coming closer to what she calls the "Roman" outlook on thinking. Arendt contends that Roman philosophy only emerged as a distinctive philosophical tradition during the centuries of its decline and fall. This is not insignificant, she suggests, as it was the experience of loss that led thinkers such as Cicero and Epictetus to turn to philosophy for consolation. For Cicero, the relevant affect for thinking is not wonder, but grief, and he saw philosophy as the *animi medicina*, what could "teach men how to cure their despairing minds" (LMT 152) and "compensate for the frustrations of politics and, more generally, of life itself" (160). Arendt adds: "Its famous watchword—which sounds almost as though it had been formulated in contradiction of the Platonic admiring wonder—became *nil admirari*: do not be surprised at anything, admire nothing" (152). What Arendt finds appealing in the Roman approach is its sensitivity to loss and rupture, but she notes a tendency in Roman philosophers to purchase consolation at the cost of relativizing the value of what has been lost. Consolation ends up sounding something like this: "In relation to the universe, the earth is but a dot; what does it matter what happens on her? In relation to the immensity of time, centuries are but moments, and oblivion will finally cover everything and everybody: what does it matter what men do?" (160).

Arendt observes that perhaps the greatest heir of the Roman approach is Hegel, whose famous saying that "the owl of Minerva only takes flight at the falling of dusk" reflects the Roman view that we are only prompted to philosophize when a certain era or experience has ended. For Hegel, the need for thinking arose "out of the disintegration of reality and the resulting *dis*unity of man and world" (153). "Out of disunity, out of being torn apart, arises thought," that is to say, "the need for reconciliation" (153). As we saw in Chapter 1, Arendt was deeply shaped by this dimension of Hegel, and she framed her own need to understand political events such as totalitarianism in terms of the reconciliation of the mind to reality. Towards the end of her life, Arendt reiterated the importance of Hegel for her thinking:

> Philosophy is a solitary business, and it seems only natural that the need for it arises in times of transition when men no longer rely on the stability of the world and their role in it, and when the question concerning the general conditions of human life, which as such are properly coeval with the appearance of man on earth, gain an uncommon poignancy. Hegel may have been right. (RJ 9)

At the same time, Arendt believed that there was the same danger of relativization in Hegel as his Roman forebears. His consolations took the form not of Stoic detachment but a philosophy of history that promises to absorb historical ruptures into a wider rational synthesis. Arendt was not so sure such syntheses were possible and she remained highly skeptical of trying to make sense of historical events through genealogical narratives. As we will see below, her vision of reconciliation as it relates to specific events of horror comes closer to that envisioned by some of her acquaintances in the Frankfurt School, who conceived reconciliation in mostly negative terms, as the ongoing task of showing where our language fails to capture the reality we seek to understand, drawing closer to that reality only in the growing awareness of the distance that remains.[8]

We can summarize by saying that in her own work, Arendt sought to combine the best insights of the Greek and Roman approaches, seeing thinking as prompted by both wonder and horror and proceeding in the mode of both affirmation and negation. For a thinker generally thought to eschew the role of emotions in politics, it is striking how central a role the affections play in her understanding of what makes us think. Indeed, Arendt rejected any strict separation between the two, preferring instead to speak of what she called "passionate thinking": "We are so accustomed to the old opposition of reason versus passion, spirit versus life, that the idea of a *passionate* thinking, in which thinking and aliveness become one, takes us somewhat aback."[9] But it was precisely passionate thinking that she sought to embody.

II. The Activity of Thinking

Let's now turn to the activity of thinking itself. That thinking might represent a highly active state was suggested by the quote from Cato above: "Never is he more active than when he does nothing, never is he is less alone than when he is by himself." For Arendt, it is the second part of this quote, the fact that we are not alone when we are by ourselves, that provides the key to understanding the first part.

Again, Arendt's guide is Socrates. Recall from Chapter 1 Arendt's fondness for his famous saying from the *Gorgias*: "it would be better for me that my lyre or a chorus I directed should be out of tune and loud with discord, and that multitudes of men should disagree with me rather than that I, being one, should be out of harmony with myself and contradict myself" (LMT 181). Arendt notes the paradoxical nature of the statement: Socrates talks of oneness, but "nothing that is identical with itself, truly and absolutely *One*, as A is A, can be either in or out of harmony with itself; you always need at least two tones to produce a harmonious sound" (183). This suggests that the oneness that Socrates has in mind is actually a harmony of two, or a "two-in-one." He is pointing to the basic reflexivity that characterizes the life of the mind in general, the fact that I can agree or disagree with myself, or will for or against myself. Arendt writes: "Mental activities themselves all testify by their reflexive nature to a duality inherent in consciousness; the mental agent cannot be active except by acting, implicitly or explicitly, back upon himself" (74). As it turns out, "difference and otherness, which are such outstanding characteristics of the world of appearances as it is given to man for his habitat among a plurality of things, are the very conditions for the existence of man's mental ego as well, for this ego actually exists only in duality" (187).[10] This inner duality is what makes thinking a genuine activity, what enables questions to be posed, answers given, and an ongoing dialogue to ensue. She writes:

> Thinking can become dialectical and critical because it goes through this questioning and answering process, through the dialogue of *dialegesthai*, which actually is a "traveling through words," a *poreuesthai dia tōn logōn*, whereby we constantly raise the basic Socratic question: *What do you mean when you say* ...? except that this *legein*, saying, is soundless and therefore so swift that its dialogical structure is somewhat difficult to detect. (185)

For Arendt, it is important to stress that we only become aware of this other self while we are engaged in the activity of thinking. When we face outward towards the world, we present ourselves not as two, but as one. Only in withdrawing from our various other activities do we meet ourselves as another. This suggests that some degree of solitude is necessary for thinking in Arendt's sense, a point of some significance that we will revisit below, when we discuss political situations in which citizens are denied such solitude.

If the self is capable of carrying on a dialogue with itself, then we should expect many of the features that characterize the Socratic dialogues to apply equally well to the self's internal dialogue. Indeed, as Arendt sees it, these dialogues can fruitfully be read not only in their plain sense as dialogues with others, but as dramatizations of the life of the mind, exteriorizing an activity that is ordinarily invisible and impossible to observe.[11] What specifically do the dialogues teach us about the nature of thinking? The first thing Arendt notes is their aporetic character. The dialogues rarely terminate in clear answers, but instead tend to run in circles. As mentioned above, Socrates often begins with ordinary phenomena or occurrences, with the happy person or a just deed, asking "What is happiness" or "What is justice?" Yet the moment he and his interlocutors begin to explore the meaning of these words, they get tangled up in knots. "These words are part and parcel of our everyday speech," Arendt writes, "and still we can give no account of them; when we try to define them, they get slippery; when we talk about their meaning, nothing stays put any more, everything begins to move" (170). The dialogue twists and turns until someone eventually confesses "I do not know" or "I know that I do not know," at which point Socrates "cheerfully proposes to start all over again" (170). As Arendt emphasizes:

> the original wonder is not only not resolved in such questions, since they remain without answer, but even reinforced. What begins as wonder ends in perplexity and thence leads back to wonder: How marvelous that men can perform courageous or just deeds even though they do not know, can give no account of, what courage and justice are. (166)

Arendt takes the various similes that have been applied to Socrates to offer further insight into the nature of thinking. He is the "gadfly" (172) whose sting rouses citizens to self-examination; the "midwife" (173) who delivers others of their opinions; and the "electric ray" (173) who, in paralyzing himself with perplexity, paralyzes those with whom he comes into contact. All of these point to thinking's role in interrupting our established routines and questioning our unexamined judgments, loosening the hold of reified concepts and getting our minds moving again. Socrates himself likens such thinking to the wind: "The winds themselves are invisible, yet what they do is manifest to us and we somehow feel their approach" (174); like the wind, we feel the impact of thinking in what it rustles and disturbs. "It is in this invisible element's nature," Arendt writes, "to undo, unfreeze, as it were, what language, the medium of thinking, has frozen into thought" (174). This includes "concepts, sentences, definitions, doctrines" (174), as well as "established criteria, values, [and] measurements of good and evil" (175). Arendt describes the dazing after-effect of thought, that "when you come out of it," you feel "unsure of what seemed to you beyond doubt while you were unthinkingly engaged in whatever you were doing" (175). The "business of thinking," she says, "is like Penelope's web; it undoes every morning what it has finished the night before" (88).

As we might expect, Arendt zeroes in on the nature of thinking by distinguishing it from a variety of other mental activities. In addition to the distinction between thinking and contemplation discussed above, Arendt also distinguishes thinking from cognition. Both are highly active mental processes, but Arendt associates cognition with the more instrumental activity of knowledge production, as opposed to thinking which represents an end in itself. The terms of the distinction should recall her distinction between work and action reviewed in the last chapter. Like work, cognition is an activity that produces an object that exists independently of the process that brought it about. It might involve deducing a conclusion from a premise, or inferring a general law from particular instances, but regardless, it produces new knowledge that can then become part of our world. Cognition for Arendt has a special association with scientific investigation and the pursuit of questions that have definite answers. Thinking, on the other hand, produces nothing so satisfying as an answer. Rather, it is our faculty for asking the unanswerable questions upon which our capacity for asking answerable questions is based. Arendt observes:

> In asking the ultimate, unanswerable questions, man establishes himself as a question-asking being ... Were man ever to lose the faculty of asking ultimate questions, he would by the same token lose his faculty of asking answerable questions. He would cease to be a question-asking being, which would be the end, not only of philosophy, but of science as well. (PP 34)

The fact that thinking does not produce results brings it closer to action. Arendt invites the comparison when she resorts to the same Aristotelian notion of *energeia* that we saw her use in the last chapter, numbering thinking among those activities, "like flute-playing, [which] have their ends within themselves and leave no tangible outside end product in the world we inhabit" (LMT 129). Like action, thinking is a kind of sheer activity, whose end is realized while we are engaged in the activity, and only so long as we remain engaged in it: "For the need to think can never be stilled by allegedly definite insights of 'wise men'; it can be satisfied only through thinking, and the thoughts I had yesterday will satisfy this need today only to the extent that I want and am able to think them anew" (88). Like action, thinking "rises out of the simple fact of being-born-in-the-world," which causes us to think "recallingly and responsively the meaning that reigns in everything that is."[12] As this need never goes away, the activity of thinking never really ends. She likens it to the sensation of being alive. We think not "for the sake of any result whatever," but because each of us is a "thinking," "musing being."[13]

While the dialogue of thinking may not result in any tangible results, Arendt insists that we not mistake the confession of un-knowing for ignorance or despair: "for the result left behind in the mind of the person ... can only be expressed as: Now I *know* what it means not to know; now I know that I do not know" (PP 33–4, my italics). Such knowledge is a kind of negative knowledge, a *via negativa* appropriate to the inexhaustibility of its subject. This is a kind of thinking that we see Arendt modeling throughout her work, whether it is when she challenges our assumptions about the meaning of freedom or questions the applicability of our traditional categories of evil. This thinking unloosens the grip of such concepts over our mind, and in the process, brings us closer to the reality we seek to understand. In this way, she seeks reconciliation, but as mentioned above, it often takes the form of a negative reconciliation, experienced in the "unfreezing" of our concepts, in the narrowing of the distance between our language and reality. In her discussion of Socrates' role as an electric ray, Arendt notes that "what cannot fail to look like paralysis from the outside—from the standpoint of ordinary human affairs—is *felt* as the highest state of being active and alive" (LMT 173). Readers of her work may find they know that sensation well.

III. The Virtue of Thinking

Socrates did not promise thinking would make anyone good, and Arendt emphasizes that thinking as such, the mind's dialogue with itself, as distinct from the exercise of practical reason (*phronesis*), "does society little good, much less than the thirst for knowledge, which uses thinking as an instrument for other purposes. It does not create values; it will not find out, once and for all, what 'the good' is; it does not confirm but, rather, dissolves accepted rules of conduct" (192). But in light of the absence of the ability to think in a criminal such as Eichmann, the question naturally arose: might the inner dialogue with the self at least condition us against some forms of evil?

In Chapter 1, we discussed one answer that Arendt provides: the desire to sustain a conversation with the self may provide an incentive against evil-doing just to the extent that one would not want to keep company with a murderer. Of course, one can do wrong and continue to keep company with oneself, but Arendt suggests it sounds something like Richard III's famous soliloquy in which he expresses love and hatred for himself, before declaring conscience a ruse of the weak. Such an internal war will not last long before the murderer eventually cuts off the conversation altogether. "Bad people," she notes, "are *not* 'full of regrets'" (191). The point is not that thinking will make us good, but that the desire to sustain friendship with oneself may be one of a variety of factors that incline us not to commit evil.

Arendt does not invest too much in the point, calling it a "moral side effect" (192). Yet she does think that there is another, more powerful way that thinking can condition us against evil, and this relates to thinking in its critical, "gadfly" role. Thinking in this mode, she says, "inevitably has a destructive, undermining effect on all established criteria, values, measurements of good and evil, in short, on those customs and rules of conduct we treat of in morals and ethics" (175). This dimension of thinking becomes particularly important under the kind of conditions discussed in Chapter 2, when thoughtless reliance upon what happens to be legal or culturally sanctioned paves a sure path to complicity in evil:

> When everybody is swept away unthinkingly by what everybody else does and believes in, those who think are drawn out of hiding because their refusal to join in is conspicuous and thereby becomes a kind of action. In such emergencies, it turns out that the purging component of thinking (Socrates' midwifery, which brings out the implications of unexamined opinions and thereby destroys them—values, doctrines, theory, and even convictions) is political by implication. (192)

The problem, of course, is that such thinking requires a degree of solitude, and it is solitude that totalitarianism's combination of terror and ideology destroys. As Arendt observes:

> We ... who have had our experience with totalitarian mass organizations whose primary concern is to eliminate all possibility of solitude—except in the nonhuman form of solitary confinement—can easily testify that if a minimum amount of being alone with oneself is no longer guaranteed, not only secular but also all religious forms of conscience will be abolished. (PP 24)

"No man can keep his conscience intact," she concludes, "who cannot actualize the dialogue with himself, that is, who lacks the solitude required for all forms of thinking" (25).

George Kateb notes that for a thinker usually focused upon joint action with our peers, this is an important admission, suggesting that our very ability to keep company with others hinges upon our ability to keep company with ourselves.[14] Arendt attributes the point to Socrates:

> The political relevance of Socrates' discovery is that it asserts that solitude, which before and after Socrates was thought to be the prerogative and professional *habitus* of the philosopher only, and which was naturally suspected by the polis of being antipolitical is, on the contrary, the necessary condition for the good functioning of the polis, a better guarantee than rules of behavior enforced by laws and fear of punishment. (24)

Although Arendt was deeply wary of thinking turned into a way of life, a *bios theoretikos*, separate from the life of political activity, this passage makes clear that she was by no means opposed to the notion of regular withdrawal from political activity. Her understanding of thinking presupposed it. For Arendt, this means friendship lies at the heart of citizenship in a double sense: political discourse and deliberation demand that we become friends with our fellow citizens, but our very ability to befriend our fellow citizens depends upon our ability to befriend ourselves. In order to contribute meaningfully to such discourse, I need to be able to carry out that dialogue with myself; conversely, to carry on a non-delusional dialogue with myself, I need regular contact with others, who interrupt and sharpen my thought.[15] In Socrates, we see the two coming together: his dialogue with the self unfolds into dialogue with others, and dialogue with others unfolds back into the dialogue with the self.

If a degree of solitude is necessary for a well-functioning political community, but is not to be identified with the *bios theoretikos*, where is it to be found? Or put in terms of the question that Cato's passage raised, "Where are we when we, normally always surrounded by our fellow-men, are together with no one but ourselves?"

IV. The Location of Thinking

In answering this question, Arendt is not in search of a particular physical location. She notes Socrates' habit "of suddenly 'turning his mind to himself,' breaking off all company, and taking up his position wherever he happened to be, 'deaf to all entreaties' to continue with whatever he had been doing before" (LMT 197). Xenophon describes an occasion when Socrates "remained in complete immobility for twenty-four hours in a military camp" (197). Evidently one can experience solitude, the "existential state in which I keep myself company," in a variety of settings, just as one can experience loneliness, the state of feeling "deserted not only by human company but also by the possible company of myself" (74), in the middle of a crowd. Let's presume that it requires some minimum degree of withdrawal from other activities that could be satisfied in many different places. Socrates' thinking, however, entails another kind of withdrawal. He remains in a military camp, but clearly withdraws to somewhere else. Where? That is the place that Arendt wants to investigate: not so much the place of the thinking subject as the region of the thinking ego. To venture there is to explore the "paradoxical condition of a living being, that though itself part of the world of appearances, is in possession of a faculty, the ability to think, that permits the mind to withdraw from the world without ever being able to leave it or transcend it" (45).

The matter turns, as Arendt sees it, on the representational nature of thought, the fact that when we think, we think not with the actual objects that we perceive with our senses, but with "invisibles," with "representations of things that are absent" (193). In Arendt's view, Augustine remains the most astute observer of the process by which the mind de-senses and de-materializes the objects of our senses, allowing us not only to think about things that are absent, but also to dwell upon things that do not originate with the senses at all. She notes that in Book 11 of *De Trinitate*, he describes a twofold transformation. When we look at an object, an image or likeness of that object is impressed upon our sight, remaining present as long as the object is present. This image "is then stored in the memory, ready to become a 'vision in thought' the moment the mind gets hold of it" (77). Arendt observes that for Augustine, this "vision in thought" (*visio cogitantis*) is not the same as the image stored in memory. As she explains, just as the likeness of a visible object is impressed upon our sight in the act of seeing, the image stored in memory impresses an image of its own upon the mind's eye in the act of thinking. When we think, we think with these "thought-objects." If Augustine is right, then every time we think, we are at least two steps removed from the immediacy of the world: once from the objects stored in our memory, and twice from the objects of our sense. This then enables the work of imagination to take over, "increasing, diminishing, altering and putting together as [the mind] pleases" (11.8).[16] As Arendt summarizes:

> It is because of this twofold transformation that thinking "in fact goes even further," beyond the realm of all possible imagination, "when our reason proclaims the infinity of number which no vision in the thought of corporeal things has yet grasped" or "teaches us that even the tiniest bodies can be divided infinitely." ... these thought-objects come into being only when the mind actively and deliberately remembers, recollects and selects from the storehouse of memory whatever arouses its interest sufficiently to induce concentration; in these operations the mind learns how to deal with things that are absent and prepares itself to "go further," toward the understanding of things that are always absent, that cannot be remembered because they were never present to sense experience. (LMT 77)

In this way, thinking "always deals with absences and removes itself from what is present and close at hand" (199). Every thought, she says, "is strictly speaking an after-thought" (78). This is why we can never think about someone while we are in his or her presence: "so long as we are with him we do not think either of him or about him ... It may, of course, happen that we start thinking about a still-present somebody or something, in which case we have removed ourselves surreptitiously from our surroundings and are conducting ourselves as though we were already absent" (78).

It is this distance that gives thinking its character of being "out-of-order," not entirely in step with common sense, which is what enables it to disrupt our established routines and open up the possibility of critical distance. While it may remove us from the world, thinking also gives us the power to make present what is absent, to summon individuals or places from across vast distances. In generalizing and abstracting, thinking also enables us to think upon things that are not limited to any one location, to move, with Socrates, from the just deed to Justice, from a courageous person to Courage. In light of this, Arendt wonders if the question of the location of thinking is wrongly put. "Looked at from the perspective of the everyday world of appearances, the everywhere of the thinking ego—summoning into its presence whatever it pleases from any distance in time or space, which thought traverses with a velocity greater than light's—is a *nowhere*" (200). If space were the only dimension in which we lived, we would perhaps have to leave the question in abeyance. "But we are not only in space," Arendt observes, "we are also in time, remembering, collecting, and recollecting what no longer is present out of 'the belly of memory' (Augustine), anticipating and planning in the mode of willing what is not yet" (201). The "thought-things" with which we think may be de-spatialized, but we still think them in temporal succession, as located in the past, or present before the mind's attention, or something we consider for the future. Perhaps, then, we do better to ask about the time of thinking.

Arendt takes the time sensation of the thinking ego to be captured in a famous parable by Kafka. In it, he depicts the struggle of a protagonist named "He":

> He has two antagonists: the first presses him from behind, from the origin. The second blocks the road ahead. He gives battle to both. To be sure, the first supports him in his fight with the second, for he wants to push him forward, and in the same way the second supports him in his fight with the first, since he drives him back. But it is only theoretically so. For it is not only the two antagonists who are there, but he himself as well, and who really knows his intentions? His dream, though, is that some time in an unguarded moment—and this would require a night darker than any night has ever been yet—he will jump out of the fighting line and be promoted, on account of his experience in fighting, to the position of umpire over his antagonists in their fight with each other. (202)

Arendt takes this description to help focus the difference between the way we experience time in the course of everyday life and when we are engaged in thought. The time sensation of everyday life, she observes, is one of relative continuity: the past passes seamlessly into the present, and the present into the future. The past is yesterday, the present today, and the future is tomorrow. In the Kafka parable, however, the past and future operate as active and even antagonistic forces weighing upon the thinking ego in the present. As Arendt sees it, the possibility of such simultaneity is a function of the same representational nature of thought discussed above: it is because we think with recollected and anticipated "thought-objects" that past and future can become simultaneous in "an immovable present," creating something like a "time gap" (207) where the ordinary distances between the tenses are suspended. As Arendt puts it, "In this situation past and future are equally present precisely because they are equally absent from our sense" (203). To be clear, the forces of past and future are only present because of the protagonist himself. In terms of the Kafka parable, "Only because man is inserted into time and only to the extent that he stands his ground does the flow of indifferent time break up into tenses; it is this insertion—the beginning of a beginning, to put it into Augustinian terms—which splits up the time continuum into forces" (BPF 11). Translated into the terms of thinking, Arendt writes:

> The gap between past and future opens only in reflection, whose subject matter is what is absent—either what has already disappeared or what has not yet appeared. Reflection draws these absent "regions" into the mind's presence; from that perspective the activity of thinking can be understood as a fight against time itself. It is only because "he" thinks, and therefore is no longer carried along by the continuity of everyday life in a world of appearances, that past and future manifest themselves as pure entities, so that "he" can become aware of a no-longer that pushes him forward and a not-yet that drives him back. (LMT 206)

In other words, it is in our mind that time is experienced as a struggle, because it is only in our mind that past and future converge as if co-present to one another. We inhabit the gap between past and future when we think, for as long as we think.

At the end of the parable, Kafka's protagonist dreams of being liberated from the struggle and inhabiting an umpire position above the fray. Arendt suggests that such a dream is unnecessary, for if it is true that the protagonist pushes back against the forces of past and future, then we should expect these forces to deflect from their original trajectory, and form something of a diagonal force extending outward from the protagonist himself: "This diagonal force, whose origin is known, whose direction is determined by past and future, but which exerts its force toward an undetermined end as though it could reach out into infinity, seems to me a perfect metaphor for the activity of thought" (209). Remaining bound by past and future, this diagonal provides a time in which to think:

> It is the quiet of the Now in the time-pressed, time-tossed existence of man; it is somehow, to change the metaphor, the quiet in the center of a storm which, though totally unlike the storm, still belongs to it. In this gap between past and future, we find our place in time when we think, that is, when we are sufficiently removed from past and future to be relied on to find out their meaning. (209)

In describing this gap, Arendt employs a number of metaphors borrowed from theological registers. She likens it to the *nunc stans*, "the standing now of medieval meditation" (LMW 12), which she says theologians used to conceptualize both God's eternity and the time sensation of meditation itself. She suspects the latter may have influenced the former:

> I am rather certain that the *nunc stans*, the "standing now," became the symbol of eternity—the *"nunc aeternitatis"* (Duns Scotus)—for medieval philosophy because it was a plausible description of experiences that took place in meditation as well as in contemplation, the two modes of thought known to Christianity. (LMT 86)[17]

In a similar vein, she appeals to Augustine's notion of *hodiernus*, or the "lasting 'todayness'" that both distinguishes God's eternity from our temporality and serves as a fitting metaphor for the way in which the three tenses of time are co-present in the mind that thinks (LMW 12). Arendt appears to have been alert to the point as far back as her dissertation, where she summarizes Augustine's description of the time sensation of thinking this way:

> It is only by calling past and future into the present of remembrance and expectation that time exists at all ... In the Now, past and future meet. For a fleeting moment they are simultaneous so that they can be stored up by memory, which remembers things past and holds the expectation of things to come. (LSA 15)

In referring to Augustine's notion of the "beginning of a beginning" above, she is also recalling his views on the natality of each human being, which provides the ontological grounds for why the protagonist in Kafka's parable disrupts "the indifferent flow of everlasting change" (LMT 207). In the activity of thinking, our ontological newness manifests itself as the unique point at which past and future meet. A final debt to the messianism of Walter Benjamin should not be overlooked. In her editorial notes to the "Theses on the Philosophy of History," she explicitly compares his notion of the messianic "Now," where time collapses, to the *nunc stans* mentioned above.[18] Pulling all of these together in a final description of the time gap of thinking, she writes: "Using a different metaphor, we call it the region of the spirit ... the path paved by thinking, the small inconspicuous track of non-time beaten by the activity of thought within the time-space given to natal and mortal men" (210).[19]

What does this all mean practically? In *Between Past and Future*, Arendt compares the position of Kafka's protagonist to the participants of the French Resistance shortly after the liberation of their country. We have discussed this example in previous chapters, so I will not repeat all of the details here. Char and his compatriots were thrown into a political situation for which nothing had prepared them. His famous aphorism, "our inheritance was left to us by no testament," was an attempt to describe their predicament, referring specifically to the fact that they had not been given a framework within which to understand and judge their experience. Char simply referred to it as our "treasure," and even while it was ongoing, he had a premonition that the treasure would be lost, not because the experience itself would come to an end, but because, without a name and a meaning, it would eventually be forgotten. Arendt observes:

Kafka's fight begins when the course of action has run its course and when the story which was its outcome waits to be completed "in the minds that inherit and question it." The task of the mind is to understand what happened, and this understanding, according to Hegel, is man's way of reconciling himself with reality; its actual end is to be at peace with the world. The trouble is that if the mind is unable to bring peace and to induce reconciliation, it finds itself immediately engaged in its own kind of warfare. (BPF 7–8)

Because he does not have a framework within which to understand the experience, Char cannot bring about the desired reconciliation, and so the meeting of the past, present, and future is experienced as a struggle: the recently completed event pushes from behind, the heirs push back from ahead, both awaiting a name, a testament that lays out what the experience was and its worth. Yet as Arendt sees it, this struggle also opens up a space in which to think, to come up with the testament for the inheritance. At one level, this requires the kind of negative thinking described above, which demonstrates how traditional categories fail to name the event; but this is also a point at which Arendt envisions a more constructive role for thought, as we experiment with new names, or apply old ones in new ways. In this case, Arendt pearl dives for the concept of "public happiness" as one way of naming Char's treasure. It is easy to assume, Arendt observes, that it is only now, in light of the unprecedented character of so many modern challenges, that such thinking has become necessary, but in fact, this just is the normal condition of thought, where the mind is always confronted with the task of reconciling past and future because past and future always converge in the mind that thinks. This means that while the thinking we do helps to narrow the gap between thought and reality, and, in turn, provides testaments for treasures so that they will not be lost, the task of reconciling ourselves to reality falls to every generation to take up as their own. As Arendt concludes:

> This small non-time space in the very heart of time, unlike the world and the culture into which we are born, cannot be inherited and handed down by tradition ... Each new generation, every new human being, as he becomes conscious of being inserted between an infinite past and an infinite future,

must discover and ploddingly pave anew the path of thought. (LMT 210)

V. Theology Between Past and Future

Arendt's work on thinking remains one of the most suggestive, if still largely unexplored, areas of her thought. The question naturally arises what such a vision of thinking might mean for the task of theology. As we have seen, Arendt herself appeals to examples from the Christian tradition in laying out her vision of thinking, citing the medieval practice of meditation and Augustine's *Confessions*. Neither provides an exact match for Arendt's thinking, yet we do not need an exact match to be provoked to consider how elements of thinking in her sense might help us better appreciate the range of ways that one might think theologically. Let me begin with meditation.

Arendt does not say much about it, but as we saw above, she alludes to the fact that its practitioners will often appeal to the metaphor of the *nunc stans*, or standing now, to describe its temporal sensation. At another point she refers to the active, searching quality of meditative investigations, likening them in their intensity to the Socratic dialogues. This searching quality, she says, is one characteristic that medieval thinkers would have cited in distinguishing meditation from contemplation.[20] While Arendt does not refer to specific figures, this description broadly corresponds to the account of meditation laid out by arguably its greatest medieval champion, Hugh of St. Victor.[21]

In *The Soul's Three Ways of Seeing*, Hugh begins just as Arendt suggests: by distinguishing meditation from contemplation. "Meditation," Hugh writes, "is the concentrated and judicious reconsideration of thought, that tries to unravel something complicated or scrutinizes something obscure to get at the truth of it."[22] "Contemplation," on the other hand, "is the piercing and spontaneous intuition of the soul, which embraces every aspect of the objects of understanding."[23] Hugh goes on to say:

> Between meditation and contemplation there appears to be this difference: meditation always has to do with things that are

obscure to our intelligence, whereas contemplation is concerned
with things that are clear, either of their nature or in relation
to our intellectual capacity. Again, while meditation is always
exercised in the investigation of one matter, contemplation
embraces the complete understanding of many, or even of
everything. Meditation is, then, a certain inquisitive power of
the soul, that shrewdly tries to find out things that are obscure
and to disentangle those that are involved. Contemplation is the
alertness of the understanding which, finding everything plain,
grasps it clearly with entire comprehension. Thus in some ways
contemplation possesses that for which meditation seeks.[24]

In Hugh's description of meditation, one can observe several features of thinking in Arendt's sense: obscurity, effort, intensity, and struggle. At one point Hugh even likens meditation to "a sort of wrestling-match [that] goes on between ignorance and knowledge" in which "the light of truth somehow flickers in the midst of the darkness of error."[25] In another memorable image, he likens meditation to "a fire in green wood," which "gets a hold at first only with difficulty; but, when it is fanned by a stronger draught and begins to catch on more fiercely, then we see great billows of black smoke arise, and smother the flame ... until at last, as the fire gradually grows, all the smoke clears, the darkness is dispelled, and a bright blaze appears."[26] Between the initial flame and consuming fire, meditation attempts to clear away the smoke, seeing through a glass darkly, in the Pauline imagery. Yet although it involves a struggle, Hugh also calls meditation "the greatest delight," recalling Arendt's observation that thinking gives one the sensation of being fully alive. As Hugh puts it, "if anyone will learn to love it very intimately and will desire to be engaged very frequently upon it, meditation renders his life joyful indeed, and provides the greatest consolation to him in his trials."[27]

Boyd Taylor Coolman explains that for Hugh, meditation can be applied to any number of matters, including the works of creation and the moral life, but it has a particularly strong association with the interpretation of scripture.[28] In the *Didascalicon*, Hugh observes that meditation "takes its start from reading but is bound by none of reading's rules or precepts. For it delights to range along open ground ... drawing together now these, now those causes of things, or now penetrating into profundities."[29] As Coolman notes, the allegorical reading of scripture is for Hugh "the quintessential intellectual practice, by which believers pursue an understanding of the mysteries of the faith, conceived of as an act of intellectual construction."[30] In Hugh's vision of meditation, we attempt to work through the various connections and apparent inconsistencies of the biblical narrative by building up a synthetic theological structure. Coolman writes:

> To give theological scrutiny to the deeper meaning of Scripture summons forth all the cognitive resources that can be mustered in its effort ... At the same time, the constructive dimension entails a degree of creative freedom ... not only in uncovering fitting, doctrinal meanings ... but even more so in the construction of the larger theological structure or synthesis of doctrine.[31]

For Hugh, it is this work of construction that makes meditation more than an academic exercise and something like a spiritual discipline, as the point is to make such an edifice the foundation of one's own mind. If ultimately more constructive than Arendt's conception of thinking, his vision similarly frames the activity of thought as tied to a space or region unique to each one of us. As Coolman puts it, meditation "entails an interiorization of theological thought, a personal appropriation of doctrine, imaged here as an act of interior construction, in which layer upon layer of doctrinal 'stones courses' are built up into a theological structure within."[32] The most famous example of this is Hugh's spiritual classic *Noah's Ark*, where he invites his readers to construct an inward dwelling place for God, an "ark" of wisdom, composed of "the works of restoration," "the condition of the universal Church," "the mysteries of the sacraments," "good works, virtues, and rewards."[33] In this way, one may temper "the instability and restlessness of the human heart" and find a stable vantage point from which to think.[34] As Coolman notes, "stabilized as an 'ark of wisdom,' the soul can now meditate on other things, especially those very external things, the 'works of creation,' which had before threatened to dissipate and disintegrate it."[35]

It is in Hugh's description of this interior structure that we find him appealing to the temporal language that Arendt notes above. In a description of the time sensation of thinking that almost exactly parallels her own, he writes:

For things have their own kind of being in the mind of man, where even those which, in themselves, are past can coexist with those yet to come. And in this respect the rational soul bears a certain resemblance to its Maker. For as in the mind of God the causes of things exist eternally without change or temporal differentiation, so also in our minds things past, things present, and things future exist together by the means of thought.[36]

When we gather the diverse works of God into our mind, we get a small taste of what it must be like to view them from God's vantage point, as we are able to make many of them present at the same time. But Hugh takes the point a step further. The sensation of time standing still that we experience when we dwell upon them is related to the enduring quality of wisdom itself. It is this dimension of meditation to which he is referring when he observes that in meditation "another world is found, over against this passing, transitory one ... There the present does not follow on the past, nor does the future supervene upon the present, but whatsoever is there, is there as in the present."[37] For Arendt, it is the meeting of past and future in the mind that offers the perspective necessary for understanding the meaning of events in the present. For Hugh, the "ark" represents more than the meeting of past and future; it is an appropriation of enduring wisdom that gives us the stability from which to think. There is, nonetheless, a shared emphasis in both thinkers upon the importance of each individual taking up the activity of thinking for him or herself: in Arendt's case, past and future only converge in the mind that thinks, and in Hugh's case, wisdom is only inwardly appropriated in the mind that meditates.

Above we noted that in her account of the time sensation of thinking, Arendt also draws upon Augustine's *Confessions*, which offers another fruitful entry point for considering what thinking in her sense might look like for theology. Arendt notes that for Augustine, we experience a respite from the fleetingness of time when we think, just to the extent that the mind can hold the images of the past and expectations for the future together in the present. Yet, as she perceptively observes in her dissertation, such simultaneity is by no means a given for Augustine. Through the force of habit, our experience of time can easily collapse into the single dimension of the past, "making today and tomorrow the same as yesterday" (LSA 83). For Augustine, we can only truly gather ourselves from dispersion and recover the unity of the various tenses of our existence when God becomes the object of our memory and expectation. In God's eternity our whole existence is present as if it were a single day, and it is in this eternal "Today" that we find the basis for gathering the pieces of our life together. In a passage that Arendt cites in *Willing*, Augustine writes:

> You are supreme and you do not change, and in you there is no "today" that passes. Yet in you our "today" does pass, inasmuch as all things exist in you, and would have no means even of passing away if you did not contain them ... How many of our days and our ancestors' days have come and gone in this "Today" of yours, have received from it their manner of being and have existed after their fashion, and how many others will likewise receive theirs, and exist in their own way? Yet you are the self-same: all our tomorrows and beyond, all our yesterdays and further back, you will make in your Today, you have made in your Today. (*Conf.* 1.6.10)[38]

For Augustine, part of dwelling upon God's eternity means coming to grips with how all the moments of our life are contained in God. Thus thinking theologically about eternity inevitably has an autobiographical dimension. If Hugh's vision of meditation entails constructing an interior dwelling place so that God might enter, Augustine's practice of confession suggests that God is already present at each moment of our lives, and part of what it means to participate in God's eternity is to comb through the "mansions of memory" (10.8.12) and turn over our every future desire to discover God's sustaining presence there.[39] In remembering, willing, and understanding God, we find the various tenses of our life coming back together, as we discover God at each point in our lives. It is in this way that the sensation of thinking is experienced as the convergence of the different tenses of time, not as opposing but reconciled forces which bring us into deeper communion with God.

While Arendt's interest in the *Confessions* is mostly limited to his insights into the time sensation of thinking, one cannot help but notice how many other features of Arendt's notion of thinking are exhibited here as well. Let me briefly mention three. First, there is the spirit of wonder that launches many of Augustine's investigations. In his discussion of memory, for example, he writes: "Enormous wonder wells up within me when I think of this, and I am dumbfounded. People go to admire lofty mountains, and huge breakers at sea, and crashing waterfalls, and vast stretches of ocean, and the dance of the stars, but they leave themselves behind out of sight" (10.8.15). Second, there is the deeply dialogical character of the work. At one level, it is a dialogue with the self in Arendt's sense of the two-in-one. We often hear Augustine addressing and posing questions to himself. To cite a few examples: "In you, my mind, I measure time. Do not interrupt me by clamoring that time has objective existence, nor hinder yourself with the hurly-burly of your impressions" (11.27.36); "Then toward myself I turned, and asked myself, 'Who are you?' And I answered my own question: 'A man'" (10.6.9); and most famously, "I had become a great enigma to myself, and I questioned my soul, demanding why it was sorrowful and why it so disquieted me, but it had no answer" (4.4.9). But, of course, as the first lines of the book announce—"Great are you, O Lord, and exceedingly worthy of praise" (1.1.1)—the work is most fundamentally a dialogue with God. As such, Augustine models that particular kind of dialogical thinking called prayer. "A theologian is one who prays," the late fourth-century monk Evagrius famously observed, "and one who prays is a theologian."[40] For Augustine, Peter Brown observes, prayer was "a recognized vehicle for speculative enquiry."[41] Indeed, the fact that his *Confessions* "were couched in the form of a prayer, far from relegating them to a work of piety, would have increased their value as a philosophical exercise: *da mihi, Domine, scire et intellegere*, 'Give me, O Lord, to know and understand' (1.1.1)."[42] Theology as prayer seems only to multiply the occasions for reaffirming our identity as question-asking beings. "Now I have a question to ask" (11.23.30)—these seven words could very well serve as a summary of the entire book. Indeed, the *Confessions* is a book full of questions. They begin as soon as the second paragraph: "which comes first: to call upon you or to praise you? To know you or to call upon you?" They continue throughout the book: "I am asking questions, Father, not making assertions" (11.17.22). "To whom should I put my question about them?" he later asks. "And to whom should I confess my stupidity with greater profit than to you, who do not weary of my intense, burning interest in your scriptures?" (11.22.28).

This brings us to the third parallel. As the Socratic dialogues do not terminate in definitive answers, many of Augustine's questions also remain unanswered. At the end of his various investigations, we find that his sense of wonder has only increased: "After saying all that, what have we said, my God, my life, my holy sweetness? What does anyone who speaks of you really say? Yet woe betide those who fail to speak" (1.4.4). Or later: "If no one asks me, I know; if I want to explain it to someone who asks me, I do not know" (11.14.17). As always with Augustine, the point is not ultimately to know God so much as to be known by Him, and as thinking is for Arendt a way of keeping company with oneself, thinking is most fundamentally for Augustine a way to keep company with God.[43] This ultimately is what we do when we think theologically. The end is the relationship, the friendship with God, which the questions and wrestling facilitate, and which final answers would effectively end. That we never arrive makes thinking an inexhaustible search, resonating with one more feature of Arendt's conception of thinking: that it is an activity that lasts as long as we are alive.

At times Arendt expresses the worry that thinking in its active sense, whether conceived as meditation or confession, plays a merely instrumental role in theology, the "handmaiden" that prepares the way for contemplation.[44] Yet as a form of prayer, Augustine's wrestlings are already a way of relating to God, already a form of participating in God, and thus can be seen as an end in itself, even as such thinking also prepares the way for an ever deeper participation in God through more contemplative modes of understanding. The vision that we find in Augustine is not one where our active searching gives way, once and for all, to contemplative rest, but a movement back and forth between the search for truth and understanding, in short, of faith seeking understanding. "The safest intent, after all, until we finally get where we are intent on getting and where we are stretching out to, is that of the seeker," he writes in *De Trinitate*. "The certitude of faith at least initiates knowledge; but the certitude of knowledge will not be completed until after this life when we see *face to face* (1 Cor. 13:12)" (9.1).

Such seeking, of course, is not merely inward. Augustine's duties as a priest and bishop of the church forced his thinking outward, and his thought was always the better for it. It is hard to imagine his distinctive voice emerging independent of the specific crises that arose during his lifetime, whether the Donatist or Pelagian controversies or the sack of Rome. In his response to these crises, we see a sensibility not unlike Arendt's own, which approaches contemporary events as "guideposts for thought," demanding a creativity worthy of the challenges of his times. The way in which Augustine strove to synthesize Greek learning and Christian doctrine in the course of articulating distinctive positions on evil, ecclesiology, history, society, grace and free will betrays the mentality of someone who found a home in the gap between past and future. Indeed, this would be the thinking space fit for a Christian who believed he lived in the time between the times, a time (*saeculum*) determined by things that are no longer and not yet.

Such creative theological thinking is what the *ressourcement* movement in twentieth-century French Catholic theology sought to recover. Also known as *nouvelle théologie*, it included such thinkers as Yves Congar and Marie-Dominique Chenu at the Dominican house of studies of Le Saulchoir in Belgium, as well as Jean Daniélou and Henri de Lubac at the Jesuit house in Fourvière, France.[45] These figures sought to cultivate a thinking more responsive to the challenges of the modern world, yet like Arendt, they believed this could only be done through a deeper engagement with the past, particularly those voices neglected by the dominant tradition of Neo-Scholasticism. Thus they advocated a "return to the sources," a program which in its execution bears a striking resemblance to Arendt's notion of pearl diving. As A. N. Williams puts it, the desire behind *ressourcement* was not "to ensconce theology in the secure fortress of a bygone era but a wish to prospect for treasure which in the earlier part of the twentieth century lay buried under the sands of neglect."[46] The specific appeal to the patristic era "lay not in the authoritative status of its theology, but its dynamism."[47] Indeed, they saw this as an era of exemplary creativity and the Fathers as the "pre-eminent witnesses of Christian novelty."[48] In returning to these sources, it was primarily the spirit of creativity that they sought to recover, not unlike Arendt's own attempt to rediscover the "original spirit" of political concepts which by her time had become empty shells. Hans Urs von Balthasar, who is frequently grouped among these thinkers, puts it this way: "If we study the past, it is not in the hope of drawing from it formulas doomed in advance to sterility or with the intention of readapting out-of-date solutions."[49] Rather, the goal is "to penetrate right to those vital wellsprings of their spirit, right to that fundamental and hidden intuition that directs every expression of their thought and that reveals to us one of the great possibilities of attitude and approach that theology has adopted in a concrete and unique situation."[50] In thinkers such as Augustine or Gregory of Nyssa, von Balthasar sought to understand their gift for "creative invention," which he says has animated theology wherever it has been most alive, whether in Paul's defense of the Gentile mission, the patristic encounter with Hellenistic culture, or Thomas' later synthesis of Augustine, Aristotle, and Islamic philosophy. Reading such thinkers against the backdrop of the present, *ressourcement* theologians also fully expected these past voices to speak in new ways. Certainly, Williams notes, "there was concern to understand [the past] on its own terms, and up to a point, for its own sake, but there was also concern to make use of it and so to carry the tradition forward."[51] In this way, the engagement with neglected voices from the tradition was ultimately seen as a way to enliven the dialogue of thinking, multiply the number of conversation partners, and thereby stir a spirit of renewal. For them, as for Arendt, "the past represents not an end, but a beginning."[52]

One could point to many other fruitful parallels to thinking in Arendt's sense, such as Vatican II's challenge to read "the signs of the times" or liberation theology's vision of theology as "critical reflection upon praxis." The challenge in either case is the same: to do the thinking that neither our predecessors nor our descendants can do for us, but which they now demand of us. In looking out on the major crises of our day, from church controversies over sexuality, marriage, and the nature of communion to broader revolutionary changes in communication and media, the changing shape of warfare, the environmental crisis, and the abiding legacies of economic, gender, and racial inequality, René Char's words have never seemed more apt: our inheritance indeed has been left to us by no testament. It now falls to us to step into the gap between past and future ourselves. In journeying through Arendt's work, we have tried to gain some experience in thinking in this gap. In Chapter 2, we took stock of the ways that many of the novel circumstances surrounding totalitarian evil continue to remain with us today, with the capacity for committing horrendous evil now extending to non-state actors and the obstacles to legal responses only having multiplied even as these responses become more urgent. In Chapter 3, we reviewed the multiple factors that contribute to the erosion of our common public world, from a consumer society that sees the world as another object to be consumed to diminished opportunities for engagement in political affairs. In Chapter 4, we took measure of the particular costs of an instrumental approach to politics that overlooks the internal goods of action and prevents the inherently unpredictable quality of political action from being born. If we found that the Christian tradition did not provide readymade solutions to these problems, we also found traditional resources speaking anew, whether it was the privation account of evil or the new beginnings promised by Augustine's theology of creation. To read Arendt is to be challenged to think through such dilemmas with the same kind of responsiveness and generativity that characterized her thinking. It is to be willing to have our thinking interrupted by these events, and to dare to interrupt these events with our own thinking. And it is to be challenged not to do it alone. For Arendt, thinking was dialogical in multiple senses. It was a dialogue with the self, yet as we saw in her discussion of Socrates above, it was also a dialogue with others, a point to which Arendt's own many, lifelong friendships attest. To do theology is to think in friendship with ourselves, with one another, and with God. It is also to think in friendship with individuals such as Arendt, without whom theology would be deprived not only of its gadfly, but someone whose voice has a way of calling theology back to its true self.

If in addressing today's challenges we find that the answers initially elude us, then we can take some comfort from the words that Augustine wrote near the end of his long study on the Trinity. After a book full of searching, indeed, after a lifetime full of searching, he wrote:

> Wait for it then, whoever you are that are listening to this; we are still looking, and no one can fairly find fault with someone who is looking for such things as this, provided that in looking for something so difficult either to know or to express, he remains absolutely firm in faith ... Let us therefore so look as men who are going to find, and so find as men who are going to go on looking. For *when a man has finished, then it is that he is beginning* (Sir 18:7). (*De Trin.* 9.1)

In thinking no less than acting, we are reminded one final time that, as Arendt liked to put it, although we must die, we "are not born in order to die but in order to begin."

Notes

1 "Hannah Arendt on Hannah Arendt," in *Hannah Arendt: The Recovery of the Public World*, ed. Melvyn A. Hill (New York: St. Martin's Press, 1979), 306.

2 Most engagement with Arendt's work on thinking has focused upon her criticisms of Christian conceptions of the *vita contemplativa*. See, for example, Bernd Wannenwetsch, *Political Worship* (Oxford: Oxford University Press, 2009), 189–206. One notable exception is William J. Richardson, SJ, "Contemplative in Action," in James Bernauer, ed., *Amor Mundi: Explorations in the Faith of Hannah Arendt* (Dordrecht, Netherlands: Nijhoff Publishers, 1987), 115–33.

3 For more on Arendt's account of thinking, see Richard J. Bernstein, "Arendt on Thinking," in Dana Villa, ed., *The Cambridge Companion to Hannah Arendt* (Cambridge: Cambridge University Press, 2000), 277–92; Elisabeth Young-Bruehl, *Why Arendt Matters* (New Haven: Yale University Press, 2006), 159–210; Jean Yarbrough and Peter Stern, "*Vita Activa* and *Vita Contemplativa*: Reflections on Hannah Arendt's Political Thought in *The Life of the Mind*," *The Review of Politics* 43:3 (July 1981): 323–54.

4 On the influence of Socrates upon Arendt, see Margaret Canovan, "Socrates or Heidegger? Hannah Arendt's Reflections on Philosophy and Politics," *Social Research* 57:1 (Spring 1990): 135–65.

5 This comes across most clearly in a passage from HC where she distinguishes thinking from contemplation: "Traditionally thought was conceived as the most direct and important way to lead to the contemplation of truth. Since Plato, and probably since Socrates, thinking was understood as the inner dialogue in which one speaks with himself (*eme emautō*, to recall the idiom current in Plato's dialogues); and although this dialogue lacks all outward manifestation and even requires a more or less complete cessation of all other activities, it constitutes in itself a highly active state ... If medieval scholasticism looked upon philosophy as the handmaiden of theology, it could very well have appealed to Plato and Aristotle themselves; both, albeit in a very different context, considered this

dialogical thought process to be the way to prepare the soul and lead the mind to a beholding of truth beyond thought and beyond speech" (HC 291).

6 In HC, Arendt suggests that Christian thinkers conferred a "religious sanction" upon the Greek conception of the *bios theoretikos*. Indeed, on nothing, she says, are Greek philosophy and Christianity in more agreement than the conviction that truth, "be it the ancient truth of Being or the Christian truth of the living God, can reveal itself only in complete human stillness" (15). If her footnotes are any indication, she thinks Aquinas is the primary culprit. Arendt notes that Aquinas, like Aristotle, defines contemplation as *quies ab exterioribus motibus* (15; II.II 179.1 ad 3), or rest from exterior movements, and he only recommends the *vita activa* because it "quiets interior passions" (15; II.II 182.3). Ultimately, she says, "every kind of activity, even the processes of mere thought, must culminate in the absolute quiet of contemplation" (15). Yet when we follow Arendt's references back to their source in the *Summa*, a more complex picture emerges. While Aquinas does state that the "contemplative life has one act wherein it is finally completed, namely the contemplation of truth," he goes on to say that the *vita contemplativa* is actually comprised of many different acts, and he gives no indication that we ever completely leave these acts behind in this life. "Some of these pertain to the reception of principles," he observes, "from which it proceeds to the contemplation of truth; others are concerned with deducing from the principles, the truth, the knowledge of which is sought; and the last and crowning act is the contemplation itself of the truth" (II.II 180.3). Moreover, while contemplation does entail rest from exterior movements, Aquinas makes clear that it does not entail the complete rest of the intellect: "the movements of intellectual operations belong to the quiet of contemplation" (II.II 180.6 ad 1). Finally, while it is true that Aquinas says the contemplative life is superior to the active life (II.II 182.1), he also says it is "better to give to others the fruits of contemplation than merely to contemplate" (II.II 188.6). The Dominican *contemplata aliis tradere* ends up looking not entirely dissimilar to the inter-relationship between the two lives that she holds up in her exemplar Socrates. For more on Aquinas' understanding of the active and contemplative lives, see Hans Urs von Balthasar, "Action and Contemplation," in *Explorations in Theology I: The Word Made Flesh* (San Francisco: Ignatius Press, 1989), 227–40.

7 For more on this, see my discussion of the fearful imagination in Chapter 2.

8 I am thinking primarily of Theodor Adorno's *Negative Dialectics* (New York: Continuum, 1973). There he writes: "if thinking is to be true—if it is to be true today, in any case—it must also be a thinking against itself" (365). It must be measured "by the extremity that eludes the concept" (365). Thinking in Adorno's sense unsettles the apparent givenness of our concepts, testing each one "until it starts moving, until it becomes unidentical with itself by virtue of its own meaning—in other words, of its identity" (156). The ultimate goal is not re-enchantment of the object, but the "disenchantment of the concept" (13).

9 Arendt, "Martin Heidegger at Eighty," in Michael Murray, ed. *Heidegger and Modern Philosophy* (New Haven: Yale University Press, 1978), 297.

10 In "Arendt and Individualism," *Social Research* 61:4 (Winter 1994), George Kateb observes: "I would like to think that Arendt is here being hospitable to the idea, intrinsic to democratic individuality, that each person is inwardly various, full of thoughts, half-thoughts, impulses, desires, reveries, insights, and occurrences that seem not to come from one center, but from the 'multitudes' contained in oneself, in Whitman's word from 'Song of Myself'" (776).

11 In her section on metaphor, she notes that we are constantly drawing on external images to describe the invisible thought process. She writes: "No language has a ready-made vocabulary for the needs of mental activity; they all borrow their vocabulary from words originally meant to correspond either to sense experience or to other experiences of ordinary life" (LMT 102).

12 Arendt, "Martin Heidegger at Eighty," 297.

13 Arendt, "Martin Heidegger at Eighty," 297.

14 Kateb, "Arendt and Individualism," 765–94. See also Roger Berkowitz, "Solitude and the Activity of Thinking," in Berkowitz and Thomas Keenan, eds. *Thinking in Dark Times: Hannah Arendt on Ethics and Politics* (New York: Fordham University Press, 2010), 237–48.

15 Critics of Arendt's thesis that thinking can condition us against evil often cite the example of Heidegger. He was, after all, one of the brightest minds of his generation, but this seemed to do him little good when it came to resisting the Nazis. Arendt takes up the question in her essay, "Heidegger at Eighty," noting that what proved to be Heidegger's undoing was not thinking as such, but his desire to turn the wonder of philosophy into an "abode," separate from human affairs. She observes that this desire "seems to me

decisive for reflecting on who Martin Heidegger is. For many—so we hope—are acquainted with thinking and the solitude bound up with it; but clearly, they do not have their residence there. When wonder at the simple overtakes them and, yielding to the wonder, they engage in thinking, they know they have been torn out of their habitual place in the continuum of occupations in which human affairs take place, and will return to it again in a little while. The abode of which Heidegger speaks lies therefore, in a metaphorical sense, outside the habitations of men" (299). She goes on to say: "We who wish to honor the thinkers, even if our own residence lies in the midst of the world, can hardly help finding it striking and perhaps exasperating that Plato and Heidegger, when they entered into human affairs, turned to tyrants and Führers ... For the attraction to the tyrannical can be demonstrated theoretically in many of the great thinkers (Kant is the great exception). And if this tendency is not demonstrable in what they did, that is only because very few of them were prepared to go beyond 'the faculty of wondering at the simple' and 'to accept this wondering as their abode'" (303). This helps illumine why Arendt was so insistent that she not be considered a professional thinker (LMT 3). And this likewise helps to illumine why she did not see Socrates as a professional thinker either (166–7). She, like him, saw thinking as a part of the life of citizenship—and an important guard against the dangers of wonder and/or thinking turned into a way of life.

16 Edmund Hill notes that the mental word is formed when we turn our attention to the remembered image. "The way the mental word is formed is by turning the attention (by an act of *cogitatio* or thought) to the object of understanding latent in the *memoria* or memory. When this is done the mental word is produced, in an act of active understanding, as a mentally visible replica or image of the object of understanding latent in the memory. It can thus be regarded as an offspring (*proles*) conceived from the parent (*parens*) memory, but this conception or generation of the mental word from the memory is only done by an act of thought." See Augustine, *The Trinity*, ed. John E. Rotelle, OSA (Hyde Park, NY: New City Press, 1991), 266.

17 Arendt contends that the medieval interpretation of the time sensation of thinking is actually a suspension of time, an "intimation of divine eternity" (LMW 12). "Such an interpretation shrouds our whole mental life in an aura of mysticism and strangely overlooks the very ordinariness of the experience itself" (12). She prefers to see the "gap" between past and future as something we experience within time, and as the normal condition of thought: "The constitution of an 'enduring present' is 'the habitual, normal, banal act of our

intellect,' performed in every kind of reflection, whether its subject matter is ordinary day-to-day occurrences or whether the attention is focused on things forever invisible and outside the sphere of human power. The activity of the mind always creates for itself *un présent qui dure*, a 'gap between past and future'" (12). I am not convinced that thinkers such as Hugh of St. Victor saw meditation as an escape from time, although I do think they saw it as a way to participate in the stability of the eternal God within time. See my discussion of meditation below.

18 In the "Theses on the Philosophy of History," Benjamin writes: "History is the subject of a structure whose site is not homogenous, empty time, but time filled by the presence of the now [*Jetztzeit*]" (261). In an editorial footnote, Arendt writes: "Benjamin says '*Jetztzeit*' and indicates by the quotation marks that he does not simply mean an equivalent to *Gegenwart*, that is, present. He clearly is thinking of the mystical *nunc stans*" (*Illuminations*, 261). For more on Arendt and messianism, see Gottlieb, *Regions of Sorrow*, 135–60.

19 Arendt does not explain what she means by "spirit" here. She may be playing upon the traditional association of the realm of the "invisibles" with the "spirit." Augustine, for example, associates reflection upon the intelligibles with the "inner man," who is "fixed with a much more assured and stable knowledge on things of the spirit" (*De Trin.* 11.1).

20 In the course of discussing how the Socratic dialogues have the effect of "unfreezing" concepts, she writes: "In medieval philosophy, this kind of thinking was called 'meditation,' and the word should be heard as different from, even opposed to contemplation. At all events, this kind of pondering reflection does not produce definitions and in that sense is entirely without results, though somebody who had pondered the meaning of 'house' might make his own look better" (LMT 171).

21 For more background on Hugh of St. Victor's conception of meditation, see Boyd Taylor Coolman, *The Theology of Hugh of St. Victor: An Interpretation* (Cambridge: Cambridge University Press, 2010); Matthew R. McWhorter, "Hugh of St. Victor on Contemplative Meditation," *The Heythrop Journal* 55:1 (2014): 110–22; Karl Baier, "Meditation and Contemplation in High to Late Medieval Europe," in Eli Franco and Dagmar Eigner, eds. *Yogic Perception, Meditation and Altered States of Consciousness* (Vienna: Verlag der Österreichischen Akademie der Wissenschaften, 2009), 325–49.

22 Hugh of St. Victor, *Selected Spiritual Writings* (Eugene, OR: Wipf & Stock, 1962), 183.

23 Hugh of St. Victor, *Selected Spiritual Writings*, 183.
24 Hugh of St. Victor, *Selected Spiritual Writings*, 183–4.
25 Hugh of St. Victor, *Selected Spiritual Writings*, 184.
26 Hugh of St. Victor, *Selected Spiritual Writings*, 184.
27 Hugh of St. Victor, *Didascalicon* 3.10, quoted Coolman, *The Theology of Hugh of St. Victor*, 165.
28 Coolman, *The Theology of Hugh of St. Victor*, 167.
29 *Didascalicon* 3.10.
30 Coolman, *The Theology of Hugh of St. Victor*, 174.
31 Coolman, *The Theology of Hugh of St. Victor*, 178.
32 Coolman, *The Theology of Hugh of St. Victor*, 179.
33 Hugh of St. Victor, *Selected Spiritual Writings*, 151–2.
34 Hugh of St. Victor, *Selected Spiritual Writings*, 45, 152.
35 Coolman, *The Theology of Hugh of St. Victor*, 186.
36 Hugh of St. Victor, *Selected Spiritual Writings*, 73.
37 Hugh of St. Victor, *Selected Spiritual Writings*, 152.
38 All citations from Augustine, *Confessions*, trans. Maria Boulding (New York: Vintage Books, 1998). Arendt mentions this passage in LMW 12.
39 Coolman states the difference between Augustine and Hugh this way: "Where Augustine turns 'inward' in order to ascend 'upward,' Hugh turns inward, not so much to ascend a ladder, as in order to construct a house, a *templum Dei*" (228). My sense is that Augustine believes God is already present, indeed, intimately present, before any such construction, and that part of the inward turn is coming to a deeper knowledge of this presence, even as one desires that it increase.
40 Quoted in Robert Wilken, *The Spirit of Early Christian Thought* (New Haven: Yale University Press, 2005), 26.
41 Peter Brown, *Augustine of Hippo: A Biography* (Berkeley: University of Berkeley Press, 1967), 159.
42 Brown, *Augustine*, 159. Arendt actually mentions prayer as an example of thinking in her sense (LMT 58, 99), although what she means by prayer and what Augustine means by prayer are two different things.
43 See Charles Mathewes' observations on Augustine and the incomprehensibility of God in "Book One: The Presumptuousness of Autobiography and the Paradoxes of Beginning," in *A Reader's*

Companion to Augustine's Confessions, eds. Kim Paffenroth and Robert Peter Kennedy (Louisville: Westminster John Knox 2003), 7–24. In *De Trinitate*, Augustine writes: "And the apostle says, *If anybody thinks he knows anything, he does not yet know as he ought to know. But anyone who loves God, this man is known by him* (1 Cor. 8:2). Even in this case, you notice, he did not say 'knows him,' which would be a dangerous piece of presumption, but 'is known by him'" (9.1).

44 See LMT 6–7 and HC 12–21.

45 For more on *ressourcement* theology, see A. N. Williams, "The Future of the Past: The Contemporary Significance of the *Nouvelle Théologie*," *International Journal of Systematic Theology* 7:4 (2005): 347–61; Marcellino D'Ambrosio, "*Ressourcement* Theology, Aggiornamento, and the Hermeneutics of Tradition," *Communio* 18 (Winter 1991): 530–55; Hans Boersma, *Nouvelle Théologie and Sacramental Ontology: A Return to Mystery* (Oxford: Oxford University Press, 2013); Gabriel Flynn and Paul D. Murray, eds. *Ressourcement: A Movement for Renewal in Twentieth-Century Catholic Theology* (Oxford: Oxford University Press, 2014); and Jürgen Mettepenningen, *Nouvelle Théologie: Inheritor of Modernism, Precursor to Vatican II* (London: T&T Clark, 2010).

46 Williams, "The Future of the Past," 351.

47 Williams, "The Future of the Past," 352.

48 Williams, "The Future of the Past," 352.

49 Hans Urs von Balthasar, *Presence and Thought: An Essay on the Religious Philosophy of Gregory of Nyssa* (San Francisco: Ignatius Press, 1955), 12.

50 Von Balthasar, *Presence and Thought*, 13.

51 Williams, "The Future of the Past," 353.

52 Williams, "The Future of the Past," 357.

BIBLIOGRAPHY

Adorno, Theodor W. *Negative Dialectics*. New York: Continuum, 1973.
Agamben, Giorgio. *Homo Sacer: Sovereign Power and Bare Life*. Stanford: Stanford University Press, 1998.
Aquinas, Thomas. *The Summa Theologica*. Translated by Fathers of the English Dominican Province. 5 vols. Notre Dame: Christian Classics, 1948.
Arendt, Hannah. "Action and 'the Pursuit of Happiness,'" delivered at the American Political Science Association, September 8–10, 1960. Hannah Arendt Papers at the Library of Congress.
Arendt, Hannah. *Between Past and Future*. New York: Viking Press, 1961.
Arendt, Hannah. *Crises of the Republic*. New York: Harcourt Brace & Company, 1972.
Arendt, Hannah. *Eichmann in Jerusalem: A Report on the Banality of Evil*. New York: Viking Press, 1963.
Arendt, Hannah. *Essays in Understanding, 1930–1954: Formation, Exile, and Totalitarianism*. Edited by Jerome Kohn. New York: Schocken Books, 1994.
Arendt, Hannah. *The Human Condition*. Chicago: University of Chicago Press, 1958.
Arendt, Hannah. *The Jewish Writings*. Edited by Jerome Kohn and Ron H. Feldman. New York: Schocken Books, 2007.
Arendt, Hannah. *Lectures on Kant's Political Philosophy*. Edited by Ronald Beiner. Chicago: University of Chicago Press, 1982.
Arendt, Hannah. *The Life of the Mind*. 2 vols. New York: Harcourt Brace Jovanovich, 1978.
Arendt, Hannah. *Love and Saint Augustine*. Edited by Joanna Vecchiarelli Scott and Judith Chelius Stark. Chicago: University of Chicago Press, 1996.
Arendt, Hannah. "Martin Heidegger at Eighty." In *Heidegger and Modern Philosophy*, edited by Michael Murray. New Haven: Yale University Press, 1978.

Arendt, Hannah. *Men in Dark Times*. New York: Harcourt Brace & Company, 1968.
Arendt, Hannah. *On Revolution*. New York: Viking Press, 1963.
Arendt, Hannah. *On Violence*. New York: Harcourt Brace & Company, 1970.
Arendt, Hannah. *The Origins of Totalitarianism*. New York: Harcourt Brace Jovanovich, 1968.
Arendt, Hannah. *The Promise of Politics*. Edited by Jerome Kohn. New York: Schocken Books, 2005.
Arendt, Hannah. "Public Rights and Private Interests." In *Small Comforts for Hard Times: Humanists on Public Policy*. Edited by M. Mooney and F. Stuber. New York: Columbia University Press, 1977.
Arendt, Hannah. *Rahel Varnhagen: The Life of a Jewess*. Edited by Liliane Weissberg. Baltimore: Johns Hopkins University Press, 1997.
Arendt, Hannah. *Responsibility and Judgment*. Edited by Jerome Kohn. New York: Schocken Books, 2003.
Arendt, Hannah, and Martin Heidegger. *Letters, 1925–1975*. New York: Harcourt, 2004.
Arendt, Hannah, and Karl Jaspers. *Hannah Arendt and Karl Jaspers: Correspondence, 1926–1969*. Edited by Lotte Kohler and Hans Saner. New York: Harcourt Brace & Company, 1992.
Arendt, Hannah, and Mary McCarthy. *Between Friends: The Correspondence of Hannah Arendt and Mary McCarthy, 1949–1975*. Edited by Carol Brightman. New York: Harcourt Brace & Company, 1995.
Aristotle. *Nicomachean Ethics*. Translated by Terence Irwin. Indianapolis, IN: Hackett Pub. Co., 1999.
Asad, Talal. *On Suicide Bombing*. New York: Columbia University Press, 2007.
Aschheim, Steven E., ed. *Hannah Arendt in Jerusalem*. Berkeley: University of California Press, 2001.
Aschheim, Steven E. "Nazism, Culture, and the Origins of Totalitarianism: Hannah Arendt and the Discourse of Evil." *New German Critique* 70 (1997): 117–39.
Augustine. *The City of God against the Pagans*. Translated by R. W. Dyson. Cambridge: Cambridge University Press, 1998.
Augustine. *The Confessions*. Translated by Maria Boulding. Vintage Spiritual Classics. New York: Vintage Books, 1998.
Augustine. *On the Free Choice of the Will, On Grace and Free Choice, and Other Writings*. Edited by Peter King. Cambridge: Cambridge University Press, 2010.
Augustine. *The Trinity*. Translated by Edmund Hill. Edited by John E. Rotelle. Hyde Park: New City Press, 1991.

Baier, Karl. "Meditation and Contemplation in High to Late Medieval Europe." In *Yogic Perception, Meditation and Altered States of Consciousness*. Edited by Eli Franco and Dagmar Eigner. Vienna: Verlag der Österreichischen Akademie der Wissenschaften, 2009, 325–49.

Balthasar, Hans Urs von. "Action and Contemplation." In *Explorations in Theology I: The Word Made Flesh*. San Francisco: Ignatius Press, 1989.

Balthasar, Hans Urs von. *Presence and Thought: An Essay on the Religious Philosophy of Gregory of Nyssa*. San Francisco: Ignatius Press, 1955.

Balthasar, Hans Urs von. *Romano Guardini: Reform from the Source*. San Francisco: Ignatius Press, 2010.

Barnouw, Dagmar. *Visible Spaces: Hannah Arendt and the German-Jewish Experience*. Johns Hopkins Jewish Studies. Baltimore: Johns Hopkins University Press, 1990.

Benhabib, Seyla. *The Reluctant Modernism of Hannah Arendt*. Lanham, MD: Rowman & Littlefield, 2003.

Benjamin, Walter. *Illuminations*. New York: Harcourt, 1968.

Benjamin, Walter. *The Arcades Project*. Edited by Rolf Tiedemann. Cambridge, MA: Belknap Press, 1999.

Berkowitz, Peter. "The Pearl Diver." *The New Republic* 44 (1999): 44–52.

Berkowitz, Roger, Jeffrey Katz, and Thomas Keenan, eds. *Thinking in Dark Times: Hannah Arendt on Ethics and Politics*. New York: Fordham University Press, 2010.

Bernauer, James, ed. *Amor Mundi: Explorations in the Faith and Thought of Hannah Arendt*. Dordrecht, Netherlands: Nijhoff Publishers, 1987.

Bernauer, James. "Bonhoeffer and Arendt at One Hundred." *Studies in Christian-Jewish Relation* 2:1 (2007): 77–85.

Bernstein, Richard. *Radical Evil: A Philosophical Interrogation*. Cambridge: Polity Press, 2002.

Bernstein, Richard. *Hannah Arendt and the Jewish Question*. Cambridge, MA: MIT Press, 1996.

Birmingham, Peg. "Arendt and Hobbes: Glory, Sacrificial Violence, and the Political Imagination." *Research in Phenomenology* 41 (2011): 1–22.

Birmingham, Peg. *Hannah Arendt and Human Rights: The Predicament of Common Responsibility*. Bloomington: Indiana University Press, 2006.

Birmingham, Peg. "Holes in Oblivion: The Banality of Radical Evil." *Hypatia* 18 (1) (2003): 80–103.

Biss, Mavis Louise. "Arendt and the Theological Significance of Natality." *Philosophy Compass* 7 (11) (2012): 762–71.
Boersma, Hans. *Nouvelle Théologie and Sacramental Ontology: A Return to Mystery.* Oxford: Oxford University Press, 2013.
Bonhoeffer, Dietrich. *Letters and Papers from Prison.* New York: Simon & Schuster, 1971.
Bonhoeffer, Dietrich. *A Testament to Freedom: The Essential Writings of Dietrich Bonhoeffer.* Edited by Geffrey B. Kelly and F. Burton Nelson. San Francisco: Harper, 1990.
Bowen-Moore, Patricia. *Hannah Arendt's Philosophy of Natality.* New York: St. Martin's Press, 1989.
Breidenthal, Thomas. "Jesus Is My Neighbor: Arendt, Augustine, and the Politics of the Incarnation." *Modern Theology* 14 (4) (1998): 489–503.
Bretherton, Luke. *Christianity and Contemporary Politics: The Conditions and Possibilities of Faithful Witness.* Oxford: Wiley-Blackwell, 2010.
Brown, Peter. *Augustine of Hippo: A Biography.* London: Faber, 1967.
Butler, Judith. *Frames of War: When Is Life Grievable?* London: Verso, 2010.
Butler, Judith. *Precarious Life: The Powers of Mourning and Violence.* London: Verso, 2004.
Canovan, Margaret. *Hannah Arendt: A Reinterpretation of Her Political Thought.* New York: Cambridge University Press, 1992.
Canovan, Margaret. "Socrates or Heidegger? Hannah Arendt's Reflections on Philosophy and Politics." *Social Research* 57 (1) (1990): 135–65.
Champlin, Jeffrey. "Born Again: Arendt's 'Natality' as Figure and Concept." *The Germanic Review* 88 (2013): 150–64.
Chiba, Shin. "Hannah Arendt on Love and the Political: Love, Friendship, and Citizenship." *The Review of Politics* 57 (3) (1995): 505–36.
Coolman, Boyd Taylor. *The Theology of Hugh of St. Victor: An Interpretation.* Cambridge: Cambridge University Press, 2010.
D'Ambrosio, Marcellino. "Ressourcement Theology, Aggiornamento, and the Hermeneutics of Tradition." *Communio* 18 (1991): 530–55.
De Crespigny, Anthony, and Kenneth R. Minogue, eds. *Contemporary Political Philosophers.* New York: Dodd Mead, 1975.
Decosimo, David. *Ethics as a Work of Charity: Thomas Aquinas and Pagan Virtue.* Stanford: Stanford University Press, 2014.
Douglas, Lawrence. *The Memory of Judgment: Making Law and History in the Trials of the Holocaust.* New Haven, CT: Yale University Press, 2001.
Dunne, Joseph. *Back to the Rough Ground: 'Phronesis' and 'Techne'*

in Modern Philosophy and in Aristotle. Notre Dame: University of Notre Dame Press, 1993.
Elshtain, Jean Bethke. *Augustine and the Limits of Politics*. Notre Dame, IN: University of Notre Dame Press, 1995.
Elshtain, Jean Bethke. *Public Man, Private Woman: Women in Social and Political Thought*. Princeton, NJ: Princeton University Press, 1993.
Euben, Roxanne Leslie. "Killing (for) Politics: Jihad, Martyrdom, and Political Action." *Political Theory* 30 (1) (2003): 4–35.
Fine, Robert. "Crimes against Humanity: Hannah Arendt and the Nuremberg Debates." *European Journal of Social Theory* 3 (3) (2000): 293–311.
Flynn, Gabriel, and P. D. Murray, eds. *Ressourcement: A Movement for Renewal in Twentieth-Century Catholic Theology*. New York: Oxford University Press, 2013.
Fulkerson, Mary McClintock. *Places of Redemption: Theology for a Worldly Church*. Oxford: Oxford University Press, 2007.
Geddes, Jennifer. "Banal Evil and Useless Knowledge: Hannah Arendt and Charlotte Delbo on Evil after the Holocaust." *Hypatia* 18 (1) (2003): 104–15.
Gottlieb, Susannah Young-ah. *Regions of Sorrow: Anxiety and Messianism in Hannah Arendt and W. H. Auden*. Stanford: Stanford University Press, 2003.
Gregory of Nazianzus. "Funeral Oration on S. Basil." In *The Fathers of the Church* Washington, DC: Catholic University Press, 1953.
Gregory, Eric. *Politics and the Order of Love: An Augustinian Ethic of Democratic Citizenship*. Chicago: University of Chicago Press, 2008.
Grumet, David. "Arendt, Augustine and Evil." *Heythrop Journal* 41 (2000): 154–69.
Hadot, Pierre. *Philosophy as a Way of Life: Spiritual Exercises from Socrates to Foucault*. Malden, MA: Blackwell, 1995.
Hauerwas, Stanley and Romand Coles. *Christianity, Democracy, and the Radical Ordinary*. Eugene, OR: Cascade Books, 2008.
Heidegger, Martin. *Being and Time: A Translation of Sein Und Zeit*. Translated by Joan Stambaugh. Albany, NY: State University of New York Press, 1996.
Herdt, Jennifer A. *Putting on Virtue: The Legacy of the Splendid Vices*. Chicago: University of Chicago Press, 2008.
Hill, Melvyn A., ed. *Hannah Arendt: The Recovery of the Public World*. New York: St. Martin's Press, 1979.
Hinchman, Lewis P., and Sandra Hinchman, eds. *Hannah Arendt: Critical Essays*. Albany: State University of New York Press, 1994.
Honig, Bonnie, ed. *Feminist Interpretations of Hannah Arendt*. University Park, PA: Pennsylvania State University Press, 1995.

Hugh of St. Victor. *Selected Spiritual Writings*. Eugene: Wipf & Stock, 1962.
Ignatieff, Michael. *The Warrior's Honor: Ethnic War and the Modern Conscience*. New York: Henry Holt and Company, 1998.
Jay, Martin. *Permanent Exiles: Essays on the Intellectual Migration from Germany to America*. New York: Columbia University Press, 1985.
Kampowski, Stephan. *Arendt, Augustine, and the New Beginning: The Action Theory and Moral Thought of Hannah Arendt in the Light of Her Dissertation on St. Augustine*. Grand Rapids, MI: William B. Eerdmans Pub. Co., 2008.
Kateb, George. "Arendt and Individualism." *Social Research* 61 (4) (1994): 765–94.
Kateb, George. "Death and Politics: Hannah Arendt's Reflections on the American Constitution." *Social Research* 54 (3) (1987): 605–16.
Kateb, George. *Hannah Arendt: Politics, Conscience, Evil*. Totowa, NJ: Rowman & Allanheld, 1984.
Kerr, Fergus. *20th Century Catholic Theologians*. Oxford: Wiley-Blackwell, 2006.
Kirsch, Adam. "Beware of Pity: Hannah Arendt and the Power of the Impersonal." *The New Yorker*, January 12, 2009, 62–8.
Krieg, Robert. *Romano Guardini: A Precursor of Vatican II*. South Bend, IN: University of Notre Dame Press, 1997.
Kristeva, Julia. *Hannah Arendt: Life Is a Narrative*. New York: Columbia University Press, 2001.
Lipstadt, Deborah E. *The Eichmann Trial*. New York: Nextbook/Schocken, 2011.
Llewelyn, John. "On the Saying that Philosophy Begins in Thaumazein." In *Post-Structuralist Classics*. Edited by Andrew Benjamin. London: Routledge, 1988, 173–91.
Luban, David. "Hannah Arendt as a Theorist of International Criminal Law." Georgetown Public Law and Legal Theory Research Paper 11–30 (2011): 1–30.
MacDonald, Dwight. "A New Theory of Totalitarianism." *New Leader* (1951): 17–19.
MacIntyre, Alasdair. *After Virtue: A Study in Moral Theory*. Notre Dame, IN: University of Notre Dame Press, 1981.
MacIntyre, Alasdair. *The Tasks of Philosophy: Selected Essays, Volume I*. Cambridge: New York: Cambridge University Press, 2006.
MacIntyre, Alasdair. *Whose Justice? Which Rationality?* Notre Dame, IN: University of Notre Dame Press, 1988.
Marsh, Charles. *The Beloved Community: How Faith Shapes Social Justice, from the Civil Rights Movement to Today*. New York: Basic Books, 2005.

Mathewes, Charles T. *Evil and the Augustinian Tradition*. New York: Cambridge University Press, 2001.
Mathewes, Charles T. "A Tale of Two Judgments: Bonhoeffer and Arendt on Evil, Understanding, and the Limits of Understanding Evil." *The Journal of Religion* 80 (3) (2000): 375–404.
Mathewes, Charles T. *A Theology of Public Life*. New York: Cambridge University Press, 2007.
May, Larry, and Jerome Kohn, eds. *Hannah Arendt: Twenty Years Later*. Cambridge, MA: MIT Press, 1996.
McGowan, John. *Hannah Arendt: An Introduction*. Minneapolis: University of Minnesota Press, 1998.
McKenna, George. "Augustine Revisited." *First Things* (April 1997): 43–7.
McWhorter, Matthew. "Hugh of St. Victor on Contemplative Meditation." *The Heythrop Journal* 55 (1) (2014): 110–22.
Mettepenningen, Jurgen. *Nouvelle Théologie: Inheritor of Modernism, Precursor to Vatican II*. London: T&T Clark, 2010.
Moran, Dermot. *Introduction to Phenomenology*. London: Routledge, 2000.
Morgenthau, Hans. "Hannah Arendt 1906–1975." *Political Theory* 4 (1) (1976): 5–8.
Moyn, Samuel. "Hannah Arendt on the Secular." *New German Critique* 35 (3) (2008): 71–96.
O'Byrne, Anne E. *Natality and Finitude*. Bloomington: Indiana University Press, 2010.
O'Donovan, Oliver. *The Ways of Judgment*. Grand Rapids, MI: William B. Eerdmans Pub. Co., 2005.
Paffenroth, Kim, and Robert Peter Kennedy, eds. *A Reader's Companion to Augustine's Confessions*. Louisville: Westminster John Knox, 2003.
Passerin d'Entrèves, Maurizio. *The Political Philosophy of Hannah Arendt*. London: Routledge, 1994.
Pieper, Josef. *Leisure, the Basis of Culture*. New York: Pantheon Books, 1952.
Rees, B. R. *Pelagius: Life and Letters*. Rochester, NY: Boydell Press, 1998.
Rieff, David. *A Bed for the Night: Humanitarianism in Crisis*. New York: Simon & Schuster, 2003.
Rieff, Philip. "The Theology of Politics: Reflections on Totalitarianism as the Burden of Our Time." *The Journal of Religion* 32 (2) (1952): 119–26.
Robinson, Jacob. *And the Crooked Shall Be Made Straight*. New York: Macmillan, 1965.
Rorty, Amélie, ed. *Essays on Aristotle's Ethics*. Berkeley: University of California Press, 1980.

Rose, Gillian. *The Broken Middle: Out of Our Ancient Society.* Oxford: Blackwell, 1992.
Rubenstein, Mary-Jane. *Strange Wonder: The Closure of Metaphysics and the Opening of Awe.* New York: Columbia University Press, 2008.
Schabas, William. *The International Criminal Court: A Commentary on the Rome Statute.* Oxford: Oxford University Press, 2010.
Scott, Joanna Vecchiarelli. "'A Detour through Pietism': Hannah Arendt on St. Augustine's Philosophy of Freedom." *Polity* 20 (3) (1988): 394–425.
Seery, John Evan. *Political Theory for Mortals: Shades of Justice, Images of Death.* Ithaca: Cornell University Press, 1996.
Smith, Ted A. *The New Measures: A Theological History of Democratic Practice.* New York: Cambridge University Press, 2007.
Stangneth, Bettina. *Eichmann before Jerusalem: The Unexamined Life of a Mass Murderer.* London: Knopf, 2014.
Stenmark, Lisa L. *Religion, Science, and Democracy: A Disputational Friendship.* Lanham. MD: Lexington Books, 2013.
Stout, Jeffrey. *Ethics after Babel: The Languages of Morals and Their Discontents.* Princeton: Princeton University Press, 1988.
Stump, Eleonore. *Aquinas.* London: Routledge, 2003.
Taminiaux, Jacques. *The Thracian Maid and the Professional Thinker: Arendt and Heidegger.* Translated by Michael Gendre. Albany: State University of New York Press, 1997.
Tanner, Kathryn. *Theories of Culture: A New Agenda for Theology.* Minneapolis: Fortress Press, 1997.
Vance, Jacob. "Twelfth and Sixteenth Century Renaissance Discourse on Meditation and Contemplation." In *Meditatio – Refashioning the Self: Theory and Practice in Late Medieval and Early Modern Intellectual Culture.* Edited by Karl Enenkel and Walter Melion. Leiden: Brill, 2011.
Vatter, Miguel. "Natality and Biopolitics in Hannah Arendt." *Revista de Ciencia Politica* 26 (2) (2006): 137–59.
Vessey, Mark, Karla Pollmann, and Allan Fitzgerald, eds. *History, Apocalypse, and the Secular Imagination: New Essays on Augustine's City of God.* Bowling Green, OH: Bowling Green State University Press, 1999.
Villa, Dana R. *Arendt and Heidegger: The Fate of the Political.* Princeton, NJ: Princeton University Press, 1996.
Villa, Dana R., ed. *The Cambridge Companion to Hannah Arendt.* Cambridge: Cambridge University Press, 2000.
Villa, Dana R. *Politics, Philosophy, Terror: Essays on the Thought of Hannah Arendt.* Princeton, NJ: Princeton University Press, 1999.
Voegelin, Eric. "The Origins of Totalitarianism." *Review of Politics* 15 (1) (1953): 68–76.

Wannenwetsch, Bernd. *Political Worship*. Oxford: Oxford University Press, 2009.
Wetzel, James. *Augustine and the Limits of Virtue*. Cambridge: Cambridge University Press, 1992.
Wilken, Robert Louis. *The Spirit of Early Christian Thought: Seeking the Face of God*. New Haven: Yale University Press, 2003.
Willard, Mara. "'Recasting the Old Questions': Theological Reliance and Renunciation in the Political Thought of Hannah Arendt" (Ph.D. diss., Harvard University, 2011).
Williams, A. N. "The Future of the Past: The Contemporary Significance of the *Nouvelle Théologie*." *International Journal of Systematic Theology* 7 (4) (2005): 347–61.
Williams, Rowan. "Politics and the Soul: A Reading of the *City of God*." *Milltown Studies* 19/20 (1987): 55–72.
Wolfe, Alan. *Political Evil: What It Is and How to Combat It*. New York: Alfred A. Knopf, 2011.
Wolin, Richard. *Heidegger's Children: Hannah Arendt, Karl Löwith, Hans Jonas, and Herbert Marcuse*. Princeton, NJ: Princeton University Press, 2001.
Wolin, Sheldon S. *The Presence of the Past: Essays on the State and the Constitution*. Baltimore: Johns Hopkins University Press, 1989.
Wolin, Sheldon S. *Politics and Vision*. Princeton: Princeton University Press, 2006.
Young-Bruehl, Elisabeth. *Hannah Arendt: For Love of the World*. 2nd edn. New Haven, CT: Yale University Press, 2004.
Young-Bruehl, Elisabeth. *Why Arendt Matters*. New Haven: Yale University Press, 2006.

INDEX

Abraham 6, 184 n.31
action 33, 157–64, 168–76
  Aristotle and 140, 143, 157, 172–3
  Augustine and 20–1, 40–1, 141–4, 152–7, 177–80
  boundlessness of 161–3
  disclosure of self through 33, 143, 157–9, 168–9
  eudaimonia and 173–5
  freedom and 160, 162–3, 171–3, 175
  habit and 169, 174–6
  irreversibility of 131 n.4, 161–3
  Jesus and 15, 141
  labor distinguished from 103, 159–60
  limits of 143, 168–76, 187 n.58
  natality and 20, 139–50, 157–64, 168–76, 177–80
  plurality and 20–1, 141, 149, 158–9, 161
  power and 158–9, 162–3
  spontaneity and 161, 165–6, 169–70
  teleology and 143, 158, 165–6, 169–74, 185 n.39, 187 n.61
  virtue and 174–6, 202–4
  work distinguished from 103, 157–8, 161–2
Adams, John 174
Adorno, Theodor 24, 26, 224 n. 8
Aeneas 178

Agamben, Giorgio 82–3
Akrill, J. I. 173
American Revolution 34, 141, 174–5
American Society of Christian Ethics 15
amor mundi 96–8, 118, 119–125, 129, 135 n.46, 139, 175, 179
anti-Semitism 11, 14, 23, 29, 146–9, 168
appetitus see Augustine, Saint, desire and
Aquinas, Saint Thomas 40, 122, 179, 220, 223 n.6
Arab Spring, the 140, 158–9
Arcades Project, The (Benjamin) 24
Arendt, Hannah, life of
  birth 13
  childhood 13–14
  death 42
  education 14–21
  Eichmann controversy 35–7
  emigration 26–7
  family 14
  internment 26
  Jewish identity 14, 22, 124, 133 n.11, 143, 146–9, 159, 168
  marriage to Heinrich Blücher 26
  naturalization 42
  Paris exile 23–4, 26

Zionism, involvement with 11, 23, 159
Aristotle 21, 39, 40, 156, 194, 220, 222 n.5
  action and 33, 157, 172–3
  contemplation and 173, 194, 223 n.6
  energeia and 172, 201
  eudaimonia and 173, 187 n.61
  friendship and 188 n.67
  Nicomachean Ethics 143, 173
  praxis and *poiēsis* distinction 25, 140, 157
  teleology and 143, 172–3, 185 n.39, 187 n.61
  virtue and 172–3
Asad, Talal 82
Aufbau 11, 28
Augustine, Saint 1–2, 17–21, 150–7, 215–19
  Arendt's dissertation on 17–20, 45 n.25, 90 n.39, 108–9, 144–6, 148, 150, 169, 186 n.54, 210, 215
  citizenship and 21, 107–8, 111, 113, 116
  City of God 6, 25, 113–15, 121–2, 141–2, 150–7, 178–9
  Confessions 7, 45 n.22, 146, 186 n.54, 192, 215–18
  creation and 18–9, 41, 141–2, 145, 150–6, 160, 170, 180, 186 n.55
  De libero arbitrio 146, 170, 183 n.21
  De Trinitate 40, 189, 205–6, 218, 221, 226 n.19, 227 n.43
  desire and 18–20, 108–9, 121, 144–6, 216
  eternal recurrence and 150–1, 153–6
  eternity and 18, 107–8, 151, 216
  eudaimonia and 108–9, 151
  evil and 51–4, 69, 75–7, 90 n.39, 183 n.21
  freedom and 40, 107, 114, 141–2, 153–6, 170, 179
  grace and 19, 40, 49 n.59, 148, 156, 167, 178–80
  habit and 186 n.54, 215
  immortality and 107, 113
  justice and 115–16, 120
  love and 17–19, 108–11, 114–16, 121–2, 148
  memory and 19–20, 145–6, 169, 205–6, 207, 210, 216–17, 225 n.16
  mortality and 144–6
  natality and 20, 143, 144–6, 150–7, 167, 169, 170, 177–80, 210
  plurality and 20
  prayer and 217
  Rome and 21, 107–8, 113, 135 n.42, 144, 177–9
  saeculum and 129, 219
  thinking and 21, 205–6, 215–19
  time and 21, 114, 208, 209–10, 215–16
  virtue and 98, 121–22, 179
  will, and the 40, 49 n.59, 69, 120, 170, 183 n.21, 186 n.54
  wonder and 217
  worldliness and 107–11, 114–15, 116–18, 135 n.42
authority 33, 107, 111, 119, 126
automation 32, 92 n.47

Balthasar, Hans Urs von 14, 219–20
banality of evil, the 35–37, 38,

51–4, 63–72, 74, 76–7, 88 n.19, 90 n.38
Basil of Caesarea 179
beauty 101, 121, 126, 133 n.12, 195
Beiner, Ronald 41, 109, 117
being 12, 16, 192–3, 223 n.6
Being and Time (Heidegger) 16, 44 n.18, 46 n.26, 144
Benhabib, Seyla 124, 127
Benjamin, Walter 4, 21, 24–7, 34, 47 n.42, 48 n.43
  Illuminations 27
  messianism and 142, 210
  Passagen-Werk, Das (Arcades Project, The) 24
Berlin salons 22, 25, 127, 146, 175
Berlin, University of 14
Bernstein, Richard 51, 55
Between Past and Future (Arendt) 12, 27, 33–4, 78, 210–12
biomedical engineering 32, 99, 131 n.4
bios politikos 181 n.14, 193 *see also vita activa*
bios theoretikos 7, 189–90, 193–95, 204, 223 n.6 *see also vita contemplativa*
Birmingham, Peg 117, 136 n.53, 138 n.73, 181 n.14
Biss, Mavis 142
Blücher, Heinrich 26
Blumenfeld, Kurt 23, 159
Bonhoeffer, Dietrich 130
Boyle, Patrick 117–18, 135 n.42, 46
Brecht, Bertolt 24, 105
Bretherton, Luke 128–9
Brown, Peter 164–5, 217
Bultmann, Rudolf 15
bureaucracy 29, 37, 38, 73, 80, 84, 96, 162, 169
Butler, Judith 82–3

Cain (and Abel) 34, 88 n.19, 178
Canovan, Margaret 12, 167–8
caritas 108–9 *see also* charity; love; neighbor, the
Cato 7, 42, 189–191, 198, 204
Char, René 27, 33, 78, 170, 173–4, 210–11, 220
charity 5, 108–12, 114–16, 126, 179
Chiba, Shin, 98, 120, 121
Christian Community Development Assoc. 129
church 97, 107–8, 111, 113, 125–30, 140, 220
Cicero 121, 196
citizenship 95–8, 119–22, 125
  Athenian outlook on 106–7
  Augustine and 21, 107–8, 111, 113, 116
  duty and 66–70
  revocation of 23, 57, 82–3
  right to have rights and, the 23, 95, 136 n.53
  see also refugees; statelessness
City of God (Augustine) 6, 25, 113–15, 121–2, 141–2, 150–7, 178–9
civil rights movement (U.S.), the 34, 140, 172
cognition 200–1
compassion 111, 132 n.9, 178 *see also* charity; love
complex space 129
concentration camps 13, 27, 29–30, 31–2, 52–3, 55–62, 64–65, 81–2, 123–5
Confessions (Augustine) 7, 45 n.22, 146, 186 n.54, 192, 215–18
conscience 58, 68, 203–4
consumer society 32–3, 96, 103–4, 221
consumerism 98, 104, 121

contemplation 190–1, 194–5, 209, 212–13, 218, 222 n.5, 223 n.6 *see also* thinking; *vita contemplativa*; wonder
Coolman, Boyd Taylor 213–14
courage 175–6, 179, 200
covenant 6, 141, 184 n.31 *see also* promising
creation 6, 41, 76–7, 141–2, 150–7
crimes against humanity 53–4, 64, 71, 72, 74, 85–6, 88 n.17, 89 n.30
"Crisis in Culture, The" (Arendt) 121, 126
"Crisis in Education, The" (Arendt) 119–20, 136 n.54, 175
Critique of Judgment (Kant) 131 n.5
Critique of Pure Reason (Kant) 14
cultura animi 121
culture 96–7, 101, 104, 121–2, 125–6
cupiditas 108–9, 121

Dante 14, 157–8
De libero arbitrio (Augustine) 146, 170, 183 n.21
De Trinitate (Augustine) 40, 189, 205–6, 218, 221, 226 n.19, 227 n.43
death *see* mortality
dehumanization 23, 29–31, 57–61, 64–5
Der Liebesbegriff bei Augustin (Arendt) *see* Augustine, Saint, Arendt's dissertation on
desire 18–20, 108–9, 121, 144–6, 169
Douglas, Lawrence 75
Dunne, Joseph 173

education 96, 119–20, 122, 123, 139, 175

Eichmann, Adolf 35–7, 51–4, 63–77, 84
evil and *see* banality of evil, the
habituation and 169
judgment of 73–5, 88 n.21
superior orders defense and 37, 69–70, 74, 85
thoughtlessness and 38–9, 54, 60, 74–6, 93 n.54, 190, 202–3
Eichmann in Jerusalem (Arendt) 12, 35–7, 42, 51, 63–71, 73, 77
Eichmann trial, the 35–7, 63–72, 85, 190
Elshtain, Jean Bethke 9 n.7, 52, 55, 76–7
emotion 111–12, 115–16, 122–5, 197–8
energeia 172, 201
enlarged mentality 14, 33, 42, 102, 112, 131 n.5
equality 116, 148–9, 162, 187 n.58
eternal recurrence 101, 150–1, 153–6, 160
eternity 209, 225 n.17
Augustine and 18, 107–8, 151, 216
Plato and 17–18, 105, 192
Euben, Roxanne 106, 135 n.41
eudaimonia 173–5
Aristotle and 173, 187 n.61
Augustine and 108–9, 151
see also public happiness
Evagrius 217
evil 35–9, 51–86, 202–4
Augustine and 51–4, 69, 75–7, 90 n.39, 183 n.21
banality of, the 35–7, 38, 51–4, 63–72, 74, 76–7, 88 n.19, 90 n.38

privation account of 51–4, 76–7, 79, 87 n.9, 90 n.39, 221
radical 14, 25, 52–3, 55–62, 63, 65, 66, 72, 79, 87 n.10
thinking as condition against 38–9, 202–4, 224 n.15
thoughtlessness and 4, 7, 36–7, 38, 69, 70, 75–6
tradition and 51–4, 61–2, 69, 72–80
existentialism 14–15, 27

fearful imagination 80–4
forgiveness 25, 33, 162–4, 166, 170, 177, 184 n.31
Founders, the (American) 25, 174–5
founding movements 25, 34–5, 141, 177–9
Frankfurt School 24, 197
fraternity 112, 133 n.12
freedom 160–2, 165–6
  Augustine and 40, 107, 114, 141–2, 153–6, 170, 179
  limits of 143, 167–71, 174–6, 187 n.58
  political 39, 106–7, 162–3, 168–76
  totalitarian repression of 30–1, 56–7, 95, 149
French Resistance, the 8, 25, 27, 33, 161, 170, 172, 173–4, 210–11 *see also* Char, René
French Revolution, the 34, 111, 141, 169
friendship 33, 39, 176, 188 n.67, 194, 202–4, 218, 221
Fulkerson, Mary McClintock 127

Gandhi, Mahatma 172
genocide 36, 64–5, 71–2, 74, 80, 82–3, 85, 89 n.30 *see also* Nazi crimes

glory 98, 106, 113, 117, 122, 135 n.41, 179
good works 110
goodness 2, 38–9, 110, 177, 202–4
Gorgias (Plato) 38–9, 198
Gottlieb, Susannah 142
grace 19, 40, 49 n.59, 91 n.43, 148, 156, 167, 176–80
gratitude 13, 20, 118, 143, 145–9, 169, 191, 195
Gray, J. Glenn 39
Greeks, the 40, 106–7, 117–18, 156, 188 n.67
Gregory, Eric 98, 112, 114–18, 122, 179
Gregory of Nazianzus 179
Guardini, Romano 14–15

habituation 37, 169, 174–6, 186 n.54
happiness *see eudaimonia*; public happiness
Hegel, Georg Wilhelm Friedrich 27–8, 40, 87 n.9, 196–7, 211
Heidegger, Martin 11, 15–17, 44 n.17
  Being and Time 16, 44 n.18, 144
  mortality and 19–20, 46 n.26, 144, 146
  natality and 144–6, 169
  Nazi party and 11, 22, 224 n.15
  thinking and 38, 224 n.15
  time and 16, 19, 144–5
  tradition and 16–7, 48 n.43
  will, the and 40
Herdt, Jennifer 121–2
Himmler, Heinrich 70
Hitler 62, 66–8
Holocaust, the 35–7, 55–72, 74–5, 82, 138 n.73, 149 *see also* concentration camps; genocide; Nazi crimes

Homer 192
homo faber 103, 162, 195 *see also* work
horror 13, 30, 35, 42, 58, 124–5
  thinking and 81–4, 191, 196–7
household, the 96, 111, 114
Hugh of St. Victor 212–15, 216
  Noah's Ark 214
Hughes, John 133 n.23
human condition, the 31–2, 49 n.53, 99–103, 144–50, 167–9
  human nature distinguished from 30–2, 49 n.52
  modern threats to 32–3, 95–6, 103–5, 148
  totalitarian rejection of 30–1
  vita activa and 32, 95, 159
Human Condition, The (Arendt) 12, 17, 20, 31–3, 37, 49 n.52, 64, 96, 117–18, 132 n.10, 135 n.42, 152, 157, 167–8, 176, 181 n.14, 189–90, 194
human rights 23, 57–8, 82–3, 95, 123, 136 n.53
Hungarian Revolution 8, 34, 140, 161

identity 102–3
  action and 33, 143, 157–9
  natality and 146–9, 168–9
ideology 29–30, 56–7, 60–1, 68, 80, 147, 149, 169, 203
Illuminations (Benjamin) 27, 226 n.18
imagination 41–2, 80–84, 93 n.54, 206
immigration 123 *see also* refugees; statelessness
immortality 2, 106–7, 113–14, 117–18, 135 n.41

imperialism 11, 29, 167
Industrial Areas Foundation 129
International Criminal Court 85–6, 89 n.30

Jaspers, Karl 11, 17, 21, 61–3, 65, 86, 90 n.38, 118
Jesus 15, 17, 110, 141, 155–6, 163–4, 184 n.31
John XXIII, Pope 15, 42, 161
judgment 14, 37, 41–2, 79, 84–6, 102, 137 n.57, 191
  Kant and 14, 67, 131 n.5
  see also Eichmann, Adolf, judgment of
justice 122–5, 136 n.53
  Augustine and 115–16, 120
  criminal 36, 61–2, 71–2, 73–5, 85–6

Kafka, Franz 207–12
Kampowski, Stephan 75–6
Kant, Immanuel 13–4, 38, 40, 170, 224 n.15
  Critique of Judgment 131 n.5
  Critique of Pure Reason 14
  Eichmann, Adolf and 67–70
  enlarged mentality and 14, 131 n.5
  radical evil and 25, 52–3, 61, 79
  will, the and 14, 40, 61, 170
Kateb, George 204, 224 n.10
Kirsch, Adam 1

labor 32, 103, 100, 107, 111, 133 n.23, 159–60
law 99, 131 n.3
  duty and 37, 66–70
  ideology and 56–7, 68, 149
  international 64–5, 71, 74, 85–6
  morality and 67–9, 73–6
Lazare, Bernard 181 n.10

libido dominandi (Augustine) 75, 113
life 32
  as cyclical process 49 n.53, 99, 101, 160
  as eternal 106–7
  as highest good 106, 111
  labor and 100, 159–60
  as linear story 101–2, 151
Life of the Mind, The (Arendt) 37–41, 51, 53, 88 n.19, 120, 156, 170, 190–212
loneliness 96, 104–5, 205
love 111–12, 120–2
  Augustine and 17–19, 108–11, 114–16, 121–2, 148
  see also *amor mundi*; charity; compassion
Love and Saint Augustine (Arendt) see Augustine, Saint, Arendt's dissertation on
Luban, David 73–4
Luther, Martin 15
Luxemburg, Rosa 8, 26, 42, 161, 175
"Lying in Politics" (Arendt) 42, 170

MacIntyre, Alasdair 78, 91 n.42, n.46, 187 n.61
Marburg University 14–17
Marx, Karl 21, 26, 87 n.9, 111
mass society 96, 104
Mathewes, Charles 52, 77, 116–17, 135 n.46, 142, 164–8, 169–71
McKenna, George 142, 150
meditation 192, 209, 212–15, 216, 218, 225 n.17, 226 n.20
memory 103, 122
  Augustine and 19–20, 145–6, 169, 205–6, 207, 210, 216–17, 225 n.16

  Benjamin and 24–6
Men in Dark Times (Arendt) 15, 42, 176
mens rea 69–70, 73–4
messianism, Jewish 142, 210, 226 n.18
miracles 139, 160, 166
modern age, the 32–3, 95–6, 103–5, 111, 189, 194–5
Montesquieu 25
mortality 32, 49 n.53, 101–2, 118, 135 n.41
  Augustine and 144–6
  Heidegger and 19–20, 46 n.26, 144, 146

natality 20, 32, 45 n.25, 49 n.53, 118, 139–50
  Augustine and 143, 144–6, 150–7, 167, 169, 170, 177–80, 210
nature 99, 101–2, 131 n.4, 160, 194–5
Nazi crimes 62, 63–5 see also crimes against humanity, genocide; Holocaust, the
neighbor, the 17–19, 109, 114–16 see also charity
Neoplatonism 17–18, 150–2
Neo-Scholasticism 14, 219
Nicomachean Ethics (Aristotle) 143, 173
Nietzsche, Friedrich 2, 21, 40, 111
Noah's Ark (Hugh of St. Victor) 214
nouvelle théologie see *ressourcement* theology
nuclear technology 12, 32, 92 n.47, 99
nunc stans 209–10, 212, 226 n.18
Nuremberg trials 61, 63, 71, 88 n.17

O'Byrne, Anne 144, 146

Oedipus at Colonus (Sophocles) 146
"On Humanity in Dark Times" (Arendt) 123, 133 n.12, 168
On Revolution (Arendt) 34–5, 132 n.9, n.10, 146, 169
On Violence (Arendt) 87 n.9, 90 n.39
Origins of Totalitarianism, The (Arendt) 11, 23, 28–31, 48 n.47, 52, 55–62, 68, 80–2, 95–6, 123–5, 181 n.14

pariah, the 22, 123, 133 n.12, 181 n.10
  Arendt as 1, 24, 112, 147–9
  conscious 147, 159
parvenu, the 146–7, 181 n.10
Passagen-Werk, Das (*Arcades Project, The*) (Benjamin) 24
Paul, Saint 40, 177, 220
pearl diving method 4, 24–6, 48 n.43, 79, 91 n.46, 141, 150–7, 211, 219
Pelagianism 164–8, 176–7
Pelagius 177
Pericles 106, 117–18
phenomenology 11, 17, 19, 28
philokalia 121
philosophy of history 27–9, 197
pity 111, 169
Plato 12–13, 162
  eternity and 17–18, 105, 192
  Gorgias 38–9, 198
  Sophist 16
  Theaetetus 12, 192
  thinking and 192–5, 222 n.5, 224 n.15
plurality 13, 20–1, 31, 123, 195
  as condition of action 32, 141, 149, 168, 193
  as condition of thought 198–9

enlarged mentality and 42, 102, 131 n.5
totalitarian attack on 53, 57, 64–5, 80, 95
poiēsis 25, 140, 157–8
polis, the 25, 105, 106–7, 113–14, 117–18, 133 n.23, 140, 188 n.67, 193–4, 204
political philosophy 11–13, 141, 162, 189–90, 193
  political theory distinguished from 12
power 34–5, 158–9, 178
  promising and 162–3
praxis 25, 33, 140, 157–8 *see also* action
private realm 99, 111, 115, 119, 133 n.23, 159, 181 n.14
privation account of evil 51–4, 76–7, 79, 87 n.9, 90 n.39, 221
promising 162–3
public happiness 25, 143, 173–4, 211
public realm 31, 96, 99, 102, 111, 113, 119, 127–8, 158–9, 176

racism 56–7, 60, 127, 147–8
radical evil 14, 25, 52–3, 55–62, 63, 65, 66, 72, 79, 87 n.10
reconciliation 12, 30, 123, 143, 202
  Hegel and 27–8, 196–7, 211
refugees 5, 23, 31, 123, 128
  normalizing 82–3
  see also immigration; statelessness
respect 176, 185 n.33
ressourcement theology 79, 192, 219–20
revolution 13, 25, 34–5, 97, 140–1, 169, 174–5

Richard III (Shakespeare) 36, 88 n.19, 203
Robespierre, Maximilien 169
Romans, the 113, 144, 177–8
    philosophy of 196
Romulus 34, 178
Russian Revolution 34, 141

saeculum (Augustine) 129, 219
Sanctuary movement, the 128
Scotus, John Duns 40, 90 n.39, 209
Schmidt, Anton 8, 161
Scholem, Gershom 63, 76, 133 n.11, 148–9, 195
science 12, 131 n.4, 201
secular, the 111, 132 n. 10
Silenus (Sophocles) 146–7
Socrates 7, 38–9, 193–4
    solitude and 203–5, 224 n.15
    thinking and 141, 194–6, 198–200, 202–5, 222 n.5
solidarity 176
solitude 199, 203–5, 224 n.15
Sophist (Plato) 16
Sophocles 146
sovereignty 141, 162–3
space for appearing 96, 99, 101–2, 104, 127, 128, 158–9 *see also* public realm
Spartacist Movement 26, 161, 175 *see also* Luxemburg, Rosa
speechlessness 12–13, 192–3
spontaneity 29–30, 59, 161, 165–6, 169–70
statelessness 23, 57, 82–4, 95, 122–3, 148 *see also* refugees, worldlessness
Stump, Eleonore 177
superior orders defense 37, 52, 69–70, 74, 85, 89 n.30

technology 12, 14, 32–3, 99, 189–90
teleology 143, 158, 165–6, 169–74, 185 n.39, 187 n.61
Tempest, The (Shakespeare) 25
temporality *see* time
tending 122, 137 n.66, 139
terror 9 n.7, 29, 55–60, 80–1, 84–5, 149, 169, 203
Tertullian 107, 131 n.7
thaumazein 12–3, 25, 192, 195
    see also wonder
Theaetetus (Plato) 12, 192
Theodosius I 178
thinking 189–92, 198–202
    Augustine and 21, 205–6, 215–19
    cognition distinguished from 200–1
    as condition against evil 38–9, 202–4, 224 n.15
    consolation and 196–7
    contemplation distinguished from 190–1, 193–4, 222 n.5
    dialogical character of 38–9, 198–200, 202–4
    freedom and 60
    Hegel and 27–8, 196–7
    Heidegger and 38, 224 n.15
    horror and 81–4, 191, 196–7
    ideology as barrier to 60
    judging and 41, 203–4
    meditation and 209, 212–15
    Plato and 192–5, 222 n.5, 224 n.15
    reconciliation and 197, 202
    representational nature of 205–7, 208
    Roman philosophy and 196
    Socrates and 141, 194–6, 198–200, 202–5, 224 n.15
    solitude and 199, 203–5
    time and 207–12, 215–16

what we are doing 12, 33, 36, 189
willing and 39–40, 186 n.57
without a bannister 72, 79, 89 n.24
wonder and 12–13, 193–5
thoughtlessness 4, 7, 33, 36–7, 38, 69, 75–6, 169, 176, 190, 203
time 117–18, 169, 207–12
   Augustine and 21, 114, 208, 209–10, 215–16
   Heidegger and 16, 19, 144–5
totalitarianism 27–31, 52–4, 55–60, 80–1, 147–50, 203–4
tradition 16–17, 28, 48 n.43, 52–4, 61, 69, 72–80, 91 n.42, n. 43, n. 46, 211

understanding 27–30, 81–5, 102, 159, 197, 202, 211
"Understanding and Politics" (Arendt) 29, 83, 151–2
University of Berlin 14
utility 101, 121, 187 n.59

Varnhagen, Rahel 22, 146–7, 159, 168, 175
Vatican II 161, 220
vengeance 163
Villa, Dana 10 n.8, 59, 68, 69, 136 n.53, 165, 185 n.39
violence 34–5, 158, 177–8
virtue 121–2, 172–3, 175–6, 179
vita activa 32, 189–90, 223 n.6 see also action, labor, work
vita contemplativa 173, 189–90, 193–5, 218, 223 n.6 see also *bios theoretikos*
Voegelin, Eric 30, 123–4

web of human relationships 158–9

Wetzel, James 75
"What is Existential Philosophy?" (Arendt) 20
"What is Freedom" (Arendt) 165, 171–2
will, the 39–41, 171, 176, 186 n.57
   Augustine and 40, 49 n.59, 69, 120, 170, 183 n.21, 186 n.54
   freedom of 39, 171–2
   Kant and 14, 40, 61, 170
will to power, the 169
Willard, Mara 79, 142
Williams, A. N. 219–20
Williams, Rowan 112–14, 117
willing *see* will, the
Wolfe, Alan 52
Wolin, Sheldon 6, 122
wonder 12–13, 192–6, 217
work 32, 96, 100, 122, 157–8, 161, 194–5
world, the 99–105, 117–18
   alienation 105, 123
   building 97, 100–1, 119–22, 125–30
   common 99–100, 102, 109, 117, 119, 122, 135 n.42, 140, 158–9, 176
worldlessness 23, 57, 82–3, 103–5, 110, 123, 133 n.12
worldliness 31, 96–7, 99–105, 109, 126, 130, 172 *see also amor mundi*
worship 126–7

Xenophon 205

Young-Bruehl, Elisabeth 87 n.10, 169
Youth Aliyah 23

Zionism 11, 23, 159

www.ingramcontent.com/pod-product-compliance
Lightning Source LLC
Chambersburg PA
CBHW050137240426
43673CB00043B/1697